SIGMUND FREUD AND ART

HIS PERSONAL COLLECTION
OF ANTIQUITIES

INTRODUCTION BY PETER GAY

EDITED BY
LYNN GAMWELL
AND
RICHARD WELLS

THAMES AND HUDSON

IN ASSOCIATION WITH
STATE UNIVERSITY OF NEW YORK
FREUD MUSEUM, LONDON

First published in Great Britain in 1989 by Thames and Hudson Ltd, London

Produced by Ed Marquand Book Design
Managing editor: Suzanne Kotz
Editor: Lorna Price
Photographer: Nick Bagguley

Typeset by The Type Gallery, Seattle
Printed and bound in Japan by Toppan Printing Co., Ltd.

Cover: Sphinx, Greek, South Italian, late 5th–early 4th century B.C.
Back cover: Freud's study, London

Photo credits: Pages 2–3, 5, 14, 152, 172, and all object photographs by Nick Bagguley, courtesy Freud Museum. Pages 1, 20, courtesy Sigmund Freud Copyrights, London. Pages 6–7 by Simon Brown for *Art & Antiques.*

Editor's note: The abbreviation "SE" is used throughout this work to refer to *The Standard Edition of the Complete Psychological Works of Sigmund Freud*, ed. and trans. by James Strachey in collaboration with Anna Freud, 24 vols. (London: Hogarth Press, 1953–74).

CONTENTS

ACKNOWLEDGMENTS

Two years ago I learned, by chance, that Sigmund Freud was a collector of ancient art, and I saw a photograph of his desk, cluttered with Egyptian, Greek, and Chinese figures. I telephoned the Freud Museum in London, and determined that the collection was, indeed, unpublished and had not left Freud's study since it was moved there, from Vienna, in 1938. And so I was inspired to organize this first scholarly publication and traveling exhibition of Sigmund Freud's personal collection of antiquities.

My initial, tentative ideas about why the founder of psychoanalysis collected these objects evolved into a focused, in-depth, interdisciplinary presentation with the critical guidance of Donald Kuspit, who acted as project adviser. A team of American and British scholars illuminated Freud's art collection with insights from archaeology, art history, classics, cultural history, the humanities, philosophy, and psychoanalysis. These specialists not only contributed text but gave advice to their colleagues from other fields in an open exchange of ideas that enriched the final publication: Martin S. Bergmann, Wendy Botting, Lucilla Burn, Dominique Collon, J. Keith Davies, Peter Gay, Donald Kuspit, Michael Münchow, Jane Portal, J. D. Ray, C. Nicholas Reeves, Ellen Handler Spitz Jonathan Tubb, and Richard Wells. My deepest appreciation to Dr. Spitz for cheerfully stepping in at a crucial time in the production of this book to offer insightful observations on the manuscript.

The advice and encouragement of many psychiatrists, psychoanalysts, and psychologists across the United States made it possible to expand the museum audience to include mental-health professionals. I extend thanks to James B. Hoyme, M.D., Medical Director, The Institute of Pennsylvania Hospital; Paul J. Fink, M.D., President, American Psychiatric Association; Homer C. Curtis, M.D., President, American Psychoanalytic Association; Zanvel A. Liff, Ph.D., President, Division of Psychoanalysis of the American Psychological Association.

The organization of this exhibition by the University Art Museum of the State University of New York at Binghamton, in cooperation with the Freud Museum, was encouraged and supported by Sidonie Smith and David Cingranelli of the office of Arts and Sciences, James Boyle of the Foundation of SUNY Binghamton, Marcia R. Craner of the Alumni Association, and Stephen Gilje and Paul

Parker of the Research Foundation. David Becker and Wendy Botting gave curatorial assistance; Cheryl McKee and Norman Nordon offered translating advice; Chris Focht provided photographic services.

The staff of the Freud Museum was extremely helpful with the conservation, photography, and research required by this project. My special thanks to Director Richard Wells, who joined me as co-curator of the exhibition and co-editor of this publication; our goal has been to make the very finest presentation of these unique objects from the Freud Museum.

I relied on the excellent guidance of Ed Marquand Book Design in all matters relating to the administration, editing, and design of this book. Due to the fine work of Ed Marquand and Suzanne Kotz, the book was transformed from an exhibition catalogue into a beautiful, intelligent publication with international distribution.

Several individuals gave me important advice about the project: Karen Brosius, K. R. Eissler, M.D., Mary Jane Matz, Romie Shapiro, Clara Diament Sujo, and Betty Turnbull.

The American tour of the exhibition and the publication were made possible by the sponsorship of CIBA-GEIGY Pharmaceuticals and the National Endowment for the Arts.

My personal efforts on this project are dedicated to Peter A. Gelker, M.D., Ph.D., and Charles Michael Brown.

Lynn Gamwell
Director, University Art Museum
State University of New York, Binghamton

When Lynn Gamwell approached me two years ago and proposed this touring exhibition and scholarly publication, the Freud Museum was newly opened and lacked a full staff; however, through collaboration with Dr. Gamwell and the State University of New York, the museum has been able to realize this ambitious project in time to commemorate the fiftieth anniversary of Freud's death.

It is thanks to the support and understanding of the Joint Committee for the Freud Museum and of the London Advisory Committee that this exceptional opportunity became a reality. On the Joint Committee, Harold P. Blum, M.D., Peter B. Neubauer, M.D., and Bernard Pacella, M.D., represent the Sigmund Freud Archives, and Hal Harvey, Professor Albert J. Solnit, and Robert Wolf (Chairman) represent the New-Land Foundation Inc. The museum has especially benefited from the specialized knowledge and broad experience of T. G. H. James, Chairman of the London Advisory Committee and formerly Keeper of Egyptian Antiquities at the British Museum.

I am especially grateful to the staff at the Freud Museum, who rose to the demands of this exhibition and publication. Erica Davies, collections manager, handled the crucially important task of assuring that the antiquities were properly prepared for their tour. Museum photographer Nick Bagguley produced the spectacular photographs that fill this book. Research on the books, documents, and objects at the museum was undertaken by J. Keith Davies, Michael Molnar, and Michael Münchow. Allison Green and Susan O'Cleary kept the transatlantic communication going. Conservators and other specialists were generous with assistance and advice: Celia Alberman, Tony Brandon, Brian Clarke, Ann De Lara, Celestine Enderley, Simon Evnine, Penny Fisher, David Fellows, Derek Gilman, Anthony Griffiths, Colin Johnson, Roger Keverne, Eric Miller, Thea Peacock, Mack Pritchard, John Roffey, Ricky Smith, and Ian Smith.

The assistance of others is gratefully acknowledged: Dr. Joanna Montgomery Byles made a scholarly contribution to the museum's work; Joe Spieler and Renée Schwartz responded when I needed them; I learned a great deal from Gwion Jones during our work on the museum's archaeological display; my London University Extra-Mural class helped me develop my ideas about Freud and his antiquities.

In the end, this exhibition and catalogue were realized because an international and interdisciplinary team of scholars and museum professionals skillfully and willingly supported this unique collaboration. On behalf of the Freud Museum, I extend my sincerest appreciation to them all.

Richard Wells
Director
Freud Museum, London

PREFACE

RICHARD WELLS

At the heart of this volume are sixty-seven antiquities collected by Sigmund Freud. They have been selected from the more than two thousand pieces that crowd Freud's extraordinary working environment at 20 Maresfield Gardens, now the Freud Museum, London. By means of this book (and the exhibition it accompanies), we aim to indicate the archaeological and aesthetic interest of the collection and to explore its significance in relation to the development of Freud's psychoanalytic work.

Immediately on arrival in England as a refugee, Freud wrote to Marie Bonaparte, with whom he had stayed in Paris en route from Vienna: "Surrounded by love for twelve hours, we arrived proud and rich under the protection of Athene" (June 8, 1938)—a gracious reference to a small, specially prized statue that Marie Bonaparte had just returned to Freud after smuggling it out of Vienna, when he had feared he might lose his entire collection. (Marie Bonaparte had also paid the ransom, a 25 percent tax, demanded by the Fascists for the release of Freud's belongings, particularly the antiquities.) Less concretely, Freud's words evoke his vision of an entire civilization, a civilization under threat once more from internal conflicts, which had erupted into the barbarism of the Nazis. During the previous world war, Freud had movingly reported on the disillusionment that the savagery and slaughter had brought to the citizen of the world, who had exchanged his native land for a foreign one in time of war, and who had relied on "unity among the civilized peoples" which had created a "new and wider fatherland." Freud reflected:

> This new fatherland was a museum for him, too, filled with all the treasures which the artists of civilized humanity had in the successive centuries created and left behind. As he wandered from one gallery to another in this museum, he could recognise with impartial appreciation what varied types of perfection a mixture of blood, the course of history, and the special quality of their mother-earth had produced among his compatriots in this wider sense.

Freud continued:

> Nor must we forget that each of these citizens of the civilized world had created for himself a "Parnassus" and a "School of Athens" of his own. From

among the great thinkers, writers and artists of all nations he had chosen those to whom he considered he owed the best of what he had been able to achieve in enjoyment and understanding of life, and he had venerated them along with the immortal ancients as well as with the familiar masters of his own tongue. (SE, 14, pp. 277–78)

Beautiful artifacts, mythological and legendary figures, sages and heroes, all from antiquity, jostle in Freud's rooms beside photographs of his scientific and medical mentors and of his female muses. To enter these rooms is to encounter the "Parnassus" and the "School of Athens" which Freud constructed for himself with such energy, turmoil, ambivalence, and playfulness from a civilization that he interpreted so profoundly—and which Freud, perhaps more than anyone, has come to represent. To engage with these items is also to register a multiplicity of points of entry to the personal and cultural matrix from which psychoanalysis itself emerged, and to which the collection of antiquities belongs.

A few months after his arrival in England, Freud was able to report:

"All the Egyptians, Chinese and Greeks have arrived, have stood up to the journey with very little damage, and look more impressive here than in Berggasse" (letter to Jeanne Lampl-de Groot, October 8, 1938).

Paula Fichtl, the Freud family maid, and Freud's son Ernst lovingly arranged all his antiquities in his reconstructed rooms in the newly acquired Maresfield Gardens exactly as they had been placed in Berggasse 19, where Freud had lived and worked for forty-seven years. The ailing eighty-two-year-old Freud was able to move in and get straight down to work for the final year of his life—Athena with pride of place among the ranks of antiquities on his desk. It is tempting to detect the goddess's influence behind the safe arrival, against all the odds, of Freud's belongings—not just the antiquities but his library, papers, and furniture, including the famous couch. Less fancifully, the desperately late rescue of Freud and his immediate family had been secured by diplomatic pressure from the United States and Britain, which offered asylum, urged on by an international group of Freud's friends and colleagues. Freud was granted his wish "to die in freedom" in England, the country whose literature and political culture he most admired. "For a while, England, the heir to Freud's remains—as Athens was to those of Oedipus—found itself the leader of the European analytic movement" (O. Mannoni, *Freud: The Theory of the Unconscious*, London, 1985, p. 175.) Wrenched from its original central European setting, psychoanalysis was to be adapted and disseminated through the English-speaking culture of Britain and the United States.

The opening in America of the exhibition *The Sigmund Freud Antiquities: Fragments from a Buried Past*, to commemorate the fiftieth anniversary of Freud's death, in exile in England, is a reminder of the geographical, cultural, and political vicissitudes of the psychoanalytic movement. It provides a stimulus to reflection on the origins, history, and future of psychoanalytic practice.

The exhibition tour also inaugurates the international exhibition program of the Freud Museum. Established in 1986, the museum is developing as a unique public resource and a forum, which participates in the work of understanding, interpreting, and publicizing the history and continuing development of psychoanalysis in all its ramifications. The exhibition illustrates the fresh perspectives on Freud's work and character that are being opened up now that his library and consulting rooms are accessible for study. Freud's collection is being investigated in detail for the first time, and can now be related to his library and manuscripts at the museum. The catalogue entries contained herein are the initial fruits of research into individual pieces, and pioneer the complex task of placing them within the overall context of Freud's life and work.

The impulse to record and remember as much as possible of the historic cultural laboratory within which Freud had made his discoveries was felt as soon as it was threatened. Freud's colleague August Aichhorn asked the photographer Edmund Engelman to make a comprehensive record of Freud's Vienna apartments in the weeks before Freud left. Some of these photographs, reprinted by Engelman himself from the original negatives, record the antiquities in their original setting.

After Freud's death on September 23, 1939, his daughter Anna continued with her own pioneering psychoanalytic work from 20 Maresfield Gardens, preserving her father's study and library intact. It was Anna Freud's wish that after her death this extraordinary legacy of turn-of-the-century Vienna in a London suburb should become a museum in honor of her father. In 1980, the Sigmund Freud Archives, a registered English charity, purchased the land and building at 20 Maresfield Gardens, with funds from the New-Land Foundation Inc. The support of the late Muriel Gardiner, the founder of the New-Land Foundation and longtime friend of Anna Freud, was crucial in establishing the museum. On Anna Freud's death in 1982, the contents of the house were bequeathed to the English charity to establish the Freud Museum, which was opened to the public on July 28, 1986. Sigmund Freud Archives Inc. and Freud Museum London Trustee Ltd. are the trustees of the registered English charity. The museum is operated through a Joint Committee of Sigmund Freud Archives and the New-Land Foundation, and managed with the assistance of the London Advisory Committee. Well over two thousand benefactors and Friends of the Museum worldwide have enabled the museum to become a cultural and educational center with an international role.

Freud's study, London.

INTRODUCTION

PETER GAY

On May 14, 1938, Sigmund Freud sat down to write his sister-in-law Minna Bernays an important letter. "In the fateful first days of next week," he told her, "the commission on which the fate of the collection depends is supposed to come here. The shipper is lurking in the background."[1] He could not be confident that he would be allowed to live out whatever time he had left in the presence of his beloved antiquities, and his agitation was showing. No wonder: many of these plaques, statuettes, and fragments had been his silent, loyal, immensely rewarding companions for decades, and the thought of having to part with them was almost too much to bear.

The Nazis had marched into Vienna two months before, and the Freud family was gradually, one by one, seeking shelter abroad, in England. Minna, in ill health and almost blind, had been the first to go; on May 5, a solicitous Dorothy Burlingham had taken her to London. And on the day that Freud went to his stripped-down study to write to her—the family were beginning to pack up their possessions—his son Martin, far less competent in dealing with the authorities than his invaluable daughter Anna, followed suit. But Freud, his wife, Martha, and Anna had not yet been issued the crucial document that would open the way to freedom. The Nazi authorities were still temporizing over the so-called *Unbedenklichkeitserklärung*, the official declaration that Freud was "innocuous"—that he had satisfied all the regulations, paid all the exactions, that an inventive and extortionate regime had been able to think up for Austrian Jews eager to depart. "We are waiting anxiously for this paper," Freud reported to Minna Bernays. It was a sign of his extreme agitation that he, normally in control of events and himself, should admit it.

During the days that followed, Freud, never one to take kindly to passivity, was forced to endure the suspense. The authorities were unpredictable and mean-spirited in the extreme. One distraction for him was being taken out for a drive, twice, to say farewell to Vienna. Always susceptible to the charm of flowers, he found delight, almost in spite of himself, in seeing the city he loved and hated aglow in its spring beauty.

Then, on May 23, he could report to Minna Bernays that he had some splendid news: "My collection has been released. Not a single confiscation, a minimal levy of RM 400"—some one hundred dollars. Fortunately, Freud went on, Hans

Demel, director of the Kunsthistorisches Museum in Vienna, who had appraised his holdings, had been very "merciful." He had estimated the value of Freud's whole collection at RM 30,000, a substantial sum, but far below the limits that would have invited the authorities to keep Freud's antiquities in Austria. In short, "The shipper can start with the packing without delay."[2] When Freud moved to his last house at 20 Maresfield Gardens in Hampstead in September 1938, he could surround himself with his cherished objects, almost as though nothing untoward had happened. They eased the year he still had left to live, for they meant a great deal to him.

But what? To discover that is to discover much about Freud the man and the psychoanalyst. "I have made many sacrifices for my collection of Greek, Roman, and Egyptian antiquities," he once wrote an admirer, the Austrian novelist Stefan Zweig, in his late years, "and actually have read more archaeology than psychology."[3] I have called this declaration "genial hyperbole,"[4] but the very exaggeration testifies to the privileged place his antiquities held in Freud's mental economy. And indeed, virtually all Freud's visitors to Berggasse 19 attest to their significance for him. When Hanns Sachs, later to become a member of Freud's intimate circle, first visited him in 1909, he noticed that while the collection "was still in its initial stages, some of the objects at once attracted the visitor's eye."[5] They were beginning to crowd every available space in his consulting room and the adjoining study at Berggasse 19. Freud's more observant analysands, like the Wolf Man, found his collection no less striking and, in fact, highly instructive. It was with the Wolf Man (as he had done before, with more than one patient) that Freud employed his collection as a master metaphor for the psychoanalytic process. "The psychoanalyst, like the archaeologist in his excavations," the Wolf Man recalled Freud telling him, "must uncover layer after layer of the patient's psyche, before coming to the deepest, most valuable treasures."[6]

As the essays in this volume abundantly show, no close student of Freud has been able to escape this convenient and powerful archaeological metaphor. It has imposed itself, rightly, because it brings together one of Freud's dominant passions—second only to his primary addiction, smoking cigars—with his fundamental commitment to digging beneath surfaces, to bringing the hidden to light, to dusting off and piecing together the encrusted fragments from a distant past, fragments often barely legible. Freud's much-quoted definition of the analyst's healing work, "Where id was, there ego shall be," read with these objects in mind, strongly suggests that the archaeological metaphor has more than metaphorical significance. It follows that anyone seriously interested in interrogating Freud's antiquities is bound to move a little closer to the solution of that larger and most interesting mystery, Freud himself—the epoch-making founder of psychoanalysis, the good nineteenth-century burgher who subverted the very style of thinking in which he was most thoroughly at home.

There is no need to pursue the implications of the archaeological metaphor here; that will be the business of the essays that follow. I want to concentrate rather on one central issue raised by what Freud called his "partiality for the prehistoric": the remarkable dialectical tension in his thought between rationality and irrationality. He saw reason and unreason, like almost everyone else, as sharply distinct, and often in severe mutual conflict. But, Freud argued, the two were not inevitably at odds. It was the task of reason to provide access to unreason, and it did so by perfecting instruments for insight partly borrowed from the enemy itself.

Freud, it is essential to remember, was a modern philosophe, a belated child of the eighteenth-century Enlightenment. His God, if he had a god, was logos. One of the most revealing papers he ever wrote, one that deserves to be required reading for anyone seeking to understand Freud, is "The Question of a Weltanschauung," the concluding essay in his *New Introductory Lectures on Psychoanalysis* (SE, 22, pp. 158–82). Does psychoanalysis require a worldview of its own? Freud asks in that paper, and replies that it does not. It is part of science, and hence the worldview of science is its appropriate domain. If Freud waded in the muck of the unconscious, of impulses to murder, rape, and incest, he did so not to celebrate but to understand and if possible conquer them. As a solid bourgeois, he believed in the virtue of self-control. While he diagnosed the superego bedeviling his educated contemporaries as being excessively punitive, while he deplored what he thought to be the hypocrisy about fundamental needs and desires in his culture, he did not invite the world to discard the responsible conscience, let alone good manners. Those self-serving and shallow readers of Freud who, especially in the 1920s, grasped at what they thought to be his teaching as proclaiming the end of all inhibitions, as issuing a license for license, fatally misread his therapeutic ideal. The abstinence he wanted to impress on his fellow clinicians was not a posture of cynicism or aloofness. If he deprecated the rage to cure as an obstruction in the work of healing neurotics, this should not be read as indifference to the suffering beings before him. His celebrated recommendation that the psychoanalyst emulate the surgeon, who puts away all human emotions as he does his sanguinary work, has served Freud badly: the metaphor was too vivid to capture his real intentions. He intended to do more than to identify, name, and diagnose the mental ills the human flesh is heir to; he intended to do something about them. Reason, to put it tersely, was at once the method of psychoanalysis and its goal.

The "reason" that Freud praised wants to be understood. It meant close observation, pitiless honesty, speculation disciplined by the frequent and faithful return to experience. This, in Freud's estimate, was the only acceptable way of being scientific about the mind. Tradition and authority and abstract reasoning, at their best, might be suggestive. They could provide hints at, but never serve as guides to, the truth. In fact, most of the time, tradition and the rest did not reach even this modest aim. Writing in the empiricist tradition launched by Francis Bacon three centuries earlier, Freud thought such ways of reasoning to be signposts pointing nowhere, or in wrong directions.

But—and here I approach the second pole governing Freud's thinking—this primacy of practical reason did not imply the denigration of the emotional dimension of the mind. How could Freud, whose psychology places the drives into the very heart of his theory, underestimate that dimension? The very point of Freud's theory of the mind, its travail and maturation, was to acknowledge the power of, and find an honored place for, the passions. In this sense, Freud's motto— "Where id was, there ego shall be"—does his enterprise somewhat less than full justice. He would have been more accurate about his therapeutic ambitions had he described successful psychoanalysis as making peace (or, more humbly, a lasting truce) among id, ego, and superego.

What is more, the emotions play a central role not merely in the psychoanalytic scheme of development but in its therapeutic technique as well. The generous, almost envious, tributes Freud paid to the psychological insights that imaginative novelists and poets can reach through aesthetic insight attest to his respect for intuition. So does the analyst's listening stance of evenly hovering attention through which the unconscious of the analyst communicates with the unconscious of the analysand. In short the passions, rightly understood and intelligently employed, are paths to understanding.

Which brings me directly to Freud's collection of antiquities. It reminds us that his view of the passions was by no means always instrumental. Collecting, as psychoanalysts have taught us, is literally a childish activity. But this does not mean that on Freud's showing it stands condemned; psychoanalysis sees the child as not merely father to the man: the child is, or at least it inhabits, the man. In *Civilization and Its Discontents* (SE, 21), once again applying the archaeological metaphor, Freud illustrated the "problem of preservation in the sphere of the mind" by reminding his readers of Rome, a modern city that still exhibits visible traces of its long and varied past: the antique Roma quadrata, Roma Septimontium, the city of the republic and the empire and of more modern buildings. That is how the mind is, and it would be futile to wish it otherwise.

Collecting stamps, or china—or Greek and Egyptian and Chinese statuettes, for that matter—partakes of, and preserves, early erotic pleasures; Freud, we are told, liked to gaze at the antiquities on his desk as he worked and, at times, moving from looking to touching, would stroke his favorites. But there is more passion to it still: collecting, as anyone who has ever collected can testify, gives power. To possess a complete collection of certain stamp issues or of one's reviews or letters to the editor is, in some intimate fashion, a way of controlling and commanding the world.

Nor, as the following essays leave no doubt, is even this all. Freud wanted to have, to control, to handle, to know, like everyone else, although in world-historical ways even more so than his fellow humans. His antiquities stood for many things in his personal life and, as his comments to the Wolf Man attest, in his work as well. In 1922, declaring himself impatient with his need to earn money, tolerate a contemptible world, and confront his growing old, he told his intimate friend Sándor Ferenczi that "strange secret longings" were rising up in him, "perhaps from the heritage of my ancestors from the Orient and the Mediterranean."[7] His antiquities, many of them from countries he had never visited and many of them originating in the region from which his remote ancestors had come, spoke to him of his Jewishness. It was, that Jewishness, something of a riddle to him: he had grown up as, and remained, a thoroughgoing unbeliever. Without regrets, he lived without a shred of Jewish ritual. Neither he, nor his family, ever attended synagogue; rather, they celebrated Christmas and Easter. And yet, as became more obtrusively obvious to him as he grew older and as anti-Semitism grew more virulent in Germany and Austria, in some fundamental way he was Jewish. The quality of that Jewishness was not yet accessible to psychoanalytic inquiry, although he was confident that some day it would be. Coveting, bargaining for, and contemplating his antiquities did not solve the question for him. They may even have made the enigma more enigmatic. After all, the krater in which his and his wife's ashes rest came from ancient Greece, a gift from Princess Marie Bonaparte, who was not Jewish.

We have not yet penetrated the full meaning of Freud's antiquities for him, although this assembly of objects helps us to make significant strides toward such an understanding. We do know that he enjoyed his collection immensely, and was deeply grateful to those friends and admirers who supplied him with new pieces. These small objects meant much to him, as I have said, and they stood for much in his life. Although sometimes, as we dissect Freud, using his antiquities as so many surgical knives to probe his mysteries, we might remember the sheer pleasure he took in those pieces. Sometimes a statue is just a statue.

NOTES

1. Freud to Minna Bernays, May 14, 1938. Freud Collection, Library of Congress. Trans. by Peter Gay.

2. Ibid., May 23, 1938. Trans. by Peter Gay.

3. Freud to Stefan Zweig, February 7, 1931. *Briefe 1873–1939*, ed. Ernst and Lucie Freud (Frankfurt am Main: S. Fischer, 1960; 2d enlarged ed., 1968), pp. 420–21.

4. Peter Gay, *Freud: A Life for Our Time* (New York: Norton, 1988), p. 171.

5. Hanns Sachs, *Freud, Master and Friend* (London: Imago Publishing, 1945), p. 49.

6. The Wolf Man, "My Recollections of Sigmund Freud," in *The Wolf-Man by the Wolf-Man*, ed. Muriel Gardiner (London: Hogarth Press, 1971), p. 139.

7. Freud to Sándor Ferenczi, March 30, 1922. Freud-Ferenczi Correspondence, Freud Collection, Library of Congress. Trans. by Peter Gay.

Freud in his study, c. 1905, with a reproduction of Michelangelo's *Dying Slave*, probably one of the "plaster copies of Florentine statues" that Freud described in his earliest recorded reference to his art collection (*Freud-Fliess*, December 6, 1896).

THE ORIGINS OF FREUD'S ANTIQUITIES COLLECTION

LYNN GAMWELL

Sigmund Freud was a passionate and well-informed collector of ancient art for over forty years. Freud's study, which contained his famous couch, desk, and library, also housed more than two thousand Egyptian, Greek, Roman, Near Eastern, and Asian objects. He bought primarily sculpture, although he owned some fragments of paintings on plaster, papyrus, and linen, and he eventually collected more than one hundred ancient glass containers and fragments. He concentrated on Egyptian art in particular—it accounts for almost half of his collection—and secondarily on Greek, Roman, and, in his later years, Chinese art.

Freud the collector, like Freud the dreamer, was overdetermined. His antiquities collection is inexhaustibly layered with meanings and associations, surrounded by endless anecdotes. I focus in this essay on the beginnings of Freud's collecting in the 1890s, and discuss three areas of meaning discernible in its origins: its relation to Freud's family, to his colleagues, and to his work. In a climate of anti-Semitism, and in reaction to the death of his father, Freud acquired an idealized image of his father and sought the remote roots of his people, the Jews, in the Near East,[1] and created a new family lineage for himself with these statues from classical, non-Semitic Mediterranean cultures.[2]

Freud's most extreme professional isolation occurred in the 1890s, the years that he began surrounding himself with antiquities. In 1899 he bought a Roman two-faced stone head of Janus, an image used in gates, its contrasting aspects looking both within and without (as Freud himself, in a sense, was beginning to do at this time), and over the years he built up an attentive audience of objects, which included an Egyptian scribe, a Greek goddess of wisdom, and a Chinese sage. Also during this decade Freud conducted his revolutionary self-analysis into unknown areas of the mind. Writing in 1901, he described himself as following the example of archaeologists in aiming "to bring to the light of day after their long burial the priceless though mutilated relics of antiquity" (SE, 7, p. 12). With this collection of antiquities, Freud populated his study with embodiments of the mental fragments from a buried past that he sought to uncover.

Once these early associations were established in the 1890s, the themes of family, colleagues, and work echo throughout the remaining decades of Freud's collecting, even after his relationship to his father was resolved, after he had

Archaeological discoveries captured the imagination of the general public in Vienna; reports of digs appeared in the popular press throughout Freud's lifetime. Here the discovery of Tutankhamun's tomb is sensationalized as "A Conspiracy Uncovered in a Grave," *Illustrierte Kronen-Zeitung*, Vienna, March 8, 1923. (Photo: Österreichisches Nationalbibliothek, Vienna)

found real colleagues, and after the realm of the unconscious had become familiar territory to him.

Freud's life spans the development of modern archaeology. When he was born in 1856, Troy was a myth, and looting ancient treasures was a profitable business; at the end of his life, in 1939, archaeology was a science, and national archaeological museums had been established in many ancient cities, including Cairo and Athens. Earlier in the nineteenth century, geologists had begun to employ stratigraphy as a dating method, and Darwin's publication of *Origin of Species*, in 1859, permitted the assumption that man has a long history.

Heinrich Schliemann's first major finds at Troy date to 1873, when Freud was an eighteen-year-old student. The legendary labyrinth of Minos was excavated on the island of Crete in 1900, the year Freud published *The Interpretation of Dreams*, when he was forty-four, and Tutankhamun's tomb was discovered in the Valley of the Kings in 1922, when Freud was sixty-six. These discoveries and others were widely reported in European newspapers; reports focused on issues that were rather trivial from an archaeological viewpoint, such as the value of the finds and disputes over their ownership. In Vienna, Freud was a daily reader of *Neue Freie Presse*, the city's most famous and liberal paper, which was unillustrated at the time of the excavations at Troy and Crete.[3] By the 1920s, when Tutankhamun's tomb was discovered, lithographs were widely used in the popular press, especially in more sensationalist papers such as *Illustrierte Kronen-Zeitung*, which dramatized the find with the headline "A Conspiracy Uncovered in a Grave." Freud first read a scholarly and well-illustrated account of an archaeological excavation in 1899, when he purchased *Ilios*, Schliemann's book on Troy.[4] Freud built an impressive archaeological library, and through his reading he became a well-informed collector (see Appendix, p. 184).

The market for antiquities changed greatly during the forty years of Freud's collecting. Simply put, in the nineteenth century antiquities traveled easily out of Egypt and Greece to European markets, but by World War I, these countries had placed increasing restrictions on the export of antiquities, in a belated attempt to retain their national treasures.[5] The European market for Chinese antiquities developed quickly in the political turmoil and grave robbing that followed the revolution of 1912, which opened China's doors to the West.[6]

The great European museum collections of antiquities were formed largely in the nineteenth century, and Freud saw several of them in the formative days of his collecting: the Kunsthistorisches Museum in Vienna, which he knew from his youth, has one of the largest and most important Egyptian and classical collections in Europe; the Louvre in Paris, whose vast ancient holdings include the *Venus de Milo* and the *Victory of Samothrace* (Freud visited Paris in 1885);[7] the Royal Museum in Berlin, which contains the Altar of Zeus from Pergamum.[8]

When we look at a private collection such as Freud's, it seems natural to assume that it belonged to someone of great wealth because these objects are so expensive today; one wonders how Freud could have afforded such a collection when he was supporting a wife, six children, and several relatives on a salary earned by treating private patients by means of a highly experimental method.

In fact, prices were low. Freud was buying in a relatively unrestricted market, and he was collecting art objects that were unfashionable, particularly in Vienna, where Baroque and Biedermeier were in vogue.[9] On the difficult topic of comparing values over time, we can be helped by Robert Lustig, the Viennese dealer who sold Freud several hundred objects from the mid-1920s to 1938, and then emigrated to New York, where he ran an antiquities dealership on Madison Avenue for about twenty-five years. According to Lustig, Greek vases could be purchased in Vienna in the 1920s for the equivalent of two hundred dollars, not five to ten thousand dollars, as they are now priced.[10]

Freud's bronze *Isis Suckling the Infant Horus* (p. 53) provides a good example of how undervalued antiquities were in Freud's lifetime, and how much their monetary and aesthetic values have appreciated over the years. Lustig found Freud's *Isis Suckling Horus* on the floor of a second-hand shop in the countryside near Vienna in the early 1930s. When he asked the price, the shop owner put the statue on a scale to weigh it, and Lustig bought it for the price of the metal.[11] Comparable Egyptian bronzes of Isis and the infant sold at auction at Sotheby's for £7 in 1899, but brought £1750 in 1987.[12]

Freud was also careful with money and a good bargainer, and he regularly set aside small amounts of extra income for his collection.[13] In a 1910 exchange with Sándor Ferenczi, his colleague in Budapest and also a collector, we find Freud's pursuit of several objects is tempered by his prudence.[14] Later in life, after his children had grown and his income was more secure, Freud continued to be conscientious about obtaining objects of quality and not overspending.[15] His careful economy, shrewd bargaining, and knowledge of what he was buying made Freud a formidable collector on a practical level.

The lack of restrictions in the antiquities market kept prices low, but also permitted forgeries to enter it easily. Freud wanted to possess original objects, in much the same spirit that he wanted to uncover the most undistorted childhood memories of his patients. He regularly had objects authenticated by local antiquities experts. For example, Dr. Julius Banko, director of the antiquities collection of the Vienna Kunsthistorisches Museum, authenticated Freud's red-figured hydria depicting Oedipus and the Sphinx (p. 95). If Freud discovered he had a fake, he got rid of it.[16] Unavoidably, some forgeries have survived in his collection, but they are few in number and include several that were authenticated by the Kunsthistorisches Museum in Freud's lifetime.[17] This is hardly surprising, as standards of authenticity and dating technology have changed over the decades.

While Freud avoided forgeries, he was comfortable with acknowledged reproductions. Over the years he bought reproductions of the marble relief *Gradiva* and of Ingres's *Oedipus and the Sphinx*. But it is worth emphasizing that Freud wanted to own authentic antiquities, which were the core of his collection.

Freud acquired his first art objects in December of 1896, two months after his father's death. To consider that he began his collection in some sense as a reaction to his father's death seems unavoidable;[18] not only the timing but also the content of Freud's early collecting suggests its strong connection with the loss of his father.

It is clear that Freud showed interest in and had the opportunity to collect in

Robert Lustig sold Freud several hundred antiquities between the mid-1920s and 1938. In this photograph from the late 1920s, Lustig stands in front of his shop on Wieblinger Strasse in Vienna, located less than a mile from Berggasse 19. (Photo: Courtesy Robert Lustig)

Freud regularly had his new acquisitions authenticated by local experts. Dr. Julius Banko, director of the antiquities collection of the Vienna Kunsthistorisches Museum, in July of 1923 wrote this authentication document for Freud's Athenian red-figured hydria (p. 95), which depicts Oedipus and the Sphinx. (Photo: Freud Museum)

the years before his father's death. In 1885, on his first trip to Paris, the twenty-nine-year-old Freud had been impressed that the home of his mentor, French psychiatrist Jean Martin Charcot, who collected Indian and Chinese antiquities, was "in short, a museum," and that the Louvre's collection of Egyptian and Near Eastern antiquities created "a dreamlike world."[19] Freud had also begun, by the mid-1890s, to use an analogy with archaeology to describe his new therapeutic procedure.[20] Granted, Freud lived in poverty during his student days, and remained poor during the early years of his marriage, but his first purchases—plaster casts and prints after Old Master works—were extremely inexpensive. When he bought his first art object in 1896, he had long since furnished a home and office; he had been married for ten years and had lived at Berggasse 19 for five. It is important, however, to keep in mind one additional element in the timing of Freud's first acquisitions. Inexpensive as these purchases were, Freud could better afford them after his father's death, when he no longer bore the financial burden of paying for his father's upkeep.[21]

During the period that his father's health failed, in the summer of 1896, Freud made his first trip to Florence.[22] Two months after Jacob Freud's death in October 1896, Freud described several artworks, which seem to be his first acquisitions, in a letter to Wilhelm Fliess: "I have decorated my study with plaster copies of Florentine statues. They were a source of exceptional renewal and comfort for me. I am thinking of getting rich in order to be able to repeat these trips. A congress on Italian soil! (Naples, Pompeii)."[23]

In this first known written reference to his art collection, Freud tells us what these objects meant to him: they were a source of exceptional "renewal"—*Erquickung* in German, or, alternately translated "refreshment," "invigoration," with a sense of "enlivenment" and "potency."[24] The word also has the overtone of "comfort,"[25] suggesting the dual reaction of release (exhilaration) and sadness (in need of comfort) that survivors often feel after death has ended the suffering of a loved one. Thus, Freud's first acquisitions brought him both renewal and comfort during his grieving, and filled his study with a sense of life in the face of death.

A clue to the identification of the "plaster copies of Florentine statues" can be seen in a photograph of Freud, taken around 1905, in his ground-floor study at Berggasse 19, in which a reproduction of Michelangelo's *Dying Slave* appears in the background (see p. 20).[26] No other known photograph of this study, which Freud used from 1891 to 1907, shows any art objects. *The Dying Slave* was probably one of the reproductions purchased in 1896 (Freud certainly wouldn't have bought more than a few such large casts to decorate his study), and these casts most likely were not moved when Freud transferred his study to the second floor in 1907: no Florentine statues appear in photos of the second-floor study, and by 1907 Freud was buying only original statues and acquiring works from only the very beginnings of the classical period.[27]

The Dying Slave is a "Florentine statue" in the sense that it is by a Florentine artist, although the original was executed in Rome. Freud would have seen it in the Louvre in 1885, eleven years before he began collecting. Freud's purchase of this reproduction in Vienna relates less to his recent trip to Florence and more to his father's death—the father who was enslaved by anti-Semitism, the coward who didn't fight back when insulted.[28] Freud's disappointment in his father was mixed with his childhood love of this gentle and generous parent. The slave in Michelangelo's construction is highly idealized, a beautiful, perfect, even hedonistic and voluptuous man, who is depicted as dying peacefully, as if going to sleep. Originally made for the tomb of Pope Julius II as a symbol of the arts,[29] this image has an aura of the culture that Freud would have given the ideal father who (unlike Jacob Freud) would have known classical literature and the arts.

Michelangelo increased the psychological tension already present in this complex symbol of death/enslavement/perfection by carving behind the slave the crouching figure of a primitive ape. He holds what appears to be a mirror, usually interpreted to refer to the classical aphorism "Ars simia naturae" (art imitates [apes] nature).[30] Working in the late nineteenth-century scientific climate created by Darwin, and in the decade of his own self-analysis, Freud may have seen in this ape, who lurks behind an ideal of humanity, new meaning for the prehistory of man and his primitive unconscious.

One cannot help but wonder what were the other "copies of Florentine statues" Freud purchased in December of 1896. Could one have been Michelangelo's *David*, the most famous and reproduced statue in Florence? As a companion to *The Dying Slave*, *David* would relate symbolically, and perhaps oedipally, to Freud himself. David was a writer (of the Psalms) and a man of humble birth who became a king; as a young Israelite, he became a hero by fearlessly slaying the Philistine giant Goliath. "Philistine" has the same connotation in German (*Philister*) and English—a common person indifferent to cultural values.

Although it seems that the Florentine statues were not moved upstairs to the

Ape carved at the base of Michelangelo's *Dying Slave* (detail). (Photo: Giraudon/Art Resource)

A color print of the rock-cut temple at Abu Simbel hung over the couch in Freud's study in Vienna. Based on a 1906 gouache by Ernst Koemer, the print was published the following year. (Photos: © Edmund Engelman; Freud Museum)

new study in 1907, Freud did acquire another prominent "father symbol" for the second-floor office, one that remained with him the rest of his life. Over the analytic couch, Freud hung a large print of the colossal Egyptian temple of Ramesses II, *The Rock-cut Temple at Abu Simbel.* [31] With his sensitivity to word associations, Freud may have appreciated the closeness of Abu to *abi*, the Hebrew word meaning 'my father,' and Simbel to the German (and English) *Symbol.* [32] If, indeed, Freud found Ramesses II, a heroic military leader and sponsor of the arts in 19th-Dynasty Egypt, a suitable "father symbol," then Abu Simbel, his colossal temple with passages deep into Mother Earth, loomed as an idealized heroic presence of Freud's Jewish-German father over his son's revolutionary couch.

At the time of Jacob Freud's death, Sigmund explicitly stated that the loss had affected him deeply. [33] Twelve years later, he wrote that he had come to realize, moreover, that this loss had prompted him to write *The Interpretation of Dreams* (1900) as part of his self-analysis (SE, 4, p. xxvi). I suggest that in addition to discovering the analytic method and writing this fundamental psychoanalytic text in the late 1890s, Freud also began collecting in response to the death of his father—first by placing an idealized statue of his father in his study, then by adding other statues from a learned and classical ancestry. [34]

In addition to Freud's struggles against anti-Semitism and his experience of the death of his father, the 1890s were years of professional isolation for him. His Jewish heritage and poverty had prevented him from having a university career in pure research, and his radical theories had alienated other neurologists. (Freud's strong attachment to Wilhelm Fliess during these years is evidence of how desperate he was for intellectual companionship.) That Freud's collection also functioned, in part, as surrogate colleagues for him is revealed in Freud's first mention of his collection in the December 1896 letter to Fliess (above, p. 24). From describing the exceptional renewal he received from the statues, Freud free-associated to wanting to meet Fliess in Italy for a "congress," in other words, for discussion and companionship.

Looking through a doorway in Freud's Vienna
consulting room, into his study, 1938.
(Photo: © Edmund Engelman)

Freud's selection and placement of his antiquities also point to their role as
audience. Almost every object Freud acquired is a figure whose gaze creates a conscious presence, and his collection is predominantly sculpture, which by its
nature has a more physical presence than painting. In describing the stone Janus
head acquired in 1899, Freud emphasized its human presence: "It looks at me
with two faces in a very superior manner."[35]

Throughout many years of collecting, Freud frequently rearranged his antiquities, but they were always located only within his study and consultation rooms,
never in his living quarters. These hundreds of human and animal figures all
faced him like a huge audience—from his desk, from cabinets, from across the
room. Freud chose in particular to confront many figures of scholars, wise men,
and scribes; some were always on his desk. He wrote thousands of manuscript
pages facing Imhotep, the Egyptian architect who, in late antiquity, was revered
as a healer. Freud's desk was also the home of the baboon of Thoth, the Egyptian
god of the moon, wisdom, and learning (p. 57), and of a Chinese sage. Several
accounts reveal that Freud treated these figures as his companions. He was in the
habit of stroking the marble baboon, as he did his pet chows, and of greeting the
Chinese sage every morning.[36]

Freud selected a bronze statue of Athena (p. 110), goddess of war, patron of the
arts, and personification of wisdom, to stand in the very center of the antiquities
on his desk.[37] Behind Athena, Freud placed a Chinese table screen (p. 129),
which would have been found on a Chinese scholar's desk along with other
objects—carved jade mountains and unusual stones—to stimulate philosophical
meditation or to inspire poetry and painting. Intended to encourage escape from
the mundane world, these meditative objects are almost exclusively unpeopled.
Freud's central focus on the human psyche, evident throughout his antiquities
collection by the predominance of human and animal forms, may have led him to
choose this unusual screen depicting a figure.

Freud's desk in Vienna, his antiquities arranged like an audience, 1938. (Photo: © Edmund Engelman)

Even after Freud's theories had gained adherents, the new psychoanalytic societies suffered from defections. Freud worked throughout his life to establish an international professional society in the face of petty disputes and professional jealousies among his followers. [38] The beleaguered founder of psychoanalysis always returned to his desk and to his dependable, silent audience, which represented for him the wisdom of the ages.

Freud first used the analogy of archaeology and psychoanalysis in the mid-1890s. Describing the case of Elisabeth von R., which he began at the end of 1892, Freud wrote:

> In this, the first complete analysis of hysteria which I undertook, I arrived at a procedure which I later elevated to a method and deliberately employed: the procedure of clearing away, layer by layer, the pathogenic psychical material, which we like to compare with the technique of excavating a buried city. (SE, 2, p. 134)

In addition to being surrogate ancestors and colleagues, the antiquities seem to have held a third meaning for Freud, that of embodying the suppressed memories he was just beginning to uncover in the 1890s. As Donald Kuspit suggests (below, pp. 133ff), the retrieved memory is like the unearthed ancient object, a metaphor Freud hints at in this comment and goes on to state explicitly in later case histories such as those of Dora (SE, 7, p. 12) and the Rat Man (SE, 10, pp. 176–77).

Surrounding himself with ancient objects in the late 1890s gave Freud a physical reassurance of the reality of the illusory, distorted, and ephemeral memories that constituted his primary data as a scientist. Returning to Freud's first recorded mention of his collection in 1896, there is another sense in which these objects from a past culture brought him *Erquickung*, a sense of life and power. Their survival was proof of a theory analogous to his own. Describing his self-analysis in 1899, Freud wrote: "I hardly dare to believe it yet. It is as if Schliemann had again dug up Troy, which had hitherto been deemed a fable."[39]

Most discussions of Freud the collector end with the postscript that Freud's ashes were placed in a Greek vase, implying that this was somehow a finale to Freud's collecting. However, there is no evidence that Freud initiated this memorial; it seems, rather, to have been a commemorative gesture arranged by Freud's family after his death.[40]

I will end instead with the moment of Freud's death. After a long illness, Freud chose to die in his study, around him his famous couch, the desk at which he had created a new theory of the mind, his library, and his lifelong collection of fragments from a buried past: his ancestors of choice, his most faithful colleagues, and the embodiments of his excavated truths of psychoanalysis.

NOTES

1. See Peter Gay, *Freud: A Life for Our Time* (New York: Norton, 1988), p. 172.

2. Discussed by Spitz, below, pp. 157–58.

3. Gay, *Freud: A Life*, p. 17. An article in *Neue Freie Presse* of July 17, 1874, reports a dispute between the Greek and Turkish governments over ownership of the relics excavated by Schliemann. Reports on the discoveries at Troy also appeared in Vienna's *Die Presse*, May 7 and July 17, 1874. My thanks to Christa Bader, Österreichisches Nationalbibliothek, Vienna, for her help in finding these and other archaeological references that appeared in the Viennese press during Freud's lifetime.

4. *The Complete Letters of Sigmund Freud to Wilhelm Fliess 1887–1904*, ed. and trans. Jeffrey M. Masson (Cambridge: Harvard University Press, 1985), May 28, 1899, p. 353 (cited hereafter as *Freud-Fliess*).

5. See, for example, Brian Fagan, *The Rape of the Nile: Tomb Robbers, Tourists and Archaeologists in Egypt* (New York: Charles Scribner's Sons, 1975), parts II and III.

6. See Jan Fontein and Wu Tung, *Unearthing China's Past* (Boston: Museum of Fine Arts, 1973), p. 16.

7. Gay, *Freud: A Life*, p. 47.

8. Ernest Jones, *The Life and Work of Sigmund Freud*, vol. 1 (New York: Basic Books, 1953), p. 189.

9. Several hundred dealers in Vienna in the 1920s and 1930s sold primarily artworks of the Renaissance, Baroque, and Biedermeier. They might handle an ancient piece as part of a larger lot or estate, but only about five dealers sold ancient antiquities exclusively (interviews with Robert Lustig, Viennese antiquities dealer, September 5, 1988, and Ruth Blumka, widow of the Viennese Renaissance and Baroque dealer Leopold Blumka, October 21, 1988). Fifty-two private collections are listed in a 1908 inventory of the artistic resources of Vienna. Only three are collections of antiquities; the remaining forty-nine are largely Renaissance, Baroque, and Biedermeier. See *Österreichisches Kunsttopographie* (Vienna: Anton Schroll, 1908), vol. 2, *Die Denkmale der Stadt Wien*, pp. 525 and 532. (This survey covered eleven of twenty-one districts in Vienna; an inventory of the remaining districts, one of which included Freud's residence, was apparently never completed because it was not published in this twenty-four-volume study of Austrian art.)

10. Interview with Lustig, September 5, 1988.

11. Ibid.

12. *Isis with Harpocrates*, bronze, 11 in. high, object 242, Sotheby's, London, auction catalogue for June 20, 1899, p. 38, price written in the margin of the copy at the Wilbour Library of Egyptology, Brooklyn Museum; *Isis and Horus*, bronze, 11 in. high, 26th Dynasty (664–525 B.C.), lot 306, Sotheby's, London, auction catalogue for May 18, 1987, prices printed in the catalogue: suggested price £1500–2000; actual auction sale £1750.

13. Jones, *Life and Work*, vol. 2 (1955), pp. 389–90.

14. Throughout 1910, Freud and Ferenczi corresponded about a minor excavation at Duna-Pentele in central Hungary, from which Ferenczi regularly got objects through a local dealer, whom he called their "treasure hunter." This impoverished inhabitant had turned entrepreneur after a Roman cemetery was discovered buried beneath local farmlands. The collectors shared the spirit of searching out quality at a good price. Their correspondence alludes to "5 clay lamps (for 1 gulden) and a small bronze vessel ... also for 1 Fl."; Ferenczi says it is supposed to be a Bronze Age piece (February 16, 1910). On February 25, 1910, he writes to Freud about "some minor objects for 20

krone... a string of beads is inside the bronze vessel, the ring is in an envelope...." He goes on to ask Freud how he feels about some "warlike objects," recently excavated belts, "Roman with gold ornamentation," at prices of 60, 100, and 150 krone. On March 3, 1910, Freud expresses his general satisfaction with the lamps and beads, not minding the price "if we please the poor fellow," but states he will not accept the expensive belts without seeing them first (Freud-Ferenczi correspondence, typewritten transcription, Freud Museum; trans. by Lynn Gamwell).

15. In a letter to Max Eitingon on February 16, 1927, after describing being fitted for a new prosthesis after oral surgery, Freud, perhaps self-conscious about exceeding his usual budget, writes: "I got myself an expensive present today, a lovely little dipylon vase—a real gem—to fight my ill humor. (Spending money is indicated not only for states of fear.)" (Freud-Eitingon correspondence, typewritten transcription, Freud Museum; trans. by Lynn Gamwell). The reference is probably to the Mycenaean stirrup jar, p. 80.

16. Freud took most of his antiquities to the Vienna Kunsthistorisches Museum for authentication. He carefully kept authentication documents for objects in the collection in his desk and bookcase; documents for thirty-six objects are preserved today at the Freud Museum. They were prepared by Dr. Julius Banko, director of the antiquities collection, in the 1920s and by Dr. Hans Demel, director of the Egyptian and Oriental collections, in the 1920s and 1930s. Both Banko and Demel authenticated objects for private dealers who sold to Freud (Frederick Glueckselig and Robert Lustig). If Freud ever discovered he owned a forgery, he gave it away, according to Robert Lustig (interview, September 5, 1988).

Lustig tells a story that illustrates some of the problems surrounding the authentication of art objects: Freud asked Lustig to get an Egyptian stone head appraised before he bought it. Lustig took it to Demel, who told him "It's a fake; don't sell it." The next day a stranger came to Lustig's shop looking for an inexpensive replica to buy; Lustig sold him the stone head. According to Lustig, several months later the stone head appeared in a Christie's auction catalogue; he added ruefully, "He stole it from me!" (interview, September 5, 1988).

There is a reference to Demel in Freud's chronicle in November 1936, which seems to record an appointment and thus confirms that the two men met to discuss the antiquities (*Kürzeste Chronik*, ed. Michael Molnar, forthcoming.) Demel is also the expert who undervalued Freud's collection in 1938, in order to reduce Freud's total assets, on which the Nazis calculated a 25 percent refugee tax. Freud had to pay this tax before he was permitted to take his household belongings, library, and antiquities collection out of Austria (Freud to Minna Bernays, May 23, 1938, Freud Collection, Library of Congress).

17. For example, Freud owned several Egyptian wooden objects, including a large boat, a group of farmers, and a standing falcon-headed figure, which Lustig bought from an Egyptian "pasha" who had married a Viennese woman and settled in Vienna. Lustig had them authenticated at the Kunsthistorisches Museum, as he did most objects before bringing them to Freud (interview, September 5, 1988). The authenticity of these wooden objects has recently been cast in doubt by experts at the British Museum. See C. Nicholas Reeves's catalogue entry, p. 58.

18. It was mentioned by Suzanne Cassirer Bernfeld in her 1951 article on Freud's collecting and his relation to antiquity, "Freud and Archaeology," *American Imago* 8:2 (1951), 127.

19. Freud expressed these ideas to Martha Bernays, writing from Paris on October 19, 1885, and January 20, 1886, in Ernst Freud, ed., *The Letters of Sigmund Freud*, trans. Tania and James Stern (New York: Basic Books, 1960), pp. 174 and 194.

20. The analogy appears in *Studies of Hysteria* (1893–95), the case history of Elisabeth von R. (SE, 2, p. 139). For a slightly later example, see Freud's preface to the Dora case of 1901 (SE, 7, p. 12).

21. An observation made by Peter Gay (personal communication, February 13, 1989).

22. Freud's biographers differ as to whether Freud actually made this trip. According to Jones, Freud spent a week in Florence in the summer of 1896 as part of "the longest holiday Freud had yet taken; he was away from Vienna for two months" (*Life and Work*, vol. 1, p. 333; as in n. 8), whereas Gay makes the reasonable point that Freud did not want to vacation too far from Vienna because his father was gravely ill, and that he took a "brief holiday" (*Freud: A Life*, p. 88). In Freud's letters, in July, he cancels a two-day trip to Berlin because his father was so ill (*Freud-Fliess*, July 15, 1896, p. 194), but then in December, after his father's death, he suggests that he has made a recent trip to Italy, which he wants to repeat (*Freud-Fliess*, December 6, 1896, p. 214). Peter Gay has conjectured that if indeed Freud did make this trip to Florence, it may have been because he thought his father might live somewhat longer after all (personal communication, September 30, 1988). In any case, Freud relied on telegrams to keep in touch whenever he was away, and he could have returned to Vienna overnight, were his father dying. In the end, Freud's somewhat inconsistent behavior—canceling one trip, then taking an even longer one—may not require more explanation

than to remember his own descriptions of his conflicted feelings toward his dying parent (*Freud-Fliess*, November 2, 1896, p. 202; Freud, "A Disturbance of Memory on the Acropolis," SE, 22, pp. 239–48).

23. Jeffrey M. Masson, ed., *Briefe an Wilhelm Fliess 1887–1904* (Frankfurt am Main: S. Fischer, 1986), December 6, 1896, p. 226; trans. by Lynn Gamwell.

24. Translations respectively by Peter Gay, *Freud: A Life*, p. 171 (as in n. 1), and by Jeffrey M. Masson, *Freud-Fliess*, p. 214 (as in n. 4), which give the sense of bringing life but miss the overtone of "comfort."

25. "Comfort" is given as a translation of *Erquickung* in a 1958 edition of *Cassell's German Dictionary*. *Erquickung* also suggests "life" as opposed to death, as does the German adjective *quick*, meaning "lively." The German *Erquickung* and *quick* share an etymological root with the English noun "quick," meaning "the living," as in "the quick and the dead."

26. The date and location of this photograph are not entirely clear. I date it to about 1905 by comparison with other photographs of Freud, noting the amount of gray in his hair, his hairline, and the cut of his beard: in *Sigmund Freud: His Life in Pictures and Words*, Ernst Freud, Lucie Freud, and Ilse Grubrich-Simitis, eds. (New York: Norton, 1978); see illus. 186 (about 1905), illus. 181 (about 1906), and illus. 193 (about 1906). The latter was used as the model for a medallion made by K. M. Schwerdtner for Freud's fiftieth birthday (1906). Assuming this date, the location would have to be Freud's ground-floor study. Martin Freud corroborates the location in his book *Glory Reflected* (London: Angus and Robertson, 1957), where he captions this photo, "My first snapshot of father in his study" (p. 24). My thanks to Inge Scholz-Strasser, secretary general of the Sigmund Freud Haus in Vienna, who after consultation with its director, Harold Leupold-Löwenthal, confirmed this date and location, again on the basis of Freud's appearance.

Confusion surrounding the date of this photograph may stem from the original prints of it, which are in the Freud Museum. There are three; two are undated, and on one is written "1905," which is crossed out, and then "1914?" in a hand other than Freud's.

This photograph is reproduced in *Sigmund Freud: His Life in Pictures and Words* (illus. 217) as being from "about 1912," with the caption "On the verandah of his home in the Berggasse, taken by one of his sons." This doesn't ring true, because this structure in 1912 was off the living room, and Freud didn't put his antiquities in the family living quarters. The photo could have been taken on a veranda in about 1905, however, because Freud's ground-floor study, located directly below the living room with attached veranda, also had one. We know from the credits listed in this publication that the caption of the photograph was written in cooperation with Freud's late son Ernst. The copyright on the photograph is held by Sigmund Freud Copyrights in London; they have no record of the origin of this dating or caption (personal communication with Tom Roberts, Sigmund Freud Copyrights, November, 1988).

27. In 1907 Freud added the following parapraxis to *The Psychopathology of Everyday Life* (1901): "There is one misreading which I find irritating and laughable and to which I am prone whenever I walk through the streets of a strange town on my holidays. On these occasions I read every shop sign that resembles the word in any way as 'Antiquities.' This betrays the questing spirit of the collector" (SE, 6, p. 110). It also betrays that between first publishing this book in 1901 and adding this observation in 1907, Freud had significantly increased his visits to dealers of original antiquities and would have been more prone to this parapraxis.

Hanging on the wall of Freud's study, as seen in the c. 1905 photograph of Freud with the reproduction of Michelangelo's *The Dying Slave*, is a second reproduction: Masaccio and Masolino's *The Healing of Aeneas* and *The Raising of Tabitha* from the Brancacci Chapel in Florence. This photograph or print after the fresco, whose subject no doubt appealed to Freud the physician, is further evidence that Freud began collecting Renaissance reproductions, and then shifted to acquiring original ancient works after around 1905. The five small tablets hanging on the wall in a vertical row on the left, and the single tablet in the upper right, are as yet unidentified.

28. Freud recounted an episode from his childhood in which his father didn't stand up against an anti-Semitic insult (see Gay, *Freud: A Life*, pp. 11–12); Freud's response to this episode is discussed by Spitz, below, pp. 156–57.

29. See Howard Hibbard, *Michelangelo* (New York: Penguin, 1975), pp. 151–52.

30. Ibid.

31. This print was published in 1907, which adds to the likelihood that Freud purchased it when he moved into his new study in this same year.

Freud owned about fifty prints, many of which depict archaeological sites, including an intaglio map of ancient Rome, an eighteenth-century etching by Piranesi from the *Veduti di Roma*, and a nineteenth-century engraving of the Acropolis at Athens.

32. This was noticed by Henry G. Fischer in "The Abu Symbol," *Psychoanalytic Quarterly* 35:4 (1966), 591. The origin of the name "Abu Simbel" for this funerary monument is not clear. My thanks to Richard Fazzini, curator of Egyptian, Classical, and Ancient Middle Eastern Art, The Brooklyn Museum, for this reference.

33. In a letter to Fliess, November 2, 1896, *Freud-Fliess*, p. 202.

34. An "ancestry of choice"; see Spitz, below, p. 157.

35. *Freud-Fliess*, July 17, 1899, p. 361.

36. According to Freud's maid Paula, who is cited by Jack Spector in *The Aesthetics of Freud* (New York: Praeger, 1972), p. 15. (The Chinese sage was later found not to be an antique Chinese work.)

37. See Bergmann, below, pp. 178–79, where this figure's role in Freud's work is discussed. After the Nazi occupation of Austria in 1938, Freud was informed that he and his family would be allowed to leave the country, but the fate of his antiquities collection and library remained uncertain for some time. During this period his friend Marie Bonaparte visited, and Freud asked her to smuggle the tiny figure of Athena out of Austria because it was his favorite piece and symbolized the whole collection to him (Jones, *Life and Work*, vol. 3 (1957), p. 228; as in n. 8).

38. See especially Gay, *Freud: A Life*, chap. 4, "Sketch of an Embattled Founder," and chap. 5, "Psychoanalytic Politics."

39. *Freud-Fliess*, December 21, 1899, pp. 391–92.

40. The origin of the idea that Freud's ashes were placed in this vase at his request is probably his letter to Marie Bonaparte thanking her for the gift of the vase in 1931: "I was very happy with it … and I can even muster some regrets that none of the beautiful urns will accompany me to my grave." Quoted in Max Schur, *Freud: Living and Dying* (London: Hogarth Press, n.d.), p. 429. This is only a whimsical expression; there is no evidence of such a request being made by Freud, for example, in his will, which makes no reference to funeral arrangements. Also, in the approximately one hundred obituary notices and descriptions of the funeral published within several months after Freud's death (preserved in the Library of Congress and the Freud Museum), the cremation of Freud's body is mentioned repeatedly but not the disposition of the ashes. Specifically, Marie Bonaparte does not mention this in her obituary published in *Marianne*, October 4, 1939. All this indicates that the ashes were placed in the vase considerably after Freud's death, an arrangement made by his family. Freud's son Ernst, an architect, designed the plinth on which the vase rests.

    The vase that holds Freud's ashes is a red-figured bell krater with a Dionysiac scene, including a kantharos (high-handled drinking cup) and a bunch of grapes, the attribute of the wine god. Although this vase type and subject are not commonly associated with burial in Greek culture, there is some evidence to suggest that for the Greeks of southern Italy in the fourth century B.C., Dionysos was worshiped primarily as a god of the underworld and the afterlife; this made Dionysiac scenes exceedingly appropriate decoration for vases designed to be placed in the grave (personal communication with Lucilla Burn, November 7, 1988).

SELECTIONS
FROM THE
COLLECTION

CONTRIBUTORS

LB   Lucilla Burn, Department of Greek and Roman Antiquities, The British Museum

DC   Dominique Collon, Department of Western Asiatic Antiquities, The British Museum

JP   Jane Portal, Department of Oriental Antiquities, The British Museum

JT   Jonathan Tubb, Department of Western Asiatic Antiquities, The British Museum

JDR   J. D. Ray, Faculty of Oriental Studies, Cambridge University

CNR   C. Nicholas Reeves, Department of Egyptian Antiquities, The British Museum

FM   Material relating individual objects to Freud's thought has been gathered from research in progress conducted at the Freud Museum by researchers including J. Keith Davies, Michael Münchow, and Richard Wells, with contributions by Ellen Handler Spitz.

CYLINDER SEAL

Mesopotamian, Sumerian (Early Dynastic III), c. 2500 B.C.
Stone, 1 1/8 × 1/2 in. (3 × 1.4 cm)
4242

Cylinder seals were developed in southern Mesopotamia (now Iraq) and southwestern Iran in the second half of the fourth millennium B.C. They replaced stamp seals as a means of marking ownership and authenticating documents because they were better able to cover large areas of clay used for sealing jars, bales of textiles, and other goods being stored or transported in large quantities. Also during this time extensive trade networks were developed, and a system of recording transactions was finally perfected—namely, the earliest known writing in a pictographic script on clay tablets.

The design on this Early Dynastic seal is arranged in two registers without a divider. Above, two long-horned quadrupeds, advancing toward the left, are followed by a lion whose tail is being grasped by a figure. This is probably a scene of animal husbandry in which a shepherd in a tufted skirt protects his flock from a predator. Lions roamed northern and eastern Iraq, and the protection of flocks, a duty assumed by the leader of each community, was frequently depicted. The most famous examples show the Assyrian kings, as shepherds of their people, engaged in lion hunts whose meaning had become purely symbolic.

The scene on the lower register is probably an agricultural ceremony. The two long-haired figures appear to be female. The seated one is either a vegetation goddess or a priestess representing her. A male attendant stands behind her and seems to be dressing her hair. The object she holds may be a plough, but it could equally be a sledge used for threshing. The scene before the seated figure may be interpreted as two figures emptying a sack onto a pile of (perhaps) grain, while a third approaches with a sack on his head. The priestess on the left seems to supervise. All the figures wear tufted skirts.

Similar scenes occur at this period on numerous seals from central Iraq and the Diyala region farther east. Often the seated figure wears a horned headdress, which was then beginning to be used to identify deities. In some cases the figures seem to be building a tiered structure reminiscent of later ziggurats, but the earliest known ziggurat is some four hundred years later. The more likely explanation is that this is one of the many agrarian festivals that took place in ancient Mesopotamia. —DC

See P. Amiet, *Glyptique mésopotamienne archaïque* (Paris, 1980), nos. 1441–69, 1482–85, especially nos. 1441 and 1463, from Tell Asmar and Ischali in the Diyala region northeast of Baghdad; for a discussion see pp. 181–86.

CYLINDER SEAL

Old Babylonian, c. 19th–18th century B.C.
Hematite, 1 × ½ in. (2.6 × 1.5 cm)
4243

The nineteenth and eighteenth centuries B.C., a period that culminated in the reign of Hammurabi (1793–1750 B.C.), saw a tremendous increase in legal, administrative, and scribal activity. More people than ever before required seals so that they could witness contracts or seal their goods and storerooms. The most commonly used seal material was hematite, a hard, fine-grained iron oxide stone. The designs on the best of these seals are remarkably consistent and depict a limited range of figures which could be combined according to certain rigid conventions.

The bearded sun god, as god of justice and omens, was frequently depicted. With his saw-toothed blade he cuts his way through the mountains of the east at dawn; generally he rests one foot on a mountain, but occasionally, as here, his attribute animal, the human-headed bull (probably a bison), is depicted instead. Before him stands a stereotyped representation of the king in ceremonial robes, holding an animal offering (probably for divination) and raising one hand. Above them are the combined symbols of the main astral bodies—sun disk, star, and crescent moon. Behind the god stands a kilted priest who has shaved his head except for a forelock. He holds a cup and a small footed bucket, and he stands on a dais, probably indicating that the scene is taking place in a temple. The suppliant goddess stands with both hands raised and intercedes before the god on behalf of the owner of the seal. The horned headdresses indicate that their wearers are deities. The king wears a round cap with a broad brim or turban, and he and the god

wear open robes to allow freedom of movement. The king's robe has a decorated border and is draped over one shoulder, whereas the god's is a pleated skirt. The goddess wears a tiered, pleated garment.

There was once an inscription in cuneiform running from the top to the bottom of the seal. The inscription was erased, perhaps by a new owner, but traces of the frame survive. Since this inscription had only two lines instead of the more common three, it is probable that it contained the names of two deities rather than the name and patronymic of the owner. The fine quality of this seal indicates that it probably came from the neighborhood of the capital city, Babylon.

Because seals were meant to be rolled out on clay, their designs and inscriptions were generally cut in reverse. The correct way of viewing the design is on the impression; it is the seal impression that is generally described in catalogues of cylinder seals. In the case of this seal, an impression was made of the impression, so that the scene is in fact back to front. Freud's collection contains about twenty cylinder seals from the ancient Near East, and he enjoyed making clay impressions of them himself.

—DC

For similar seals, see D. Collon, *Catalogue of Western Asiatic Seals in the British Museum, Cylinder Seals III: Isin/Larsa and Old Babylonian Periods* (London, 1986), especially nos. 328–71 and pp. 25, 30, 34–35, 37, 48, 138. On Freud's impressions of seals, see Helga Jobst, "Freud and Archeology," *Sigmund Freud Haus Bulletin* (Vienna) 2:1 (1978), p. 47.

FEMALE FIGURE

Syrian, Middle Bronze Age, c. 2000–1750 B.C.
Clay, h. 4 ⅝ in. (11.7 cm)
3725

This terracotta is typical of a large group of figurines current in the Orontes Valley of central Syria during the early part of the Middle Bronze Age (c. 2000–1750 B.C.). Numerous examples have been found in well-dated, excavated contexts at sites such as Hama, Qatna, Qadesh, and also at Tell Mardikh (Ebla). The group as a whole includes both male and female figures, differentiated on the basis of overall proportions and style of headdress. Anatomical sexual features such as penises are rare, but many of the females have clearly depicted pubic triangles and/or small applied breasts. Although neither genitals nor breasts are represented on this example, the general shape of the body, especially the treatment of the hips, strongly suggests that it is female.

Further support for this attribution comes from the headdress. Male figures of this Orontes Valley group usually have low pointed caps, whereas the females, as in this case, tend to have elaborate high headdresses with a number of piercings. Several examples have been found in which these holes were used for the suspension of small copper or gold rings.

The function of these figurines is difficult to establish. It certainly cannot be assumed that they formed part of some cult or fertility ritual because fertility figures customarily have exaggerated sexual attributes, and many, if not most, of the Orontes figurines show no representation of the genitalia at all. The contexts in which the majority of these figures have been found seem to be purely domestic rather than religious or funerary. Thus it is more reasonable to interpret these terracottas as ornaments or perhaps even playthings; figurines of this type have frequently been found associated with model beds, chariots, and carts.

—JT

For similar examples, see Leila Badre, *Les Figurines anthropomorphes en terre cuite à l'age du bronze en Syrie* (Paris, 1980).

AMENOPHIS I AND AHMOSE-NOFRETIRI

Egyptian, New Kingdom (18th Dynasty), probably reign of
Amenophis III, 1390–1353 B.C.
Steatite, 3 1/2 × 3 1/4 in. (9 × 8.3 cm)
3072

The main figure of this fragmentary dyad is the deified Amenophis I, who is shown wearing a short Nubian wig, kilt, and armlets and clutching a flail in his right hand. He is seated beside his mother, the deified queen Ahmose-Nofretiri, who wears an elaborate vulture headdress, close-fitting garment, and broad collar. Mortise holes in the top of the head of each figure were probably intended for the attachment of headdress embellishments. The back of the dyad is incised with two opposed pairs of columns of hieroglyphs, one double column relating to each figure. The text behind the king reads: "The good god, son of Amun,... / King of Upper and Lower Egypt, Djeserkare...." That behind the queen may be translated: "The god's wife, born of the god, the king's wife ... / his mother, the mother of the king, Ah[mose-Nofretiri...."

After their deaths, both Amenophis I, second king of the 18th Dynasty (r. 1514–1493 B.C.), and his mother Ahmose-Nofretiri, wife of King Ahmose I (r. 1539–1514 B.C.), were worshiped as the divine patrons of the vast Theban necropolis. They enjoyed particular popularity among the official necropolis work force, which was based at the village of Deir el-Medina. The reason for the attention paid to the couple is not at all clear, although it was previously speculated that Deir el-Medina had been founded during the reign of Amenophis I. Both Amenophis I and his mother appear to have shared a common place of burial at Dra Abu'l Naga, in a tomb first prepared for Ahmose-Nofretiri and later extended to receive a second burial. In 1913–14 this tomb was cleared for the fifth Earl of Carnarvon by Howard Carter, the archaeologist best known for discovering the tomb of Tutankhamun in 1922.

The Freud statue, which perhaps comes from a small domestic shrine, is related to a group of statuettes in glazed steatite representing Ahmose-Nofretiri herself or Queen Tiye, consort of Amenophis III, the pharaoh in whose reign this piece was probably carved.
—CNR

This queen-mother affectionately and intimately grouped with her king-son may have appealed to Freud, a firstborn and favored child. "If a man has been his mother's undisputed darling he retains throughout life the triumphant feeling, the confidence in success, which not seldom brings actual success along with it" (SE, 17, p. 156).

Freud avidly followed reports of excavations throughout his life and surely would have known about Howard Carter's excavation of the tomb of Amenophis I and Ahmose-Nofretiri. The author of the Oedipus complex may have been intrigued by their burial arrangement—mother and son lying together for eternity in a common tomb.
—FM

On Amenophis I and Ahmose-Nofretiri, see W. Helck et al., *Lexikon der Ägyptologie* (Wiesbaden, 1972–), I, cols. 102–109, s.v. "Ahmose Nofretere" (M. Gitton), and ibid., cols. 201–203, s.v. "Amenophis I" (E. Hornung), with references. On the burial of Amenophis I and Ahmose-Nofretiri, see C. N. Reeves, *Valley of the Kings: The Decline of a Royal Necropolis* (London, forthcoming), pp. 3–5. For related sculptures, see C. Aldred, "Ahmose-Nofretari Again," *Artibus Aegypti. Studia in honorem Bernardi V. Bothmer a collegis amicis discipulis conscripta* (Brussels, 1983), pp. 7–14.

HEAD OF OSIRIS

Egyptian, Third Intermediate Period, 1075–716 B.C., or later
Bronze, h. 7 in. (18 cm)
3128

Osiris was a complex deity, woven into the Heliopolitan cosmogony as the firstborn son of Geb and Nut, and possessing an essentially dual role in the religion of ancient Egypt. Perhaps originally worshiped as a god of fertility, Osiris only gradually accrued to himself—by assimilation with various local gods such as Andjety, Khentimentiu (Foremost of the Westerners, i.e., the dead) and Sokar—the trappings of a mummified god-king, ruler of the underworld and lord of resurrection. By the end of the 5th Dynasty (2520–2360 B.C.) the king, in life the embodiment of Horus, was equated in death with Osiris. This latter identification was in due course extended to all Egyptians, bestowing on them for the first time the opportunity for an independent existence in the next world and ensuring for Osiris a timeless and unbounded popularity.

According to legend (a number of versions of which exist, the fullest by Plutarch), Osiris was a terrestrial king whose popularity and success aroused the jealousy of his brother, Seth. Seth determined to seize the throne for himself, and with a number of accomplices, he prepared a magnificent chest, the dimensions of which tallied closely with the measurements of his brother. During the course of a banquet held in the king's honor, Seth had this coffer dragged in, and he offered to present it as a gift to the one whom it fit most closely. When Osiris came to lie down within the box, Seth and his followers immediately nailed shut the lid, sealed it with molten lead, and cast the chest into the Nile. Carried out to sea, the box eventually washed up at Byblos on the Lebanese coast, where it was found by Isis, the dead king's widow. Brought back to Egypt, the body fell into Seth's hands and was cut into fourteen pieces and scattered the length and breadth of the country. According to one version of the tale, Isis sought out the pieces and buried each where she found it; other texts tell how the dismembered portions of the body were reassembled as the first mummy. The corpse was reanimated by Isis, "the great magician," by the beating of her wings (she had taken the form of a kite), and upon the mummy of Osiris the goddess was able to conceive the child Horus.

This well-modeled head of Osiris, broken from a large hollow-cast figure in bronze, wears an atef crown now lacking its separately modeled plumes and perhaps a solar disk. The head was further embellished with a uraeus, the sacred cobra of Egypt (of which only the tang now remains) and an attached beard (again lost). The eyes and the straps of the beard (and, doubtless, the missing beard and the plumes and disk of the atef) were formerly inlaid, presumably with semiprecious stones, such as carnelian and lapis lazuli, faience, or brightly colored glass.

In its complete state, the figure to which this head was once attached must have been an imposing object. If not a cult figure as such, it had clearly been presented to the god by a particularly rich and pious worshiper. The vast majority of ex-voto offerings of this sort appear to have been produced during the Late Period (716–332 B.C.) and after, although the overall style of the present piece, its size, and the lavish use of inlays may reflect a somewhat earlier date.

—CNR

On Osiris, see W. Helck et al., *Lexikon der Ägyptologie* (Wiesbaden, 1972–), IV, cols. 623–33, s.v. "Osiris" (J. G. Griffiths), with the references there cited. The standard works on Egyptian bronzes are G. Roeder, *Ägyptische Bronzewerke* (Glückstadt, 1937), and idem, *Ägyptische Bronzefiguren* (Berlin, 1956).

HEAD OF A KING PROTECTED BY
THE HORUS FALCON

Egyptian, New Kingdom (18th Dynasty), probably reign of
Amenophis III, 1390–1353 B.C.
Steatite, originally glazed, h. 3 ³/₈ in. (8.6 cm)
3362

This head from the figure of a king wears the *nemes* headcloth surmounted by the double crown of Upper and Lower Egypt; behind perches a falcon with a solar disk on its head, its wings (now broken) bent in a gesture of protection. The king's face (the mouth and nose of which have suffered damage) is relatively well carved, with eyebrows and cosmetic lines in relief and separated by an incised line. The ears are large and well modeled. Short straps running part way up each side of the face indicate the presence of a beard, now broken away.

Despite certain stylistic peculiarities, such as the shortened form and odd positioning of the straps of the beard, the authenticity of this patinated steatite head is not open to serious doubt. The material, as much as the style, suggests that it is a product of the reign of Amenophis III, one of the richest and most powerful kings of the 18th Dynasty, father of the heretic Amenophis IV-Akhenaten (r. 1353–1336 B.C.) and in all likelihood the grandfather of the boy-king Tutankhamun (r. 1332–1323 B.C.).

The statuette of which this head originally formed a part is of a distinctive type that occurs sporadically from the Old Kingdom on, one of a relatively small number of royal figures in which the symbolic protection of the god Horus, who was immanent in the king, is given concrete expression. The most famous instance of this type is the "diorite" statue of Chephren of the 4th Dynasty (2640–2520 B.C.), found in his valley temple at Giza in 1858 and one of the masterpieces of Egyptian art. What was perhaps a close parallel to the Freud figure is shown in two dimensions in the chapel of Ipuy at Thebes (private tomb no. 217), which dates from the time of Ramesses II (1279–1213 B.C.). A fragmentary scene in this tomb shows the deified king Amenophis I—perhaps the intended subject of the Freud head—carried by priests in a palanquin. The form of the falcon, with its bent wings and solar disk, is almost identical, but the head of the figure is lost.

—CNR

For the steatite figures of the reign of Amenophis III, see J. Vandier, "Une Statuette de la reine Tiy," *Monuments et mémoires, Foundation Eugène Piot* 54 (1966), pp. 7–23; C. Aldred, "Ahmose-Nofretari Again," *Artibus Aegypti. Studia in honorem Bernardi V. Bothmer a collegis amicis discipulis conscripta* (Brussels, 1983), pp. 7–14. On the Chephren statue, see E. L. B. Terrace and H. G. Fischer, *Treasures of Egyptian Art from the Cairo Museum: A Centennial Exhibition 1970–1971* (London, 1970), no. 6, pp. 41–44. For the scene from the tomb of Ipuy, see N. de G. Davies, *Two Ramesside Tombs at Thebes* (New York, 1927), pl. XLI: 23.

IMHOTEP

Egyptian, Late Period, 716–332 B.C.
Bronze, h. 4 ³/₄ in. (12 cm)
3027

Imhotep, the deified vizier of King Djoser of the 3rd Dynasty (2705–2640 B.C.), is best known today as the architect of the Step Pyramid at Saqqara, the world's first large-scale stone building. He was held in high esteem less as an architect, however, than as a sage, and scribes habitually poured a libation to his memory before they began to write. In more recent antiquity, Imhotep was revered as a healer and magician, and from the Late Period on (after 716 B.C.) shrines were dedicated to his worship in temples at Philae, Thebes, Saqqara, and elsewhere. In later times he was recognized as the son of Ptah (god of craftsmen) and a woman named Khereduankh. The deification of Imhotep was completed when, with the arrival of the Greeks in Egypt, he came to be identified with Asklepios, the classical god of medicine.

This figure of Imhotep was cast in bronze by the lost-wax method; the eyes are inlaid, probably with electrum (an alloy of silver and gold). The god is shown seated, wearing a close-fitting cap and a short, pleated kilt, and holding a partially unrolled though uninscribed papyrus on his knees. Imhotep's feet rest upon an uninscribed square base. The figure may have been presented at a shrine of the god by a pilgrim seeking relief from illness or offering thanks. The original throne, from which the bronze has now been separated, may have been inscribed with the pilgrim's name and a dedication to the god.

—CNR

Freud may have especially favored this figure because of Imhotep's identification during classical times with the Greek god of healing, Asklepios. In *The Interpretation of Dreams*, Freud refers to this deity as being associated with the healing power of dreams:

> In Greece there were dream oracles, which were regularly visited by patients in search of recovery. A sick man would enter the temple of Apollo or Aesculapius, would perform various ceremonies there, would be purified by lustration, massage and incense, and then, in a state of exaltation, would be stretched on the skin of a ram which had been sacrificed. He would then fall asleep and would dream of the remedies for his illness. These would be revealed to him either in their natural form or in symbols and pictures which would afterwards be interpreted by the priests. (SE, 4, p. 34n)

—FM

On Imhotep, see W. Helck et al., *Lexikon der Ägyptologie* (Wiesbaden, 1972–), III, cols. 145–48, s.v. "Imhotep" (D. Wildung).

AMON-RE

Egyptian, probably Late Period, 716–332 B.C.
Bronze, h. 8 ³/₈ in. (21.2 cm)
3138

Because of the vast numbers of figures offered to the gods as gifts by devout pilgrims, particularly during the Late Period and Greco-Roman times, temple repositories had periodically to be cleared out and the old offerings buried in the vicinity of the god's shrine. Such caches, frequently stumbled upon by diggers, are the source of most divine figures encountered today in private and public collections.

Corrosion deposits built up over the years of burial have only recently been removed from this particular bronze, revealing the incised detail of its surface. Now attached to a modern wooden base, the figure of the god Amon-Re is shown in human form, wearing a short wrap-over kilt, his left foot to the fore. His right arm is held down by his side, and his left arm is bent at the elbow, originally to grasp a staff, now lost. On his head the god wears his characteristic flat-topped crown with tall double plumes and large solar disk; on his chin he carries the divine beard.

The name Amun, "the hidden one," conveys some impression of the god's universal and all-pervading nature. A creator god, his elevation to the status of king of the gods and lord of the thrones of the Two Lands (Egypt) is first attested in the reign of Sesostris I (1918–1875 B.C.); during the course of the Middle Kingdom (1987–1640 B.C.) "Amun" appears as a component of several royal names. The god's prestige was further increased during the New Kingdom (1540–1075 B.C.) by association with the sun god Re. As a result of this syncretism the king became son of Amun, and the monarch owed his very existence to the god's impregnation of the royal mother. By the time of the Greeks, the god Amon-Re was identified with Zeus.

The city of Amun (Egyptian *niwet Amun*, the "No-Amon" of the Bible) was Thebes, the east bank of which boasts two magnificent and well-preserved temples dedicated to the god's worship, at Luxor and Karnak. Numerous other monuments offer evidence of his preeminence, not only within Egypt but also beyond the frontiers—notably in Nubia, where the god's popularity continued for several centuries after the decline of Egyptian political influence in the area.
—CNR

For a discussion of some of the possible meanings of this statue in the context of Freud's life and work, see below, Spitz, pp. 154ff.
—FM

On Amun, see W. Helck et al., *Lexikon der Ägyptologie* (Wiesbaden, 1972–), I, cols. 237–48, s.v. "Amun" (E. Otto), and the references there cited.

PTAH

Egyptian, Late Period, 716–332 B.C., or later
Bronze, h. 6 ³/₄ in. (17.1 cm)
3036

This well-modeled figure of the god Ptah, cast solid by the lost-wax method, has a variegated green patina. The god is shown in characteristic form, with a close-fitting cap, broad collar, *menit* counterpoise (collar counterweight), and a square-cut false beard. His hands, protruding from the ridge-backed shroud he wears, clutch a *was* scepter, the hieroglyph for "dominion." The figure is mounted on a modern ebony base, which obscures the tang and replaces the ancient bevel-fronted *maat* base upon which the god is traditionally depicted.

Ptah stands apart from the other important gods of ancient Egypt in that he was first and foremost a local god — that of Memphis, a royal residence and the administrative capital of Egypt. He was variously represented as having created the world by thought and speech alone; as the divine patron of craftsmen and artists, Ptah was equated by the Greeks with Hephaistos. He was later worshiped as the principal figure of the Memphite triad, his partners being the lion-headed goddess Sekhmet and the junior member Nefertum, god of the sacred lotus.

As with the greater number of such figures, this bronze was presumably presented at a shrine of the god by a suppliant.

—CNR

On Ptah, see W. Helck et al., *Lexikon der Ägyptologie* (Wiesbaden, 1972–), IV, cols. 1177–180, s.v. "Ptah" (H. te Velde).

SPHINX AMULET

Egyptian, Late Period, 716–332 B.C.
Egyptian faience, h. 1 ³/₈ in. (3.6 cm)
3830

The traditional Egyptian sphinx, with its lion's body and human head (more bizarre forms had little more than a human face, or the head of a ram or falcon), was a curious mix of brute strength and contemplative intelligence. Despite its ominous presence, it was throughout Egyptian history a power for good, a guardian creature closely associated with the king. Usually male (although not infrequently female), the creature could be represented in a number of poses: couchant with its paws stretched out in front, seated, standing, or walking. It has been suggested that the term "sphinx" originated from an Egyptian expression, *shesep ankh*, which means "living image."

This green faience amulet in the form of a seated sphinx has hair arranged in cruciform fashion. The type is evidently female, although here it is shown without breasts. Broken across the legs and repaired, the creature is seated on a rectangular base, rounded at the rear, a suspension loop behind the head.

The most famous Egyptian sphinx is the colossal sculpture carved from a limestone outcrop in the necropolis at Giza. Carved initially in the image of King Chephren of the 4th Dynasty (2640–2520 B.C.) (whose pyramid complex it guards), during the New Kingdom the Giza sphinx was worshiped as a representation of the sun god Harmachis—Horus in the horizon—and associated with the Semitic deity Hauron.
—CNR

On Egyptian sphinxes, see W. Helck et al., *Lexikon der Ägyptologie* (Wiesbaden, 1972–), V, cols. 1139–147, s.v. "Sphinx" (C. M. Zivie).

VULTURE

Egyptian, Late Period, 716–332 B.C., or later
Bronze, h. 1 ¾ in. (4.3 cm)
3783

This small vulture, cast in bronze by the lost-wax method, makes contact with a rectangular base at the feet and tail. It has a suspension ring, now worn through, on the back.

The Egyptians identified the vulture with a number of deities, including Nekhbet of Elkab, the principal tutelary goddess of Upper Egypt, whom this small bronze piece was probably intended to represent. In hieroglyphic script, the vulture stands as the sign for *mut* (mother), which is the name given to another vulture goddess, Mut, one of the maternal guardians of pharaoh. A member of the Theban triad of gods, Mut was the consort of Amun and mother of Khons. Her cult center was located at Karnak in that area of the temple known as Ishru. Unlike Nekhbet, Mut is more usually represented in human form as a woman wearing a vulture headdress surmounted by the double crown of Upper and Lower Egypt.

Although amulets of a size appropriate for wear were a common feature of ancient Egyptian life, Freud's vulture is more probably to be recognized as a small votive bronze offered at a shrine by a visiting pilgrim.
—CNR

"It would be interesting to enquire how it could be that the ancient Egyptians came to choose the vulture as a symbol of motherhood." So began Freud's discussion of the Egyptian vulture deity and the ancient concept of an androgynous mother-goddess. Basing his discussion on ancient Greek authors such as Plutarch, Freud wrote that the Egyptians regarded the vulture as a symbol of motherhood, believing that only female vultures existed and that they could be impregnated by the wind. Thus the vulture goddess Mut, both in her sexual self-sufficiency and her occasional representation with male as well as female attributes, was a goddess who possessed both maternal and masculine characteristics (SE, 11, pp. 88–89, 94).

The context of Freud's inquiry into the Egyptian vulture is his essay "Leonardo da Vinci and a Memory of His Childhood." His interpretation is based, in part, on a well-known mistranslation of a passage from Leonardo's notebooks in which the artist wrote of a *nibbio* coming to his cradle when he was an infant. In the German text that Freud used, the Italian word *nibbio* is incorrectly translated as "vulture" instead of "kite" (SE, 11, p. 61, editor's note). There is a debate as to the significance of this mistranslation to the validity of Freud's interpretation of Leonardo.
—FM

On Nekhbet and Mut, see W. Helck et al., *Lexikon der Ägyptologie* (Wiesbaden, 1972–), IV, cols. 366–67, s.v. "Nechbet" (M. Heerma van Voss), and cols. 246–48, s.v. "Mut" (H. te Velde).

ISIS SUCKLING THE INFANT HORUS

Egyptian, Late Period (26th Dynasty), 664–525 B.C.
Bronze, h. 8 ½ in. (21.5 cm)
3037

The goddess Isis, offspring of Geb and Nut and sister-wife of Osiris, represented above all else the wifely and motherly virtues that the Egyptians held dear. Following the death of Osiris and his eventual resurrection as lord of the underworld, Isis took refuge in the marshes of Chemmis in the Delta. Here she gave birth to their son, rearing him in secret, protecting him by her magical powers that he might in due course avenge the murder of his father.

In this bronze figure, Isis wears a tripartite vulture headdress surmounted by the horned disk of her close associate, the cow goddess Hathor, and a simple, close-fitting, ankle-length garment. Harpocrates (Horus the child), to whom the goddess offers her breast, is naked (in keeping with his youth) except for a broad collar and close-fitting cap and sidelock; physically, however, he is represented not as a child but, in typical Egyptian fashion, as a miniature adult.

As the mother of Horus, Isis was also the mother of pharaoh and the guarantor of royal succession. Always a goddess of importance in Egypt, during the later periods of pharaonic rule the worship of Isis was especially popular. Under the Romans, her cult spread throughout the empire, and she came to be regarded as the goddess par excellence. *Isis lactans* is seen by some as a natural prototype for the Christian image of the Madonna and Child.

The Freud bronze, which is of particularly fine quality, was cast by the lost-wax technique. Although it may have been employed as a domestic cult figure, it is more likely to have been intended for dedication at a shrine of the goddess. Figures of metal, stone, wood, or faience were commonly offered to the gods by devout pilgrims who hoped by their gifts to secure divine favor—here, perhaps, in view of the goddess's maternal associations, in anticipation of or thanks for a painless birth. Such figures were commonly inscribed with the name of the deity and the name and filiation of the votary, either upon the base or (as perhaps here) upon an original plinth, now lost.

—CNR

For the goddess Isis, see W. Helck et al., *Lexikon der Ägyptologie* (Wiesbaden, 1972–), III, cols. 186–203, s.v. "Isis" (J. Bergman), with references.

DONATION STELE

Egyptian, Ptolemaic Period, dated 301 B.C.
Limestone, h. 20 7/8 in. (53 cm)
4581

This extremely interesting limestone stele has a commemorative inscription and the characteristic round top and division into registers.

In the upper register is the winged disk of the sun, the emblem of the solar god Horus, which extends its protection over the scenes below. The sun is flanked by two uraei, the sacred cobras of Egyptian kingship, which wear the crowns of southern or Upper Egypt (right) and Lower Egypt (left). This emblem is common on Egyptian stelae of all periods.

The middle register, largest of the three, is intended to symbolize the religious meaning of the entire stele. On the right stands the figure of a pharaoh wearing one of his many ritual crowns; in his hands he presents the hieroglyph denoting a field, or agricultural land. This motif was originally designed to commemorate endowments of land but was rapidly applied to religious donations in general. The cartouche containing the name of the king is damaged and seems to be uninscribed, but we know from the accompanying text in the lower register that he is in fact Ptolemy, the general of Alexander the Great, who seized control of Egypt when Alexander died in 323 B.C. and later declared himself pharaoh.

The style of the figures and the hieroglyphs are typical of this period, as is the method of carving in relief. The high value originally attached to the stele is shown by traces of gold leaf, which once decorated the upper registers.

Four gods face the person of the king and are clearly intended as the recipients of the donation. From right to left these are: the sky god Amun, wearing two vertical plumes on his head; his consort Mut, wearing the double crown of Upper and Lower Egypt; their son the moon god Khonsu, who is here identified with the god Horus in an unusual form, shown with the crescent and disk of the new moon upon his head; and Horus of Mesen, a solar deity, described here as "the noble winged scarab who presides over the Lower Egyptian Thebes."

The gods pictured in the middle register make it very likely that the object originated in the city of Semabehdet, otherwise known as the Lower Egyptian Thebes, the modern Tell Balamun in the northern Delta. Inscriptions from this site are extremely rare and add to the interest of this stele.

The lowest register, somewhat damaged, contains an inscription in demotic, the shorthand script regularly used in Egypt for everyday purposes during the Late Period. The six lines of text record a date, the month of Pakhons in the fourth year of Pharaoh Ptolemy (July, 301 B.C.). The text then mentions a chapel, which is to be assigned in perpetuity, together with its endowment income and its divine images, to one Amenhotep, son of Khahor. Nothing else is known of this man, but another major inscription of Ptolemy, issued while he was still nominal governor of Egypt, records that large tracts of land in the northern Delta, which had been confiscated when Egypt was a province of the Persian Empire, were returned at this time to the native priesthood, doubtless to secure their loyalty to their new overlord. The Freud stele, which probably once stood in the chapel to which it refers, records a small episode in this process, the attempt by the first Greek-speaking ruler of Egypt to secure a power base among the literate classes of his newly acquired province.

—JDR

There are references to this stele in Dimitri Meeks, *State and Temple Economy in the Ancient Near East* (Leuven, 1979), p. 684, no. 10, and in Adel Farid, *Fünf demotische Stelen* (diss. Würzburg, 1985), II, *Bibliographie der demotischen Inschriften*, p. 200.

BABOON OF THOTH

Egyptian, Roman Period, 30 B.C.–A.D. 395
Marble, h. 8 ½ in. (21.5 cm)
3133

The cult center of Thoth, the ibis-headed lunar god and patron of all things intellectual, particularly writing, was Hermopolis Magna (modern el-Ashmunein) in Middle Egypt. As scribe of the gods, Thoth had charge of the scales at the Weighing of the Heart ceremony, conducted after death to establish the merit and virtue of the deceased (see p. 63). The baboon (*hedj wer*, the Great White One), one of the old gods of Hermopolis Magna whose worship the ibis god supplanted, was recognized as the spirit of Thoth. Thoth frequently appears in baboon form seated atop the balance, from which vantage point he could announce to Osiris that the dead man was indeed "true of voice."

The baboon of Thoth is here shown in a characteristic squatting pose with his front paws resting upon his knees and with the lunar crescent and disk upon his head. This figure's function is not immediately apparent. During the New Kingdom (1540–1075 B.C.) smaller examples of the type evidently formed part of composite group representations of a scribe in the presence of his god. Here, however, the baboon more probably represents an independent offering, perhaps originally set in a contrasting base dedicated at a shrine of Thoth by a pilgrim of the Classical Period, when the god was enjoying renewed popularity owing to his identification with the Greek god Hermes.

—CNR

As god of intellectual pursuits, the baboon of Thoth may have held a special appeal for Freud because of its conflation of instinct and intellect. One of Freud's missions, after all, was to reveal the profound influence of instinct—sexuality and aggression—on man's intellectual achievements.

This deity, the inventor of hieroglyphs, also reminds us of Freud's interest in the Egyptian language. In "The Antithetical Meaning of Primal Words" (1910), Freud discussed the work of nineteenth-century philologist Karl Abel and compared the antithetical meaning of certain Egyptian words with a similar phenomenon in dreams—that of the symbolic representation of an idea by its opposite. Freud noted that "we psychiatrists cannot escape the suspicion that we should be better at understanding and translating the language of dreams if we knew more about the development of language" (SE, 11, p. 161).

—FM

On Thoth, see W. Helck et al., *Lexikon der Ägyptologie* (Wiesbaden, 1972–), VI, cols. 497–523, s.v. "Thot" (D. Kurth).

FALCON-HEADED FIGURE

Forgery, 19th century A.D.
Gessoed and painted wood, h. 8 ⅝ in. (22 cm)
3124

This striding, falcon-headed deity, whose skin is painted red-brown, wears a low, wrap-over kilt in white, with red and black pendant uraeus serpents at the front; his plain tripartite wig (longer at the front than at the back) is painted a dark blue-green. The arms appear to have been carved separately and pegged on; on the undersurface of each foot is a tenon for insertion into a separate base.

This bizarre figure is probably intended as a representation of the falcon-headed Horus, son of Isis, who avenged the murder of Osiris, king of the underworld (see p. 40). Like a number of pieces in Freud's collection, the falcon-headed god is of relatively modern manufacture, of a type still produced in Egypt today using traditional methods and frequently employing ancient materials. It was perhaps one of a group of wooden pieces purchased by Freud from the dealer Robert Lustig in 1931 or 1932. Lustig acquired the figures from the nineteenth-century descendants of an Egyptian "pasha" who had settled in Vienna.

Forgery in Egypt has a long history. One of the earliest known imitations is a green stone *shabti* figure (now in the Ashmolean Museum, Oxford) brought back from Egypt during the seventeenth century. Locally produced fakes of this early date are rare, however, and it is only with the advent of the nineteenth century that such copies became common. Napoleon's expedition to Egypt in 1798 prompted a renewed interest in the land of the Nile, an interest further stimulated by J.-F. Champollion's deciphering of hieroglyphic script in 1822 and the establishment of the first Egyptian museum at Ezbekia in 1835. From this time on, with the burgeoning tourist trade, forgeries of Egyptian antiquities proliferated, although their general naiveté would today deceive only the most inexperienced of collectors.
—CNR

Falcon-headed humans appeared in an anxiety dream that Freud had as a child and analyzed some thirty years later in *The Interpretation of Dreams*:

> In it, I saw my beloved mother, with a peculiarly peaceful expression on her features, being carried into the room by two (or three) people with birds' beaks and laid upon the bed. I awoke in tears and screaming and interrupted my parents' sleep. The strangely draped and unnaturally tall figures with birds' beaks were derived from the illustrations to Philippson's Bible. I fancy they must have been gods with falcons' heads from an ancient Egyptian funerary relief. (SE, 5, p. 583)

Freud may have been drawn to this falcon-headed Horus because it represents the confluence of many delicately interwoven themes—the mother, death, Judaism.
—FM

On Horus, see W. Helck et al., *Lexikon der Ägyptologie* (Wiesbaden, 1972–), III, particularly cols. 14–25, s.vv. "Horus" (W. Schenkel), "Horus and Seth" (H. te Velde), and "Horusmythe" (J. G. Griffiths). On the subject of forgeries of Egyptian antiquities, see S. Schoske and D. Wildung, *Falsche Faraonen* (Munich, 1983); an excellent survey of the topic, by H. G. Fischer, will appear in the Macmillan *Dictionary of Art* (London, forthcoming).

PATAIKOS FIGURE

Egyptian, Late Period, 716–332 B.C.
Egyptian faience, h. 3 ½ in. (9 cm)
3809

This finely modeled blue Egyptian faience figure represents Pataikos, the bandy-legged, brachycephalic dwarf divinity. Shown naked except for a close-fitting cap, he stands on a square base, and there is a suspension loop behind his neck.

Pataikos, whose name is a Greek form of the Egyptian Ptah-Sokar, was a manifestation of Ptah, creator god of Memphis. He was a common household deity, showing affinities with both Bes and Harpocrates, particularly during the Late Period. Pataikos was a popular subject for amulets, more complex and slightly earlier versions of which are shown with a scarab beetle on the head, clutching a serpent in either hand, and with the feet resting on two crocodiles.

Dwarfs—both the pathologically deformed as well as pygmies of the sort brought as a gift for King Pepi II by the explorer Harkhuf during the 5th Dynasty (2520–2360 B.C.)—were a common feature not only of Egyptian religion but of court life. Some achieved wealth and relatively high office, such as the dwarf Seneb, well known from his tomb statue and false door (now in the Cairo Museum), who during the Dynasty (2640–2520 B.C.) was appointed as chief of all the dwarfs in the palace and as priest in the funerary cults of kings Cheops and Dedefre.

The material of Freud's Pataikos figure, Egyptian faience, bears no more than a superficial resemblance to faience proper, the tin-glazed earthenware of Faenza in Italy. Egyptian faience consists of a ground quartz core with an alkaline glaze; it was produced throughout the ancient Near East from the fourth millennium B.C. on.
—CNR

On Pataikos, see W. Helck et al., *Lexikon der Ägyptologie* (Wiesbaden, 1972–), IV, cols. 914–15, s.v. "Patäke" (J. G. Griffiths); for dwarfs in ancient Egypt, see ibid., VI, cols. 1432–435 s.v. "Zwerg" (K.-J. Seyfried). On Egyptian faience, see A. Kaczmarczyk and R. E. M. Hedges, *Ancient Egyptian Faience* (Warminster, 1983).

WALL RELIEF DEPICTING A COURT OFFICIAL

Forgery, in the style of the Egyptian New Kingdom
(late 18th Dynasty), c. 1353–1292 B.C.
Limestone, h. 25 in. (63.4 cm)
4379

This finely carved fragment of sunken relief depicts a kneeling courtier with his arms raised in adoration, a subject commonly found decorating the door jambs of the tomb chapel. The figure displays strong Amarna influence, both in physiognomy and costume, and is reminiscent of the sort of work produced during and in the wake of the Amarna period, between the reigns of Akhenaten and Horemheb.

Its quality notwithstanding, the authenticity of the piece is open to serious question. The overall proportions of the figure (in particular the length of the upper torso and the narrowness of the hips) are unconvincing, with some confusion in the drapery of the arms and in the fall of the kilt below the navel. Other details are, in sum, equally disconcerting: the strands of the wig lack a common source at the crown; the curls on the inner edge of the wig fail to continue into the fringe of hair covering the brow, causing the wig to appear to sit too high; the eye is over-large, positioned too close to the nose, and the contour line between eye and eyebrow badly positioned and rather short; the lips are poorly modeled, and the stubby beard perhaps not entirely appropriate to the figure; the two folds of flesh in the neck beneath the chin, which ought at this period to be present on a principal figure, are absent; the peculiar "flap" at the neck of the man's shirt is clearly a mis-construed tie-opening. The shape of the block accommodates the figure with suspicious neatness, without any evidence of a text. Both the back and left-hand edge of the block have been cut in modern times. The cutting is exceptionally neat and markedly different from the hesitant, uneven sawing usually encountered in blocks that have been reduced in size (for ease of transportation) for sale on the art market.

The Freud relief is nevertheless an exceptionally subtle work, well above the quality of fakes normally encountered. It brings to mind the work of the Berlin Forger, Oxan Aslanian, one of the best (known) producers of spurious Egyptian pieces. Aslanian was an Armenian based in Egypt, Berlin, and finally Hamburg, and was working at about the time Freud was putting his collection together. Some of his most successful creations were executed in the Amarna style, as several photographs of his work preserved in the Staatliche Sammlung Ägyptischer Kunst in Munich reveal.

—CNR

The writer is grateful to Cyril Aldred, J. R. Harris, and other colleagues for their comments on this piece. On the Berlin Forger, see S. Schoske and D. Wildung, *Falsche Faraonen* (Munich, 1983); R. Krauss, "Zwei Beispiele für Echtheitsuntersuchungen an Äegyptiaca," *Jahrbuch Preussischer Kulturbesitz* 23 (1986), pp. 153–73.

HEAD OF A WOMAN

Egyptian, Middle Kingdom (12th Dynasty), 1938–1759 B.C.
Basalt, h. 2 ½ in. (6.3 cm)
3307

This small, fragmentary representation of a woman originally formed the right-hand figure of a group statue, probably a funerary dyad depicting the lady standing beside her husband. She wears a long, striated, tripartite wig and a simple, close-fitting dress (which in the complete figure would have extended down to the ankles), its broad shoulder straps concealing the breasts. The face is competently modeled, with narrow, far-set eyes and a broad nose (now chipped). As is characteristic of sculpture of this date, the ears are large, their size further emphasized by the style of the wig.

The vast majority of minor sculptures of this type seem to have been purchased "off the shelf" and associated with the owner by means of an appropriate identifying text, which could be either incised or added in paint. The features of such sculptures offer less the portrait of an individual than a portrayal of the Egyptian ideal, which in the case of women was demure, passive, and physically appealing.

Although the ancient Egyptians regarded the sexes as equal before the law, the roles of men and women differed fundamentally. The Egyptian woman had her place, which was first and foremost as wife and mother. Despite occasional instances of female literacy and the minor part played by women in temples, the basis of a woman's world was the family home. Much of her time was expected to be spent indoors, hence the yellow skin color commonly found in sculpture and relief, in contrast to the red skin of the field-working male.

—CNR

On women in ancient Egypt, see S. Schoske and D. Wildung, *Nofret—Die Schöne*, 2 vols. (Munich, 1984), with the bibliography there cited.

HEART SCARAB

Egyptian, New Kingdom (18th–19th Dynasty), 1540–1190 B.C.
Serpentine, 1 × 1 5/8 × 2 1/4 in. (2.4 × 4 × 5.6 cm)
4004

For the Egyptians the scarab beetle (*Scarabaeus sacer*) was closely associated with the concept of resurrection and rebirth: it lays its eggs in a ball of dead matter, dung, from which new life was subsequently seen to emerge. The scarab is today one of the most frequently encountered amulets from ancient Egypt.

The majority of Egyptian scarabs are small (less than 1.5 cm in length), usually made of glazed steatite, and commonly set as bezels in finger rings. This particular specimen, carved in gray-green serpentine, is somewhat larger and of the type commonly referred to as a heart scarab. It has a realistically modeled back with "pecked" prothorax and striated elytra (wing cases), and the flat base carries seven horizontal lines of incised hieroglyphic text, reading from right to left.

This text, taken from Chapter 30B of the Book of the Dead (see p. 76), may be translated: "Recitation by the Osiris Kenro: / O my heart of my mother! O my heart of my mother! O my heart of / my coming into being! Do not stand up / against me as a witness / before the guardian of the balance! / The Osiris, the standard-bearer / Kenro." Kenro, whose title is a military one, appears to be otherwise unattested. To judge from the style of his heart scarab, however, he lived during the 18th or, more probably, the 19th Dynasty.

The heart scarab was a common article of funerary equipment, intended to prevent the heart (for the Egyptians the seat of all emotions and the source of all physical action, including speech) from testifying against its owner at the final judgment, the Weighing of the Heart.

In this ceremony, the heart was placed in one pan of the scales to be balanced against the feather of Maat, goddess of truth and justice, which rested in the opposing pan. With the heart in place on the balance, the deceased recited a declaration of innocence before the divine tribunal of forty-two assessors. If there was no imbalance, the deceased was proclaimed "true of voice" and received into the underworld by Osiris. If the scales did not balance, his chances of entry into the hereafter would be lost: he would be thrown to "the Eater"—a composite monster, part crocodile, part lion, and part hippopotamus—to die a second death.

The rubric to Chapter 30 of the Book of the Dead, reads: "To be inscribed on a scarab made from nephrite, set in fine gold with a chain of silver and placed at the throat of the deceased." In practice, however, any green stone might be used—such as the gray-green serpentine employed here—and the scarab wrapped unmounted in the mummy bandages, close to the heart it was intended magically to bolster.

—CNR

For the relevant chapter from the Book of the Dead, see the translations of T. G. Allen, *The Book of the Dead, or Going Forth by Day* (Chicago, 1974); R. O. Faulkner, *The Ancient Egyptian Book of the Dead*, ed. Carol Andrews (London, 1985). For heart scarabs generally, see M. Malaise, *Les Scarabées de coeur dans l'Égypte ancienne* (Brussels, 1978). The rank of standard-bearer is discussed by A. R. Schulman, *Military Rank, Title and Organization in the Egyptian New Kingdom* (Berlin, 1964), pp. 69–71.

SHABTI FIGURE OF SENNA

Egyptian, New Kingdom (18th Dynasty), Tuthmosis III–
Amenophis II, 1479–1400 B.C.
Limestone, h. 9 in. (23 cm)
3271

Mummified figures recognizably of the type referred to as *shabti*, *ushabti*, or *shawabti* first appeared singly in tombs toward the end of the Middle Kingdom (1987–1640 B.C.), when they were clearly intended as substitutes for the dead person. Later their role broadened, and they came to be regarded as deputies of the deceased, whose job was to carry out on his behalf in the next world any menial agricultural tasks that he might be called upon to perform. This change in function was reflected, during the middle years of the 18th Dynasty, by the introduction of figures clutching agricultural implements—a pick, a hoe, and usually a rope suspending a basket slung over the left shoulder—with which these tasks were to be accomplished. By the Third Intermediate Period (1075–716 B.C.), *shabtis* are encountered often several hundred to a burial, equipped with their own *reis* (overseer) figures to supervise each group of ten workers. Carved from stone during the earlier periods, the range of materials employed in the production of *shabti* figures later widened to include wood, pottery, glass, bronze, and Egyptian faience, the most commonly used material of all.

This limestone *shabti* of a man has a tripartite wig decorated with thickly applied dark blue-green paint with vertical yellow stripes. The sensitively modeled face has large ears and a squared beard. The hands are crossed on the chest above seven horizontal bands of cursive hieroglyphic text in black. The hieroglyphs are now faded; that the owner's name was Senna, however, is confirmed by the text of an identical *shabti* in Bologna.

Shabti figures are commonly inscribed, as here, with a version of Chapter 6 of the Book of the Dead (see p. 76), which translates: "O *shabti* allotted to me! If I be summoned or if I be detailed to do any work which has to be done in the realm of the dead, if indeed obstacles are implanted for you therewith as a man at his duties, you shall detail yourself for me on every occasion of making arable the fields, of flooding the banks, or of conveying sand from east to west: 'Here am I,' you shall say."
—CNR

Freud was fascinated by the way in which the dead continue to influence the living, that is, to live on intrapsychically—in mummified form, one could almost say—and to work for and on the living mind. Freud discovered a different kind of life after death: the coercion of the commands, prohibitions, fears, and wishes of the deceased on the minds and actions of those who live on.
—FM

For the relevant chapter of the Book of the Dead, see T. G. Allen, *The Book of the Dead, or Going Forth by Day* (Chicago, 1974); R. O. Faulkner, *The Ancient Egyptian Book of the Dead*, ed. Carol Andrews (London, 1985). For *shabtis* generally, see J.-F. and L. Aubert, *Statuettes égyptiennes. Chaouabtis, ouchebtis* (Paris, 1974); H. Schneider, *Shabtis: An Introduction to the History of Ancient Egyptian Funerary Statuettes*, 3 vols. (Leiden, 1977). For the Bologna *shabti* of Senna, cf. S. Curto, *L'Egitto antico nelle collezioni dell'Italia settentrionale* (Bologna, 1961), p. 112, no. 174, pl. 54.

SHABTI FIGURE OF DJEHUTYEMHEB

Egyptian, New Kingdom
(late 18th–19th Dynasty), c. 1323–1190 B.C.
Indurated limestone, with head of gessoed and painted wood,
h. 8 ¼ in. (21 cm)
3269

This high-quality *shabti*—of a man, despite its rather foppish appearance—is unusual in that it was a composite figure, with a finely worked body of hard white stone and a carved and gessoed wooden head painted in black, red, and yellow. The original position of the figure's crossed arms (which were presumably modeled separately in wood, like the head) is shown by traces of red on the chest. Whether the figure originally carried tools is uncertain. The feet (now missing) were no doubt also produced in wood and attached in a manner similar to that of the arms. The figure wears an elaborately pleated costume with flared sleeves and square-fronted apron. The front of the apron carries three columns of hieroglyphs, which still preserve traces of their original dark fill. This text, obscured in places by encrustation, identifies the owner as "overseer of cattle in the temple of Re, Djehutyemheb" (apparently over an earlier name which had been erased), followed by the usual extracts from Chapter 6 of the Book of the Dead (see p. 76).

The so-called costume of daily life worn by this figure was a common feature of *shabtis* of late 18th and 19th Dynasty date, and was later adopted for the *reis* or overseer *shabtis* supplied to supervise the worker figures.
—CNR

On the apron of this *shabti*, remnants of earlier, imperfectly erased hieroglyphs are still visible—a condition consonant with Freud's view of mental life as a stratification of meanings. He discussed the idea of layers of inscription and attempts at effacement in his short paper "A Note Upon the 'Mystic Writing-Pad'" (SE, 19, pp. 227–34).
—FM

For the relevant chapter of the Book of the Dead, see T. G. Allen, *The Book of the Dead, or Going Forth by Day* (Chicago, 1974); R. O. Faulkner, *The Ancient Egyptian Book of the Dead*, ed. Carol Andrews (London, 1985). For *shabtis* generally, see J.-F. and L. Aubert, *Statuettes égyptiennes. Chaouabtis, ouchebtis* (Paris, 1974); H. Schneider, *Shabtis: An Introduction to the History of Ancient Egyptian Funerary Statuettes*, 3 vols. (Leiden, 1977).

SHABTI OF IMHOTEP BORN OF BASTETIRDIS

Egyptian, Late Period (30th Dynasty), 380–342 B.C.
Egyptian faience, h. 8 in. (20.3 cm)
3351

This well-modeled *shabti* figure of pale green Egyptian faience has a body of characteristic mummy form and wears a striated tripartite wig and divine beard. The *shabti's* hands, which protrude from the close-fitting shroud, clutch in the right a pick, and in the left a hoe and basket rope; the basket itself is suspended behind the left shoulder. Nine horizontal bands of hieroglyphic text cover the front and sides of the lower torso and legs. The continuity of the text is interrupted by a dorsal pillar; the feet rest on a square base.

The text is taken from Chapter 6 of the Book of the Dead (see p. 76), and in it the owner is named as a priest: "the god's father Imhotep, born of Bastetirdis." Other *shabtis* of the same man, a contemporary of the 30th Dynasty, are in Leiden and Frankfurt. Like Freud's example, these would have been interred in the tomb of Imhotep, which was probably situated in the vast Saqqara necropolis. Freud possessed a closely similar *shabti* of Imhotep's brother, Wahibreemakhet, born of Bastetirdis (FM 3464), conceivably acquired at the same time. It is possible that the two men shared a common place of burial.

—CNR

For the Leiden *shabti* of Imhotep, see H. Schneider, *Shabtis: An Introduction to the History of Ancient Egyptian Funerary Statuettes* (Leiden, 1977), vol. II, no. 5.3.1.9, pp. 156–57, with vol. III, pl. 57. For the Frankfurt *shabti*, see *Ägyptische Kunst im Liebighaus* (Frankfurt am Main, 1981), no. 30. For Wahibreemakhet as a probable brother of Imhotep, see Schneider, loc. cit. For three Leiden *shabtis* of Wahibreemakhet, see ibid., vol. II, nos. 5.3.1.55–57, pp. 164–65, with vol. III, pls. 58 and 67.

MUMMIFIED FALCON

Egyptian, Late Period, 716–332 B.C., or later
Gessoed and painted wood, 3 ³/₈ × 2 ¹/₄ × 6 ⁵/₈ in.
(8.6 × 5.7 × 17.2 cm)
3285

This painted figure, which takes the form of a mummified falcon, has a red body and a white head and chest. Details of the eyes are picked out in black and red; a schematized collar in blue is at the front, with its *menit* counterpoise (to balance the weight of the heavy bead collar) on the back. A mortise hole on top of the head was probably intended for the attachment of a double-plume ornament with solar disk, a regular feature of such figures; here, however, it is lost.

Freud's falcon represents the funerary deity Sokar, lord of Rostau (the entrance to the underworld), the preeminent deity of the Memphite necropolis, who is closely associated with the creator god Ptah (see p. 48).

The figure is of a type usually found mounted on the vaulted lids of wooden pedestal or corner-post coffins of the 25th Dynasty (750–656 B.C.) and on the somewhat later shrine-shaped canopic boxes (intended to contain the viscera of the deceased, which the Egyptians removed from the body and embalmed separately) of Ptolemaic times (332–30 B.C.).

—CNR

On Sokar, see W. Helck et al., *Lexikon der Ägyptologie* (Wiesbaden, 1972–), V, cols. 1055–74 (E. Brovarski), with the references there cited.

FALCON RELIQUARY

Egyptian, Late Period, 716–332 B.C.
Bronze, 5 3/4 × 2 5/8 × 7 in. (14.7 × 6.6 × 17.6 cm)
3484

This bronze coffin for a sacred animal takes the form of a rectangular box with cavetto cornice, sealed at one end and still preserving its ancient contents. The box is surmounted by a well-modeled falcon with detailed feathering, feet, broad collar, and eyes, standing on a rectangular base that was cast as part of the box. The falcon represents Horus in his original manifestation as lord of the sky; he wears the double crown of Upper and Lower Egypt, an allusion to Horus's victory over Seth and his succession to the throne of the living (see p. 40).

During the later dynasties, animal cults were especially popular in Egypt, and pilgrims who wished to make an offering to the gods were able to purchase in the temple precincts ritually killed and mummified creatures—from falcons, ibises, crocodiles, dogs, and cats, to shrews, fish, and scarab beetles. These animals, frequently bred in captivity on the temple estates, were often packed into an appropriately shaped container, as here, which could then be offered as an ex-voto in the pilgrim's name. The mummies were interred by the thousands in rambling underground galleries such as those discovered at Tuna el-Gebel in Middle Egypt and the Sacred Animal Necropolis at Saqqara, just outside Cairo. This particular coffin may have come from any one of the sites where falcon worship was common, including Buto, Giza, Saqqara, Abydos, and Kom Ombo.

These manifestations of divinity were often dealt with in a rapid, and apparently careless, production-line manner. Modern examination of several well-bandaged and ostensibly intact animal mummies has shown them to be drastically incomplete, composed of little more than a handful of old bones, or else miraculously overendowed.

—CNR

On Horus, see W. Helck et al., *Lexikon der Ägyptologie* (Wiesbaden, 1972–), III, particularly cols. 14–25, s.vv. "Horus" (W. Schenkel), "Horus and Seth" (H. te Velde), and "Horusmythe" (J. G. Griffiths). On Egyptian animal worship, see H. S. Smith, *A Visit to Ancient Egypt: Life at Memphis and Saqqara (c. 500–30 B.C.)* (Warminster, 1974).

HUMAN-HEADED BIRD

Egyptian, Ptolemaic Period, 332–30 B.C.
Gessoed and painted wood, h. 5 ½ in. (14 cm)
3286

The surface of this human-headed bird is covered with a thin layer of gesso and painted. The tripartite wig and beard are black; the breast is yellow with feathering in black; the feet are red; the wings are green with details in black and red; facial details are in black on a yellow background.

This type of figure, commonly encountered perched at the rounded summits of Ptolemaic wooden funerary stelae, represents the *ba* (individuality) of the deceased, one of the aspects into which a person divided at death. The accompanying aspects were the body itself and the *ka*, or life force. Unlike the body, the *ba* was not a prisoner of the tomb. Very much independent, it took the form of a bird in order to revisit the land of the living and partake of the pleasures left behind.

—CNR

For the *ba*, see W. Helck et al., *Lexikon der Ägyptologie* (Wiesbaden, 1972–), I, cols. 588–90, s.v. "Ba" (L. V. Žabkar); S. D'Auria, P. Lacovara, and C. H. Roehrig, eds., *Mummies and Magic: The Funerary Arts of Ancient Egypt* (Boston, 1988), esp. pp. 43–45 (J. P. Allen).

MASK FROM A COFFIN

Egyptian, New Kingdom (19th Dynasty), 1292–1190 B.C.
Gessoed and painted wood, 9 5/8 × 7 3/8 in. (24.5 × 18.7 cm)
4384

For the ancient Egyptian, the coffin, whether carved in stone (when it is more properly referred to as a sarcophagus), beaten from sheet metal, pegged together from planks of wood, or molded in cartonnage (see p. 75), was the deceased's eternal home and his ultimate protection from hostile elements. Small rectangular boxes, produced during the Early Dynastic Period (2965–2705 B.C.) for contracted burials, developed during the succeeding Old Kingdom (2705–2225 B.C.) into massive sarcophagi designed to receive a full-length mummy. Anthropoid coffins, human-form containers that could double as substitutes for the mummy, appear to have developed from the cartonnage head coverings of the First Intermediate Period (2180–1987 B.C.). From the 12th Dynasty on (after 1938 B.C.), they became the most usual type, often contained within a larger coffin or sarcophagus of rectangular form or nested (as with Tutankhamun) one or more within another in the manner of Russian dolls.

This wooden face mask, one of three in Freud's collection, was originally pegged (perhaps with an intervening layer of linen) to the lid of an anthropoid coffin. The surface of the mask is gessoed and painted. The colors have darkened considerably, but the face appears to originally have been a creamy yellow with the eyes detailed in red, white, and black; the lips and nostrils are outlined in red. A dowel in the chin provides evidence for the original presence of a beard, which conveniently identifies the otherwise anonymous owner as a man. The floral fillet, with its large, central lotus flower (the stem of which would have continued over the head), appears to have been originally executed in red and dark blue-green. Remains of the right ear may be discerned, separately applied in plaster.
—CNR

For a comprehensive and up-to-date discussion of the subject, see J. H. Taylor, *Egyptian Coffins* (Aylesbury, in press).

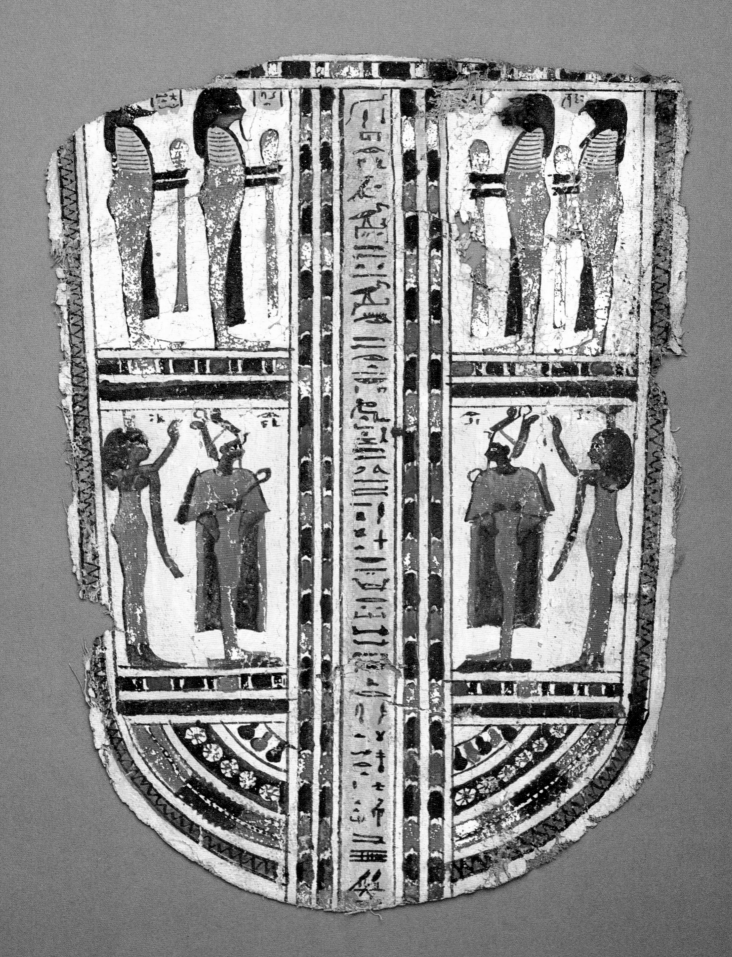

FRONTAL COVERING OF A MUMMY

Egyptian, Ptolemaic Period, 332–30 B.C.
Cartonnage, 15 × 9 ½ in. (38 × 24 cm)
4936

Wood of any size and quality has always been scarce in Egypt, and a popular alternative for the preparation of certain items of funerary furniture was cartonnage—a form of board made up of alternating layers of linen (or papyrus) and glue, molded around a form and gessoed to receive the painted design. Masks or headpieces of cartonnage occurred as early as the First Intermediate Period (2180–1987 B.C.). During the Third Intermediate Period (from the 22nd Dynasty on, after 944 B.C.), one-piece cartonnage cases made an appearance, split at the back to allow the insertion of the mummy. Perhaps during the 26th Dynasty (664–525 B.C.) and certainly by Ptolemaic times (332–30 B.C.) these cases were replaced by a series of separate cartonnage elements, including mask, broad collar, frontal panels, and foot case and sandals.

This particular piece of cartonnage, prepared for the mummy of a woman, would have been placed over the legs. Its surface decoration is divided by a column of hieroglyphs, which may be rendered: "Recitation by the Osiris Tadjehuty, true of voice, daughter of Djehutyan, true of voice, engendered by the lady of the house Tasheret[en]hap, true of voice: May Anubis who is in his bandages, lord of the Sacred Land, come to you; may he give to you a goodly burial upon the west in the district of the Coptite nome." The dog-headed Anubis, who had assisted Isis, "the great magician," in the embalming of her husband Osiris, is here called upon to perform a similar service for the lady Tadjehuty.

The colored vignettes at the upper left and upper right of the cartonnage contain named representations of the four sons of Horus (shown with red bodies and loops of linen, yellow collars, green faces—green being the color of fertility—and black hair). These minor deities, whose role was the elimination of hunger and thirst, are: Duamutef, the dog-headed genius responsible for the embalmed stomach of the deceased; Imsety, the human-headed protector of the liver; Hapy, the baboon-headed guardian of the lungs; and Qebhsenuef, the falcon-headed guardian of the embalmed intestines. The lower left and right vignettes depict Osiris, lord of the underworld, protected respectively by Isis and her sister Nephthys, the two principal mourners at the god's funeral. Each figure is shown, again, with green flesh and red costume.

A single line of hieratic (a cursive form of the hieroglyphic script) is written in black on the back of the panel. Presumably a delivery docket, it records that the cartonnage was "destined for the district of Coptos."
—CNR

Freud saw dreams as being analogous to hieroglyphs in that both communicate through imagery. "If we reflect that the means of representation in dreams are principally visual images and not words, we shall see that it is even more appropriate to compare dreams with a system of writing than with a language. In fact the interpretation of dreams is completely analogous to the decipherment of an ancient pictographic script such as Egyptian hieroglyphs" (SE, 13, p. 177).
—FM

On the development of cartonnage, see W. Helck et al., *Lexikon der Ägyptologie* (Wiesbaden, 1972–), V, cols. 434–68, s.v. "Sarg NR-SpZt" (A. Niwiński); S. D'Auria, P. Lacovara, and C. H. Roehrig, eds., *Mummies and Magic: The Funerary Arts of Ancient Egypt* (Boston, 1988), pp. 166–68 (J. H. Taylor), with the references there cited. On the four sons of Horus, see *Lexikon der Ägyptologie*, III, cols. 52–53, s.v. "Horuskinder" (M. Heerma van Voss), with references.

MUMMY BANDAGES WITH VIGNETTES FROM THE

BOOK OF THE DEAD

Egyptian, Ptolemaic-Roman Period, c. 100 B.C.–A.D. 200
Linen; 3441 (top): 4 $\frac{1}{2}$ × 15 in. (11.5 × 38 cm),
3327 (bottom): 4 $\frac{3}{4}$ × 21 $\frac{5}{8}$ in. (12 × 55 cm)

The Book of the Dead was a collection of magical spells, with accompanying vignettes, intended to enable the deceased to pass through the underworld in safety and to achieve a carefree existence in the hereafter. Excerpts from it (never the full repertoire) are commonly found buried with the dead, written on rolls of papyrus, vellum, or leather, on the wrappings of the mummy, and on the walls of the tomb chamber or on individual items of funerary furniture.

These two fragments of inscribed, medium-quality linen come from the wrappings of a mummy. The first (top), probably from the beginning of the document, is painted in black with an outline representation of the god Osiris, lord of the underworld. The mummiform god wears the atef crown and is shown seated upon his throne within a shrine, his body enclosed within a close-fitting shroud from which his hands protrude to clutch a crook and flail, the twin symbols of kingship; offerings of food, drink, and flowers are placed before him. Two columns of cursive hieroglyphs between the god and the offerings read (right to left): "Recitation by Osiris, Foremost of the Westerners [i.e., the dead], the great god, / lord of Abydos, lord of eternity, ruler of forever." The speech that this text anticipates is not present.

The second fragment of inscribed linen (bottom) is of similar quality and perhaps from the same mummy. It contains a vignette showing the procession to the tomb and the deceased adoring the god Re-Horakhty. The text, written from right to left in hieratic, is taken from Chapters 1, 2, and the beginning of Chapter 3 of the Book of the Dead—the "spells of going out into the day." According to Dr. R. A. Caminos, who has studied these linen fragments, the owner's name is given as Pakhasu, and that of his mother as Taremetjnetbastet. Neither Pakhasu nor his mother appear to be attested from other sources. Palaeography and overall style, however, suggest that they flourished between c. 100 B.C. and A.D. 200, if not a little later.

—CNR

For the relevant chapters from the Book of the Dead, see T. G. Allen, *The Book of the Dead, or Going Forth by Day* (Chicago, 1974); R. O. Faulkner, *The Ancient Egyptian Book of the Dead*, ed. Carol Andrews (London, 1985). For Books of the Dead on linen, see particularly R. A. Caminos, "The Rendells Mummy Bandages," *Journal of Egyptian Archaeology* 68 (1982), pp. 145–55; S. Pernigotti, *Tomba di Boccori. Il libro dei morti su bende di mummia* (Pisa, 1985–).

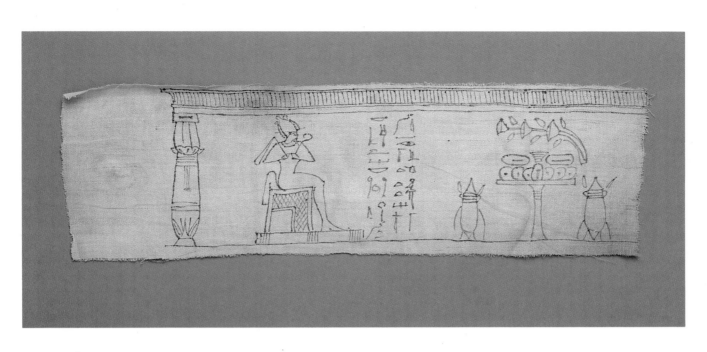

MUMMY PORTRAIT

Egyptian, Roman Period, c. A.D. 250–300
Tempera on wood, 13 ³/₈ × 9 in. (34 × 23 cm)
4946

This portrait, in classical style, represents a balding, middle-aged man seated face-front and wearing a white tunic decorated with two embroidered bands. The painting is of a type produced in Egypt between the first and fourth centuries A.D. employing one of two basic media: encaustic (pigmented beeswax) and tempera (watercolor). These portraits are usually found bound in place over the face of the owner's mummy, in an interesting combination of foreign artistic tradition and native religious practice. At least one such portrait has been found in its ancient frame, indicating that, in the earlier period at least, such paintings were commissioned for display while the owner was still alive.

Freud acquired his mummy portrait from the collection formed by an Austrian dealer, Theodor Graf. Graf was associated with several important archaeological discoveries made in Egypt during the latter years of the nineteenth century. In November 1887, Graf took delivery of a large consignment of portrait panels executed in encaustic and tempera, stripped from mummies that had been uncovered only a short time before in the cemetery of ancient Philadelphia, er-Rubaiyat, in the Faiyum. Of the more than three hundred mummy portraits that were to pass through Graf's hands, some ninety-six were put on display in Berlin in 1889. The exhibition was a great success and subsequently traveled to many of Europe's major museums. In 1893 the collection was shown at the World's Fair in Chicago.

In the several catalogues of the Graf collection produced during these years, the present mummy portrait is listed as no. 53. It is described in the 1922 (Buberl) edition with Freud's ownership and its purchase price (600 florins) noted.

—CNR

The Freud portrait is published as no. 482 in K. Parlasca, *Repertorio d'arte dell'Egitto greco-romano. Serie B—Vol. II. Ritratti di mummie* (Rome, 1977), p. 88, with pl. 117, fig. 2, where full references will be found. The definitive edition of the Graf portraits is that of P. Buberl, *Die griechisch-ägyptischen Mumienbildnisse der Sammlung Th. Graf* (Vienna, 1922), which Freud owned. The standard discussion of mummy portraits is that of K. Parlasca, *Mumienporträts und verwandte Denkmäler* (Wiesbaden, 1966); see also A. F. Shore, *Portrait Painting from Roman Egypt* (rev. ed., London, 1972), and D. L. Thompson, *Mummy Portraits in the J. Paul Getty Museum* (Malibu, 1982).

STIRRUP JAR

Mycenaean, Late Helladic IIIB, c. 1300–1200 B.C.
Terracotta, h. 6 in. (15 cm)
3757

This beautifully shaped vase reaches its widest diameter some distance below the shoulder. It rises as a narrow cylinder from its small, flat, and spreading foot. It then gradually swells out before drawing in again to the flattish shoulder, from which rise the double stirrup handle, with its false spout, and the actual spout. The rounded form is accentuated by the decoration of concentric bands of orange glaze, closely spaced near the foot, more sparsely above it, and most concentrated near the shoulder, just below which the rings are varied with a band of broken zigzags. The upper surface of the stirrup handle is decorated with concentric rings, matching the set under the foot, and the shoulder bears five stylized papyrus heads, each formed from three semicircular strokes, one hook, and two rows of dots. This simple decoration articulates and emphasizes the stirrup jar's taut, elegant form, with which it is in perfect harmony.

This vase belongs to the period of the great Mycenaean palaces. Vases of this type were very probably found at Mycenae by Freud's hero Heinrich Schliemann when he excavated there in the mid-1870s.
—LB

This vase is published and discussed by C. and H. Weiss, "Ein Blick in die Antikensammlung Sigmund Freud," *Antike Welt* 16 (1985), pp. 44–45. For the type of vase and its decoration, see A. D. Lacey, *Greek Pottery in the Bronze Age* (London, 1967), pp. 199, 215; for the stylized papyrus heads, see A. Furumark, *Mycenaean Pottery: Analysis and Classification* (Stockholm, 1941), p. 293, fig. 45, no. 130 (slightly more angular than this one); for a vase very similar in shape and decoration, but again with more angular flowers, see Stefan Hiller, *Mykenische Keramik* (Mainz, 1975), pl. 25, no. 242.

HORSE AND RIDER

Greek, Archaic Period, c. 550 B.C.
Terracotta, h. 4 ⅛ in. (10.3 cm)
3723

This highly stylized figure of a horse and rider merges man and animal into one entity. The apparently legless rider, who clings with both hands to the horse's mane, seems to grow from the horse's back. The horse is boldly decorated with stripes and slashes; his eye is strongly marked and on his chest three rows of dots above a wavy line are perhaps a schematic indication of a harness.

Horses of this kind, with or without riders, were a popular product of the coroplasts' workshops of Boeotia in the sixth century B.C. Like most terracotta figurines, they are generally found in graves, where they were laid as gifts and perhaps to provide comfort to the dead. Although their significance is not altogether clear, models and carvings of horses and horsemen were always popular in ancient Greece in graves or on tombstones. They may well have been intended to underline the heroic character of the dead person as a warrior or hunter.

—LB

Freud used the metaphor of riding to speak of the ego riding the forces of the id:

> The functional importance of the ego is manifested in the fact that normally control over the approaches to motility devolves upon it. Thus in its relation to the id it is like a man on horseback, who has to hold in check the superior strength of the horse; with this difference, that the rider tries to do so with his own strength while the ego uses borrowed forces. The analogy may be carried a little further. Often a rider, if he is not to be parted from his horse, is obliged to guide it where it wants to go; so in the same way the ego is in the habit of transforming the id's will into action as if it were its own. (SE, 19, p. 25)

This figure is an especially apt image for this metaphor because Freud conceived the ego as differentiating out of the id, and hence, horse and rider are joined into one composite body.

—FM

For very similar examples of horsemen, see R. A. Higgins, *Catalogue of Terracottas in the Department of Greek and Roman Antiquities, British Museum* (London, 1954), I, nos. 782–86, pl. 105. For a brief discussion of the type, see R. A. Higgins, *Tanagra and the Figurines* (London, 1987), p. 78.

CORINTHIAN BLACK-FIGURED

ALABASTRON

Greek, Archaic Period, c. 600 B.C.
Terracotta, h. 11 ¹/₈ in. (28.2 cm)
3699

The overall impression given by this large alabastron (oil or perfume flask) is of a rich, abstract tapestry, but in fact, there is a central subject, a winged "mistress of animals," standing frontally but with her head turned to the left. She wears a beautiful, finely patterned tunic, with its details incised and touches of added red and white. She has a large head, broad shoulders, and long arms. She wears a long-sleeved tunic over another garment; the tunic is richly bordered and has a central decorative panel of incised zigzags and white spots; the undergarment is striped vertically in red, black, and white. On her head she wears a polos, the tall headdress often worn by goddesses in the Archaic Period (c. 600–480 B.C.), and in each hand she holds the neck of a swan. The wings of the swans extend around the vessel and almost touch at the back, and the field is filled with a dense thicket of ornaments: large rosettes, palmette bunches, and lotus buds.

The vase painting of Corinth in the sixth century B.C. was characterized by scenes of animals, some real, some fantastic, prowling through dense thickets of ornaments. Many of the monsters, animals, and semi-human figures originated in the Near East. The winged mistress of animals shown here is thought to derive from various Near Eastern mother-goddesses, whom the Greeks associated with the huntress goddess Artemis.

This vase presents a typical alabastron profile, the contours swelling out strongly below the slender neck, then tapering to the rounded base. The decoration of black and red, with touches of faded grayish white, shows to perfection on the characteristic Corinthian pale yellow-brown clay. The vertical edge of the rim is decorated with a simple broken meander, and the neck has vertical rays above a band of checker pattern formed by setting short vertical black rays between horizontal bands of golden glaze. Under the base is a large rosette framed by rays and lines.

This vase is carefully painted, and in general the shape, size, and style suggest it belongs to the early Corinthian period.

—LB

For Corinthian vases of similar shape and size, see London GR 1861.10-24.15 and 1869.4-4.11, both decorated with a winged male figure. For the mistress of animals on Corinthian vases, see H. Payne, *Necrocorinthia* (Oxford, 1931), pp. 78–79; for a more general discussion of the mistress of animals in Archaic Greek art, see Chr. A. Christou, *Potnia Theron. Eine Untersuchung über Ursprung, Erscheinungsformen und Wandlungen der Gestalt einer Gottheit* (Thessaloníki, 1968), and R. Laffineur, *L'Orfèvrerie Rhodienne orientalisante* (Paris, 1978), pp. 32–45, with good bibliography.

ATHENIAN BLACK-FIGURED LEKYTHOS

Gela Painter
Greek, Archaic Period, c. 500–480 B.C.
Terracotta, h. 12 ³/₄ in. (32.5 cm)
3679

This large cylinder lekythos (oil or perfume flask) bears a figure scene of two warriors on horseback. Doric columns frame the scene on the left and right. The warriors move to the right, armed with shields, spears, and helmets, and wearing short tunics and mantles. Beside their horses walk a dog and a bitch. The crests of the warriors' helmets break through into the meander border above the scene, and in the field are letters of the Greek alphabet, principally *nu*'s, scattered at random. Added red is used for the mane of the second horse and the tail of the first, for the crest of the leading warrior's helmet, for the rims of both their shields, and for the spots on their mantles; these last are also decorated with incised crosses.

It is likely that the warriors are female, presumably Amazons; if they were men, one would expect them, in the Archaic period, to be shown bearded. Black-figure vase painters covered women's skin with white slip, which was fragile and tended to wear off. Usually it is possible to detect, as here, where the exposed areas of flesh are rather greenish, differing in tone from the other black areas. This is noticeable, for example, on the near legs of both riders, now hardly standing out against the black of the horses' flanks. Had they been male riders, the legs would probably have been incised. The same greenish tinge to the black occurs where one would expect to see a shield device on the shield of the leading rider.

This large lekythos has a short neck, a very plump and heavy cylinder, a thick fillet between foot and body, and an elegantly profiled, stepped foot. The lip, handle, lower part of the body, and upper surface of the foot are decorated in black glaze, which has partly peeled off the lower parts of the body, while the other areas are reserved (unglazed).

The neck rises from a ring of tongues; on the shoulders are three linked multipetaled fan palmettes, with two dots between each, and a large open bud hanging on either side of the handle. The figure scene is bordered by a meander band running to the right between one black line above and two below; the lower border is formed by a single glazed ground line in the reserved area of the figure scene, and in the black glaze below it are two narrow red lines.

The figure scene is on the whole rather carelessly painted, although more care has been taken with the horses and dogs than with the human figures. The distinction between the sexes of the dogs is an interestingly realistic detail.

This vase has been attributed to the Gela Painter, a prolific painter of lekythoi who was named after the Sicilian colony of Gela, where more than forty vases by his hand were found. The size and shape of the vase are those he favored, and the form of the palmette decoration is highly idiosyncratic. The subject of the figure scene occurs elsewhere in his work, and the letters sprinkled in the field are characteristic. Typical, too, is the interest shown in animals and the more careless rendering of human figures. The framing columns are also a frequent feature of his scenes.

—LB

For a careful analysis of this vase with attribution to the Gela Painter, see C. and H. Weiss, "Ein Blick in die Antikensammlung Sigmund Freud," *Antike Welt* 16 (1985), pp. 46–48. For the Gela Painter see E. Haspels, *Attic Black-figured Lekythoi* (Paris, 1936), pp. 78ff and 205ff (this vase belongs to group IIIb, pp. 80–81); J. D. Beazley, *Attic Black-figure Vase-painters* (Oxford, 1956), pp. 473ff and 699ff; J. M. Hemmelrijk, "The Gela Painter in the Allard Pierson Museum," *Bulletin Antieke Beschaving* 49 (1974), pp. 117–58.

ATHENIAN BLACK-FIGURED LEKYTHOS

Haimon Painter (Workshop)
Greek, Classical Period, c. 490–470 B.C.
Terracotta, h. 6 ³/₈ in. (16.2 cm)
3683

This small chimney lekythos presents the Sphinx, facing right, seated on a column capital or altar between two seated and two standing elders of Thebes, all leaning on sticks. There are dots in the field, intended as sketchy imitations of inscriptions. White was added to highlight certain areas: the details of the altar, the Sphinx's head and wings, the outlines of the folding stools of the elders, and the fillets around their heads.

This lekythos has an elongated neck and mouth, a flat shoulder, and a stepped foot. On the shoulder are two sketchy rows of buds, and below the shoulder, which is articulated by a single black line, is a sketchy meander running to the right above two black lines. Below the figure scene are three narrow reserved lines.

The shape of the vase and the careless style of the painting, with the elongated, small-headed figures, indicate an attribution to the workshop of the Haimon Painter. Both the style and the iconography find close parallels in the work of the Painter and his associates, although the fake letters in the field would be unusual for the Painter himself.

—LB

See J. M. Moret, *Oedipe, la sphinx et les Thébains* (Geneva, 1984) for two very similar pieces with virtually identical scenes: Louvre CA 1705 (pl. 29.1–4), which is assigned to the related Pholos Group, and Frankfort VF b 305 (pls. 27.1–2), attributed to the Haimon Painter. For the Haimon Painter, see E. Haspels, *Attic Black-figured Lekythoi* (Paris, 1936), pp. 130–41.

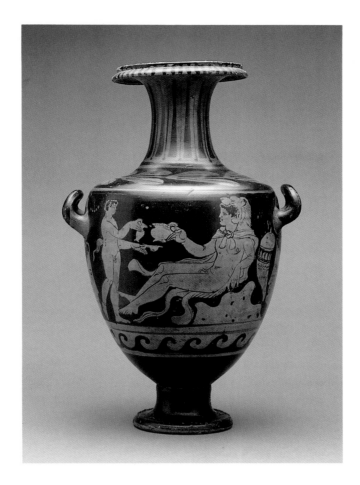

RED-FIGURED HYDRIA

Foundling Group
Greek, Classical Period, from Campania, c. 360–330 B.C.
Terracotta, h. 13 in. (33 cm)
4400

The figure scene on this small hydria shows Herakles on the right, reclining on a rock and attended by a satyr. Herakles is naked except for his lion skin, which he wears pulled up over his head, the paws tied on his chest. He holds out a mug to be filled by the satyr, who carries a jug and a strainer, which he seems to be offering to the hero. Behind Herakles is a large overflowing cornucopia. All the vessels bear traces of encrustation, which suggests that they were once painted either white or gold. In the field above are three festoons of dots, also once white or gold, of which only shadows now remain.

This rather elongated hydria has a long neck and a tall, spreading foot. The overhanging rim is decorated with rays sketchily rendered; the neck bears a rough tongue pattern. On the shoulder is a veined laurel wreath running to the right; probably it was originally embellished with white or gold spots set above and below the central stem where each pair of leaves branches off, now marked only by shadows in the glaze. Below the vertical handle is a palmette complex, which extends with trumpet-shaped flower buds at each side across to the horizontal handles. Under each handle is a female head. Below the figure scene, encircling the vase, is a band of wave pattern moving to the right.

—LB

This vase is listed by A. D. Trendall, *The Red-figured Vases of Lucania, Campania and Sicily*, 3d suppl., cons. (London, 1983), p. 181, no. 113a. For Campanian vases, see A. D. Trendall, *The Red-figured Vases of Lucania, Campania and Sicily* (Oxford, 1967), pp. 189–561.

ATHENIAN RED-FIGURED LEKYTHOS

Achilles and Phiale Painters (Workshop)
Greek, Classical Period, c. 450–440 B.C.
Terracotta, h. 14 ³/₄ in. (37.4 cm)
3700

This large cylinder lekythos is of elegant design and manufacture. The figure scene shows a winged woman pursuing a youth to the left. Under a black-bordered mantle, the woman wears a finely pleated chiton with full, baggy sleeves. Her hair is arranged under a *kekryphalos* (headband), and she wears earrings. She stretches out her right hand to the youth, who moves off to the left while looking back at his pursuer. He is dressed in a large mantle, also black-bordered, which hangs to his feet and leaves his right shoulder bare. On his head he wears a wreath of red-painted leaves, and he carries a lyre.

Judging by the context of the pursuit and the predatory gesture of her right hand, the winged woman must be Eos, goddess of dawn. According to legend, Eos was of an amorous disposition, and in art of the fifth century B.C. she is frequently shown pursuing a youth, either Kephalos or Tithonos. Kephalos is usually shown as a hunter; this youth's lyre makes it more likely that he is Tithonos, a prince of Troy. The abduction of Tithonos had a tragic ending, for when Eos persuaded Zeus to grant her lover immortality, she forgot to ask also for the gift of eternal youth. Thus it became the fate of the unfortunate Tithonos to grow ever older and more decrepit, yet powerless to die.

This lekythos has a long neck, separated from the lip by a slight jog and rising from a sloping shoulder. The cylinder is almost vertical for much of its length, tapering sharply to the narrow fillet above the small, neat foot. The neck, handle, and lip are black-glazed, as is the upper surface of the foot and most of the body, on which the figures are reserved in the red-figure tech-nique. The shoulder is decorated in the older black-figure technique, with the pattern in black upon a clay ground; the vertical edge of the foot is also reserved. The black glaze is generally lustrous but is in parts slightly smoky with a greenish tinge. These areas are probably ghosted imprints of other vases fired near this lekythos in the same kiln.

The base of the neck is marked by an ovolo (egg pattern), and on the shoulder are three black palmettes, the central one pointing down, with an elongated central petal, the outer two pointing toward the handle. All three are circumscribed by scrolls, with double curls in place of the more usual lotus buds flanking the central palmette. The figure scene is bordered below by a band of simple meander running to the right, and above by a meander band in which three meander squares alternate with one upright crossed square.

The shape and pattern decoration of this vase enable its assignment to the workshop of the Achilles and Phiale Painters. A more precise attribution is difficult; it is near the work of the Phiale Painter and his associates, but the figures are stiffer and sketchier. The eye in particular is very casually rendered with four brief strokes, that of the brow extended to the edge of the nose.

—LB

See C. and H. Weiss, "Ein Blick in die Antikensammlung Sigmund Freud," *Antike Welt* 16 (1985), pp. 48–51. For Eos, see *Lexicon Iconographicum Mythologiae Classicae* (Zurich and Munich, 1981–), III, s.v. "Eos" (C. Weiss). For the Achilles and Phiale Painters, see E. Simon, *Die griechische Vasen* (Munich, 1978), pp. 136–40.

ATHENIAN WHITE-GROUND LEKYTHOS

Reed Painter
Greek, Classical Period, c. 420–400 B.C.
Terracotta, h. 11 ⅛ in. (28.3 cm)
3711

This white-ground lekythos shows a youth (left) and a woman (right) facing each other across a funerary stele. The youth, wrapped in a red mantle that leaves his chest and arms bare, leans on a stick. The woman is dressed in a black peplos with red borders; her face and hair, like those of the youth, are rendered in red outline and wash. In her left hand she carries a shallow basket from which dangle three fillets or sashes; her right hand reaches toward the stele. The stele is tall with a stepped base and crowned with an ovolo molding, surmounted by an acanthus leaf acroterion, which breaks through the meander border above. The stele is hung with sashes like those in the basket, and to emphasize that the scene is set in a graveyard, another tomb monument is drawn (rather awkwardly) behind the first.

This lekythos is of standard late fifth-century B.C. shape and size. The neck, lip, and handle are black-glazed, as are the lower part of the body and upper surface of the foot. The vertical edge of the foot is covered in a red wash; the shoulder and upper body of the vase bear a white slip on which the figures are painted in matte red outlines, then filled in with washes of solid color, principally red and black. The shoulder is decorated with a palmette design in dilute brown glaze with touches of added red, now very worn. The upper edge of the cylinder wall is bordered with a band of meander with occasional saltire crosses, very sketchily executed in dilute glaze, between double and more solid glaze lines above and below.

White-ground lekythoi were made to contain the perfumed oil given as a gift to the dead; some of them have an inner container so that the vase could appear full at less expense. Nearly all were made as grave goods, and this accounts in part for their extreme fragility and the fugitive nature of their coloring, much of which was applied after firing. Their subject matter is often funerary, visitors at a tomb being the most popular theme. Sometimes the scenes show lekythoi standing on the steps of a tomb, or else carried in baskets like the one shown here. Often there are just two people in the scene, and it is generally difficult to tell the deceased from the mourner. This ambiguity is paralleled on the contemporary sculptured tombstones of Attica. In this case, however, it seems likely that the woman is bringing an offering to the tomb of the dead youth.

On the grounds of shape, pattern-work, style, and subject, the vase may be attributed to the Reed Painter, a prolific painter of white-ground lekythoi. The reeds that are the key characteristic of his work are absent here, but typical of his hand is the woman's head, with delicate profile and luxuriantly curling red hair. Typical, too, are the form of the stele, the appearance of the second monument behind it, the abundance of fillets, and the attitude of the youth—all features readily observed on the Reed Painter's many vases.

—LB

This vase is unpublished, unless it is ARV 1379, 62, Paris Market Segredakis, described by J. D. Beazley, *Attic Red-figure Vase-painters* (Oxford, 1963) as "youth and woman at tomb (youth leaning on a stick to right, woman in peplos moving left with basket)." Freud owned at least one other object that had originated with the Parisian dealer Segredakis, notably the bronze Venus considered here (see p. 112), purchased by Marie Bonaparte; she may have presented Freud with other antiquities from the same source. For the Reed Painter and his workshop, see D. C. Kurtz, *Athenian White-ground Lekythoi* (Oxford, 1975), pp. 58–68. A very similar scene appears on one of the Reed Painter's London vases, GR 1873.8-20.303 (vase D 73).

SPHINX

Greek, South Italian, late 5th–early 4th century B.C.
Terracotta, h. 7 1/4 in. (18.5 cm)
4387

In the Greek legend of Thebes, the Sphinx was a monster, half-lion and half-woman, who destroyed those who could not answer her riddle: "What is it that walks on four legs in the morning, on two at noon, and on three in the evening?" Oedipus answered that it was Man, who first crawls on all fours, then walks upright, and in old age needs a stick as a third leg.

This figurine is apparently solid, and was originally covered in white slip, now discolored. The clay, where visible, is orange. The Sphinx sits solidly on her haunches, facing ahead. On her head is the tall polos headdress; her wavy hair is drawn back from her forehead and fastened in a bun at the back. Her breasts are prominent, her legs and paws sturdily modeled. Her body is slim, and her wings are precisely modeled and neatly curled above her back.

The provenance and date of this piece are suggested by its clay and style.

—LB

For similar examples of Greek terracotta sphinxes, see F. Winter, *Die Antiken Terrakotten* (Berlin, 1903), III, part i, p. 230, no. 5 (two in Ruvo and one in Berlin, not otherwise published).

ATHENIAN RED-FIGURED HYDRIA

Apollonia Group
Greek, Classical Period, c. 380–360 B.C.
Terracotta, h. 9 in. (22.8 cm)
3117

The scene on this small hydria (water jar) shows Oedipus seated before the Sphinx. Oedipus (right) is seated on his mantle, which covers a rock. Naked except for the *pilos* (cap) on his head, he leans on the pair of spears held in his right hand. His left hand seems to make a conversational gesture toward the Sphinx, who sits bolt upright facing him. Her seat is a curiously rendered rock, shown as if with a black core. Her face and body are white, the body decorated with spots of brown glaze presumably representing fur. Her wings are reserved in the red ground, with details added in black glaze; her tail is also reserved. Behind her stands a youth, presumably a companion of Oedipus, also armed with two spears and with a mantle over his shoulders.

This hydria has an elongated neck, a wide rim, and a relatively narrow body drawn in to an elaborate stepped foot. The overhanging edge of the rim is decorated with a carelessly executed ovolo, and the same pattern encircles the vase below its widest point to form the ground line for the figures. The vertical handle rises from a complex of palmettes and lotus buds, which extends around to the horizontal handles of the vase.

—LB

For Freud, no myth attained a greater explanatory power in relation to psychoanalysis than that of Oedipus and the Sphinx. The influence of his classical education on the development of his thinking is readily apparent in the crystallization of his ideas on the human condition in the famed "Oedipus complex." Reviewing his dreams and self-analysis, and drawing on his knowledge of Greek tragedy, Freud observed patterns of experience within himself that he believed universal in human behavior:

I have found, in my own case too, being in love with my mother and jealous of my father, and I now consider it a universal event in early childhood. . . . If this is so, we can understand the gripping power of *Oedipus Rex*, in spite of all the objections that reason raises against the presupposition of fate . . . . The Greek legend seizes upon a compulsion which everyone recognizes because he senses its existence within himself. Everyone in the audience was once a budding Oedipus in fantasy and each recoils in horror from the dream fulfillment here transplanted into reality, with the full quantity of repression which separates his infantile state from the present one. (SE, 1, p. 265)

On Freud's fiftieth birthday and in recognition of the key role that the Oedipus legend had played in the development of psychoanalysis, Freud's colleagues presented him with a medallion bearing a portrait of Freud on one side, and Oedipus and the Sphinx on the other, with the quote from Sophocles, "He who knew the famous riddle and was a most powerful man."

—FM

On this vase, see C. and H. Weiss, "Ein Blick in die Antikensammlung Sigmund Freud," *Antike Welt* 16 (1985), pp. 50–51. For a similar scene on a vase of comparable date and style, in which Oedipus, in the company of another youth, prepares to answer the Sphinx, seated on similar rocks (present whereabouts of this vase are unknown), see J. M. Moret, *Oedipe, la sphinx et les Thébains* (Geneva, 1984), pl. 55; For the Apollonia Group, see J. D. Beazley, *Attic Red-figure Vase-painters* (Oxford, 1963), 1482, and K. Schefold, *Untersuchungen zu den Kertscher Vasen* (Berlin and Leipzig, 1934), pp. 102–104.

FIGURE OF A WOMAN

Greek, Hellenistic Period, from Tanagra, c. 300–250 B.C.
Terracotta, h. 6 ¹/₈ in. (15.5 cm)
3925

This is a perfect example of a Tanagra figure. Although such figures were mass-produced in antiquity, today scholars and collectors unite in their praise. This woman demonstrates the Hellenistic interest in the individual and human, rather than the ideal and heroic. Even though virtually nothing is known about the social conditions of third-century Boeotia, figures such as this seem to provide a vivid glimpse of the women of Tanagra going about their daily lives.

This figure is of fine, pale orange clay. It was made in two molds; the base was made separately. There are traces of white slip over most of the figure, and red on the hair.

The woman stands with her weight on her right leg, her head turned to the left. She wears a mantle drawn tightly over a chiton and muffling her right arm; in her left hand she holds a fan. Her hair, under her conical sun hat, is drawn back in the "melon" style and tied in a bun. She also wears earrings.

—LB

For the history and terracottas of Tanagra, see R. A. Higgins, *Tanagra and the Figurines* (London, 1987). For a figure whose body may derive from the same mold as this one, see F. Winter, *Die Antiken Terrakotten* (Berlin, 1903), III, part ii, 54:7 (Athens 1112); compare also London GR 1875.3-9.1 (C 247).

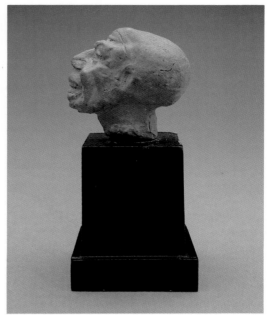

GROTESQUE HEADS

Greek, Hellenistic Period, 100 B.C.–A.D. 100
Terracotta, each: h. 1 ⁵⁄₈ in. (4 cm)
3752, 3747

These two small grotesque heads were broken from figures of a man and a woman. Both have hideously large noses, ears, and mouths set in sagging, wrinkled skin. The female head differs from the male in its head covering; otherwise there is very little to distinguish them.

The exact significance of such grotesque heads is not clear, although thousands survive from ancient Greece. Perhaps they represent dwarfs or persons with other deformities who may have been objects of curiosity in the Hellenistic courts. Elaborate tableau and mime performances were an important element of Hellenistic court entertainment and may have included dwarfs. Judging from contemporary art and literature, the Hellenistic mind certainly displayed an extreme interest in physical deformity in all its various forms; the evidence does not permit us to conclude whether this interest was morbid or sympathetic.

—LB

For examples of similar grotesque heads from Smyrna, see S. Mollard-Besques, *Musée du Louvre. Catalogue raisonné des figurines et reliefs en terre-cuite grecs, étrusques et romains* (Paris, 1972), III, part 1, pls. 292–329; for examples very close to these, see especially pls. 295e and 321i.

HEAD OF A WOMAN FROM A RELIEF

Greek, Classical Period, early 4th century B.C.
Pentelic marble, h. 4 ³/₄ in. (12 cm)
4520

This marble head has been broken from a large piece of sculpture worked in high relief. The angle of the relief is such that the head would have appeared in three-quarter view to the right. The face of this young woman is beautifully designed and realized: the contours of the cheeks and forehead run smoothly one into the other; the chin is firm and rounded, the nose long and finely cut, the eyes set at a perfect angle. The smooth, polished surface of the skin is emphasized by its juxtaposition with the rough and wavy hair, which is parted in the center of the forehead, drawn back, and tied in a knot on the neck.

This head is extremely Classical in style. The marble is Pentelic, like the marble of the Parthenon, and the head itself is very likely to have come from an Athenian grave relief. Such reliefs generally show either two or three figures: the dead person and one or more relatives. The figures are shown in attitudes of great stillness and silent, dignified grief. As with scenes on white-ground lekythoi, it is frequently impossible to decide who is the mourner and who the person mourned. It is certainly impossible to decide to which category this head belongs, for her downcast gaze would suit either.

Many would consider this piece the single most aesthetically pleasing and valuable article in Freud's collection. It is certainly the most truly Classical.

—LB

For a description of grave reliefs of this type, see M. Robertson, *A History of Greek Art* (Cambridge, 1975), pp. 365–72, pls. 121–24.

EROS

Greek, Hellenistic Period,
probably from Tanagra, c. 300–250 B.C.
Terracotta, h. 3 3/8 in. (8.5 cm)
3897

This Eros was made to appear suspended in flight, as is
suggested by the pierced projection between his wings,
and by his pose. His left leg is forward, wings raised, his
right arm brought across his chest; his missing left arm
was perhaps outstretched. Around his head is a narrow
band, and draped across his lower body is a scanty mantle. A band, perhaps for amulets, crosses his chest from
his right shoulder. On his feet are boots.
—LB

For this type, see F. Winter, *Die Antiken Terrakotten* (Berlin,
1903), III, part ii, pp. 320–22.

EROS

Greek, Hellenistic Period, 3rd–2nd century B.C.
Terracotta, h. 4 in. (10 cm)
3912

This childlike figure of Eros is shown with his right leg slightly forward. His wreathed head is set to one side, and both his arms are muffled in his mantle, which is drawn up to expose his genitals.

The clay of this figurine is red; it was originally coated in white slip. Traces of gold are visible at the top of the wings and on the wreath, blue on the mantle, and red on the hair.

Aspects of this figure, particularly the coy pose, the affected set of the head, and the sweet smile, cast doubt on its authenticity. If genuine, both the color and texture of the clay and the style of the figurine suggest it was made in Boeotia.

—LB

For a similar piece, see S. Mollard-Besques, *Musée du Louvre. Catalogue raisonné des figurines et reliefs en terre-cuite grecs, étrusques et romains* (Paris, 1963), II, pl. 62c, MYR 7.

EROS

Greek, Hellenistic Period, from Myrina, c. 150–100 B.C.
Terracotta, h. 15 in. (38 cm)
3880

This spectacular terracotta Eros is shown flying forward, his left leg in front of the right, his head turned to the right but both arms bent to the left. He appears to have been carrying something, for not only are his hands unfinished, but their attitude demands an object, possibly a lyre or other musical instrument, a common attribute of figures of this type. His whole posture is, in fact, remarkably contorted and complex.

The clay varies in color from pale orange on the body to deep pinkish red on the wings. Both wings carry a coroplast's monogram in the shape of a large *kappa*. The figurine was originally coated in white slip, now partly worn off. Traces of blue appear on the lower feathers of both wings, and traces of gold on the upper edge of the right wing only; traces of red may be seen on the hair and wreath.

—LB

Freud identified the basic life instinct as Eros, as opposed to Thanatos, and he described the evolution of civilization as "the struggle between Eros and Death, between the instinct of life and the instinct of destruction, as it works itself out in the human species" (SE, 21, p. 122). In defining Eros as the life instinct or the libido, Freud referred to the classical concept of love:

> We are of the opinion, then, that language has carried out an entirely justified piece of unification in creating the word "love" with its numerous uses, and we cannot do better than take it as the basis of our scientific discussions and expositions as well. By coming to this decision, psychoanalysis has let loose a storm of indignation, as though it had been guilty of an act of outrageous innovation. Yet it has done nothing original in taking love in this wider sense. In its origin, function, and relations to sexual love, the "Eros" of the philosopher Plato coincides exactly with the love force, the libido of psychoanalysis. (SE, 18, p. 91)

Freud's collection includes at least six statues of the god of love. Although this Eros held a musical instrument, others depicted in contemporary Hellenistic wall paintings carry bows—a reminder that Eros, in a fusion of the forces of aggression with the libido, causes his victims to fall in love by attacking them.

—FM

The body and legs of this Eros are almost certainly from the same mold as a figurine in the Louvre, MYR 60, see S. Mollard-Besques, *Musée du Louvre. Catalogue raisonné des figurines et reliefs en terre-cuite grecs, étrusques et romains* (Paris, 1963), II, pl. 42b; the head and wreath resemble a similar figure, also in the Louvre (MYR 56, in Mollard-Besques, loc. cit., pl. 42e). For other similar figures, see F. Winter, *Die Antiken Terrakotten* (Berlin, 1903), III, part ii, pls. 342 and 344.

ARTEMIS

Greek, Hellenistic Period, from Myrina, 2nd century B.C.
Terracotta, h. 9 7/8 in. (25 cm)
3273

The goddess Artemis, huntress and patroness of wild creatures, is recognizable by her hunting dress of short tunic, mantle, and boots with turned-down flaps. She is shown in rapid movement to the right, her right arm flung out ahead, while her left, wrapped in the mantle, hangs at her side. On her head she wears a diadem. Her tunic is pressed back against her thighs as though blown by a violent wind, and it is fastened with a broad girdle at her waist; her mantle cascades over her arm. Her hair is drawn back and arranged in a bun, and the features of her face are very crudely rendered.

The clay of this figurine is bright red and very coarse. The decoration consists of white slip, with rose-madder on the mantle and near the hem of the tunic. The figurine was made in two molds, front and back, with the join visible at the side; the back is fully modeled, with a large, round vent.

In its style and also in the type of clay, this piece strongly resembles a figurine of unknown provenance in the British Museum, again representing Artemis, this time seated on an altar with her arm around a deer. The British Museum piece has been attributed to Myrina.

—LB

Images of androgynous, childless women intrigued Freud. Artemis, like Athena, is chaste and masculinized. Both are virgin goddesses of aggression: Artemis is goddess of the hunt, armed with arrows; Athena is goddess of war and holds a spear. It is interesting to note that whereas Freud interpreted the action in the *Oresteia* of Aeschylus as a turning from matriarchy to patriarchy (SE, 23, p. 114), the plot is set in motion by the rage of Artemis, and the play is brought to an end by the proclamation of Athena. So the brutal battles between the sexes and generations that are fought out among the human characters in this drama are, in fact, controlled by phallicized women who possess enormous power and who live, as it were, outside of human time.

—FM

For the British Museum example, GR 1884.11-10.1 (D 158), see H. B. Walters, *A Catalogue of Terracottas in the Department of Greek and Roman Antiquities at the British Museum* (London, 1903), pl. xxxvii.

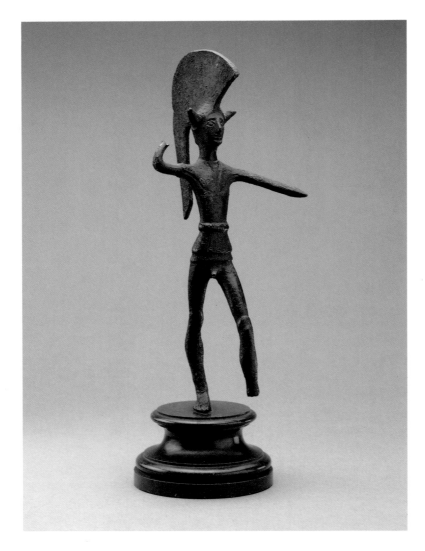

WARRIOR

Italic, Umbrian, c. 500–450 B.C.
Bronze, h. 8 ¼ in. (20.8 cm)
3135

Warrior figures of this type are commonly found as dedications in Umbrian and Etruscan sanctuaries, placed there presumably either in thanks for or in hope of victory. This slender, stylized figure of a warrior strides forward with left leg advanced and right hand raised to hold or throw a spear (now lost). He wears a helmet with a long crest, its details finely incised, and with upturned cheekpieces that reveal his rather crude features—large nose and eyes, small mouth, firm chin. His short cuirass is incised with decorative patterns; below is the skirt of his tunic, too short to cover his genitals.

—LB

Compare this figure with others such as *British Museum Catalogue of Bronzes*, no. 444, and Boston, MFA 52.186, from the Todi Group, illustrated and discussed by M. Comstock and C. Vermeule, in *Greek, Etruscan and Roman Bronzes in the Museum of Fine Arts, Boston* (Boston, 1971), pp. 166–67, no. 191. For these warriors as a class, see E. Richardson, *Etruscan Votive Bronzes* (Mainz, 1983), pp. 192ff.

ENGRAVED MIRROR

Etruscan, late 4th–early 3rd century B.C.
Bronze, 9 ⁵/₈ × 6 ¹/₂ in. (24.5 × 16.6 cm)
3082

Thousands of Etruscan mirrors survive today, many engraved, like this one, with a scene from mythology or daily life. Many of the subjects are at least mildly erotic; favorites are scenes of female adornment, showing a mirror in use, and scenes of the goddess of love. The undecorated, slightly convex backs of bronze mirrors were highly polished to reflect well the images of their owners, who, evidence suggests, were principally women.

Mirrors seem to have been an essential possession for any Etruscan woman of status. Scenes on the mirrors suggest that, for women, personal adornment, love, and fertility were closely associated with the idea of immortality of the soul. It is perhaps for this reason that so many mirrors accompanied their owners to the grave; most Etruscan mirrors have been found in tombs. Essential for a woman's adornment in life, they were equally crucial for the survival of her soul after death.

The scene on this mirror consists of four figures, standing apparently on rocks. In the center is an armed warrior with his arm around the woman at his side. The warrior wears a helmet and a corselet, and a mantle

hangs loosely around his arms. The woman is naked apart from a mantle falling around her hips, a necklace, and a headdress. Framing the scene on the left is another warrior, leaning on his spear, with his shield beside him on the ground. On the right is the goddess Athena, armed with helmet, spear, and shield.

The identity of the three characters to the left of Athena is not altogether clear. Two might represent the Dioscuri, the divine twins Castor and Pollux, and the third either their sister, Helen of Troy, or Venus. However, the proprietary gesture of the man beside the woman makes it perhaps more likely that the scene shows either the abduction of Helen by Theseus, accompanied by Peirithous, or the recovery of Helen after the sack of Troy by her husband, Menelaus, with another warrior. All these subjects are represented on Etruscan mirrors.

—LB

For an excellent survey of Etruscan mirrors, their origins, development, subject matter, function, and significance, see N. Thompson de Grummond, *A Guide to Etruscan Mirrors* (Tallahassee, 1982).

BALSAMARIUM

Etruscan, 3rd century B.C.
Bronze, h. 3 ³/₄ in. (9.4 cm)
3029

This container for perfumed oil, incense, or ointments, hollow cast in several parts, is in the form of two joining heads set back to back. The heads are those of a satyr and a maenad, male and female followers of Dionysos, god of wine. Satyrs are mischievous and amorous creatures, part-man, part-beast; maenads are their female counterparts, who symbolize impulse and abandon. Both heads are carefully modeled and finished. The maenad wears a twisted fillet around her hair, a band across her forehead, and a torque around her neck. Her features are plain but strongly marked—a straight nose, prominent eyes, large mouth, and full chin. The satyr's face is characteristically ugly, with sharply slanting eyebrows, deeply lined forehead, large ears, snub nose and curly hair, moustache, and beard. He also wears a twisted fillet around his head, and a bunch of grapes hangs in the center of his forehead. At the side where the two heads join is a cluster of grapes on a vine leaf.

Bronze vases such as this are fairly commonly found in Etruscan tombs of the third century B.C. Some may have been used to perfume the air, for many of them have chains, or, like Freud's, pierced lugs for the attachment of chains, by which they must have been suspended. Others may simply have held cosmetics. Some of these vases are shaped in the form of just one head, usually female, but very often they have the double-head arrangement seen here, and the most popular combination is of satyr and maenad heads. The attraction of this arrangement lay perhaps in its juxtaposition of opposites—beautiful and ugly, female and male.
—LB

Freud, the profound dualist, owned several two-faced figures. As early as 1899 he possessed a stone Janus head, and he kept this double-headed balsamarium on his desk in his later years. Dualism runs throughout Freud's thinking, appearing in such fundamental dichotomies as the pleasure principle versus the reality principle, Eros versus Thanatos, and libido versus aggression, and in Freud's notion of the dream mechanism of reversal—the representation of an idea by its opposite.

Likewise, central to this object is the notion of the basic bisexuality of all human beings, which Freud discussed in his fundamental work, "Three Essays on the Theory of Sexuality," of 1905 (SE, 7, pp. 135–243).
—FM

On these objects in general, with numerous excellent illustrations, see S. Haynes and H. Menzel, "Etruskische Bronzekopfgefässe," *Jahrbuch des römisch-germanischen Zentralmuseums Mainz* 6 (1959), pp. 110–27. For parallels, see *British Museum Catalogue of Bronzes*, nos. 756–58; and D. G. Mitten and S. Doeringer, *Master Bronzes from the Classical World* (Mainz, 1968), no. 225. A very similar piece was recently sold on the New York market; see Sotheby's *Antiquities and Islamic Art*, New York, May 29, 1987, lot 90.

ATHENA

Roman, 1st or 2nd century A.D.,
after a Greek original of the 5th century B.C.
Bronze, h. 4 ⅛ in. (10.4 cm)
3007

This solid-cast figurine of Athena presents the goddess of wisdom and war in a frontal pose, with her left hand raised to hold a spear, now lost. In her lowered hand she carries a patera (libation bowl) decorated with a petal design. Her head is bent and turned a little to the right; her left leg is straight, the right bent at the knee in the classical contrapposto stance. She wears a helmet of Corinthian type set back on her head; the crest is long and reaches well below her shoulders. Her peplos is belted over the overfall and open down the right side; above it she wears her usual attribute, a rectangular aegis (breastplate) with featherlike scales and a crudely featured gorgoneion, a representation of the gorgon Medusa's head, here lacking its usual fringe of snakes. The back of the figure is as carefully worked as the front, with the drapery falling in irregular columnar folds.

The overall style of this piece, combined with specific features such as the simplified form of the aegis and the decoration of the patera, suggests it is a Roman work, probably provincial, of the first or second century A.D.; the pose, however, very probably derives from a Greek original of the fifth century B.C.

—LB

Freud displayed his attachment to this bronze Athena, goddess of war and patron of the arts, by placing her in the center of his desk and by selecting her as the sole piece to be smuggled out of Austria in 1938, when the loss of his entire antiquities collection was threatened.

In a short manuscript dated 1922 (SE, 18, p. 273f), Freud discussed the sexual symbolism of the decapitated, serpent-tressed head of Medusa, which Athena customarily wears on her breastplate. According to Freud, decapitation represents castration, and the horrifying decapitated head of Medusa symbolizes the female genitals, which lack a phallus. He also noted that the horror of this image of castration is mitigated by the ring of snakes surrounding Medusa's head because the snakes symbolically replace the penis. Freud described the head of Medusa:

> This symbol of horror is worn upon her dress by the virgin goddess Athena. And rightly so, for thus she becomes a woman who is unapproachable and repels all sexual desires—since she displays the terrifying genitals of the Mother. Since the Greeks were in the main strongly homosexual, it was inevitable that we should find among them a representation of woman as a being who frightens and repels [a male] because she is castrated. (p. 274)

This statuette and Freud's manifest attachment to it illustrate his commitment to a construction of female sexuality in terms of its relation to a male norm. Athena is a masculinized female whose lacks are manifest: her spear is missing, the Medusa on her breastplate displays no snakes, she has no phallus. In the last half century, Freud's construction of the female gender in terms of the lack of a phallus has been much debated and revised (see below, Spitz, pp. 160–61, n. 46).

—FM

For an Athena of the same period and in the same pose, but of a slightly more sophisticated style, see P. C. Bol and T. Weber, *Frankfurt Liebighaus. Bildwerke aus Bronze und Bein aus minoischer bis byzantinischer Zeit* (Melsungen, 1985), pp. 125–29, no. 62, with a full discussion and bibliography of the type. For two similar but cruder Athena figurines of uncertain date in Sparta, see *Lexicon Iconographicum Mythologiae Classicae* (Zurich and Munich, 1981–), II, Athena 185, pl. 726.

VENUS

Roman, from France or the Rhineland, 1st or 2nd century A.D.
Bronze, h. 5 in. (12.5 cm)
3471

Venus was the goddess of love and beauty in the classical world. Here, she stands in a relaxed position, her left foot just behind her right. Her head is turned slightly to her left; in her right hand she holds out a strand of her hair, while in her left hand she holds a mirror into which she stares. There is a diadem around her head, and her legs are covered by a garment draped below her hips and tied in a knot at the front. The goddess has narrow shoulders, a long torso, and small breasts. The contours of her body are simply but smoothly rendered.

Such statuettes are found in considerable numbers throughout the territory of the Roman Empire. This piece was probably made in a Roman province.
—LB

This Venus, holding a mirror, recalls Freud's notion that women are characterized by narcissism. The woman's cathexis of her whole body and her desire for it to be beautiful, he believed, was an attempt to compensate for the lack of a phallus. This Venus admiring herself in a mirror may have held special interest for Freud in his theorizing about women. In his essay "On Narcissism," Freud states:

> Women, especially if they grow up with good looks, develop a certain self-contentment which compensates them for the social restrictions that are imposed upon them in their choice of object [of affection]. Strictly speaking, it is only themselves that such women love with an intensity comparable to that of the man's love for them. (SE, 14, pp. 88–89)

—FM

For one of many similar figures, see R. Fleischer, *Die römischen Bronzen aus Österreich* (Mainz, 1967), pls. 42–43, no. 74.

FRAGMENT OF A WALL-PAINTING

Roman, 1st century B.C.–1st century A.D.
Plaster, h. 7 5/8 in. (19.5 cm)
3976

This fragment shows a sphinx seated against a deep pinkish orange background. At the bottom is a border of running scrolls between horizontal lines, all executed in dark brownish black. The sphinx sits upright, her long tail curling up behind her. Her raised left paw holds a spray of ivy leaves tied with a white ribbon. Her body is outlined in dark brown and filled in with white, now worn so that the pink background shows through. Areas of dark shading suggest the shadowy underside of her body and legs. Her hair is brown, as are her eyebrows, eyes, and mouth. Her hair is drawn away from her face and tied loosely at the back of her neck.

This fragment undoubtedly belongs to a larger composition; it seems highly likely that a second sphinx or other animal sat facing this one, perhaps holding the other end of the ivy chain. The context is hard to reconstruct; the figure could have belonged either in a mythological landscape painting or in an architectural scene. It is probably impossible to determine the original location of the fragment, but the style and coloring recall the paintings of the cities and villas of Campania of the first centuries B.C. and A.D.

—LB

For an introduction to Roman painting, see J. Liversidge, "Wall Painting and Stucco," chap. 4, in M. Henig, ed., *A Handbook of Roman Art* (Oxford, 1983).

FRAGMENT FROM THE LID OF

A SARCOPHAGUS

Roman, A.D. 160–210
Marble, 10 × 37 in. (25.4 × 94 cm)
4381

This fragment comes from the right-hand end of the parapet that ran along the front of the gabled lid of a sarcophagus. The relief frieze represents the mourning Trojans carrying the ransomed body of their leader Hector. The story of the slaying of Hector by Achilles, in revenge for the death of his friend Patroclus at Hector's hand, is part of the legend of Troy and is recounted in Homer's *Iliad*. (Freud also owned the left-hand fragment of this frieze.)

After Patroclus' funeral, the distraught Achilles dragged the body of Hector around Patroclus' tomb at dawn for eleven days, refusing to yield the corpse to Hector's grief-stricken father, Priam, king of Troy. This refusal constituted not only an unusually cruel revenge but was also a gesture that affronted the gods and custom, as a proper burial was essential to the hero's entry into the afterlife. Eventually the gods resolved that Achilles should be made to relinquish Hector's

body to his family. Priam, accompanied by a single herald, drove through the night to the Greek camp with a cart full of treasure and made his way unobserved to Achilles' tent. There he knelt before Achilles and asked him to think of his own father. Achilles, softened by his appeal, accepted the ransom and surrendered the body. So Hector was returned to Troy, where he was buried with due ceremony and mourning.

In this relief, the body of Hector originally would have occupied the central position. His body is of heroic proportion, about a third again as large as the other figures. It is carried by two Trojans, identified by their typical Phrygian caps. One Trojan stoops beneath the weight of Hector's legs, and the other strains to support his trunk. Two Trojans walk in front, one carrying two vessels, and both looking back toward the body; on the far side walks a third Trojan. Behind the corpse comes an animated group of four figures: two women, a young boy, and an older man. The disheveled women are shown in attitudes of extreme grief and despair, while the older man, more restrained, looks down at the young boy as if to comfort him. The scene on the sarcophagus fragment recalls Homer's account of the arrival of the body of Hector in Troy (*Iliad*, 24.706ff).

It is tempting to identify the figures to the right of the corpse on the sarcophagus fragment as Hector's parents, his wife, and their young son. However, three other known fragments—one possibly part of this sarcophagus lid (now lost), two others of the same subject—seem to indicate that when complete, the relief panel may have shown Priam on the left, kneeling before Achilles, with the body of Hector carried from the right toward the pair by a party of mourning Trojans. The vessels carried by the Trojan on the far left of the extant fragment could perhaps be seen as part of the ransom brought by Priam to Achilles. Such an arrangement confuses the logical sequence of events, for Priam had first to gain Achilles' consent to his demand before the body could be delivered to Hector's kinsmen, who in any case would have had no place in the Greek camp. One might argue further that the body should have been carried away from Achilles rather than toward him. However, for the artist to have neglected the strict demands of narrative in favor of juxtaposing the two most striking episodes in the story is hardly surprising.

The type of sarcophagus to which this fragment belongs and the style and subject of the relief suggest its date and that it was made in Rome. The Emperor Hadrian (A.D. 117–138) initiated a revival of Roman enthusiasm for all things Greek, and during the reigns of his successors, the Antonine emperors, the fashion for burial rather than cremation (which had previously been the custom) promoted the production of large numbers of expensively made sarcophagi, many of them decorated with scenes from Greek mythology. By commissioning such a coffin, some wealthy Roman, a senator perhaps, would demonstrate his familiarity with Greek religion, culture, and literature. Unlike many of the Greek myths represented on Roman sarcophagi, the ransoming of Hector is a highly appropriate subject for the decoration of a funeral monument: after a heroic life and death, the body is restored to its kin for the necessary rituals of mourning and burial.

—LB

The route by which this relief, which is in two fragments, came into Freud's collection has been reconstructed by Dr. Alfred Bernhard-Walcher of the Vienna Kunsthistorisches Museum. See the letter from Dr. Bernhard-Walcher, working from notes of the late Fritz Eichler, former director of the Kunsthistorisches Museum, Vienna, to S. Neufeld, February 6, 1987, in the Freud Museum, London. Both fragments surfaced on the Rome antiquities market and, through several dealers' hands, were brought to Vienna in the 1920s. The right-hand fragment was bought in 1930 by an unidentified woman, who must have given or sold it to Freud. The left-hand fragment was sold directly to Freud in 1930. On the left-hand fragment see C. Robert, *Die Antiken Sarkophag-Reliefs* (Berlin, 1890–1919), III, pt. 3, p. 551, no. 58 (i). On the third fragment (currently lost), see G. Koch, "Verschollene mythologische Sarkophage," *Archäologischer Anzeiger*, 1976, p. 103, nos. 7, 8, and especially 6. For a discussion of the type of scene and references for the other extant fragments, see G. Koch and H. Sichtermann, *Römische Sarkophage* (Munich, 1982), p. 130 and n. 46.

UNGUENTARIUM

Roman, c. A.D. 150–250
Glass, h. 6 1/8 in. (15.5 cm)
3594

This free-blown glass perfume bottle varies in color from white to gray, with patches of iridescent blue and green. Its wide, flattened rim and slightly swelling mouth are set above a long, narrow neck, which flares out sharply into the wide, low body. The body is gracefully profiled; its underside is slightly concave.

This unguentarium was made in the eastern Mediterranean, possibly Cyprus.

—LB

For this type of bottle, see C. Isings, *Roman Glass from Dated Finds* (Gröningen, 1957), p. 98, form 82A; for similar examples, see J. Hayes, *Roman and Pre-Roman Glass in the Royal Ontario Museum* (Toronto, 1975), nos. 518ff.

GRAPE FLASK

Roman, 3rd century A.D.
Glass, h. 5 ³/₄ in. (14.7 cm)
3550

This glass flask, which would have been used for perfume or oil, was made in a two-part mold with vertical seams. It is grayish green in color, with touches of bright iridescent green. It has a wide, flattened rim above a long neck, which rises from a collar set above the ovoid body; the underside of the flask is slightly concave. The surface of the body is decorated with an overall pattern of stylized "grapes," with a vine leaf set in the center top of each side. This flask was probably made in Syria or Palestine.

—LB

For similar examples, see J. Hayes, *Roman and Pre-Roman Glass in the Royal Ontario Museum* (Toronto, 1975), no. 91, or S. B. Matheson, *Ancient Glass in the Yale University Art Gallery* (New Haven, 1980), no. 279.

JAR

Roman, c. A.D. 50–150
Glass, h. 7 5/8 in. (19.5 cm)
4394

This beautifully shaped, round-bodied jar has a rim that is flattened on top and folded downward and outward. Of free-blown glass, green in color with brownish areas, it contains cremated human bones.

Jars of this shape are generally found in the western provinces of the Roman Empire, and it seems likely that they were manufactured in Italy, southern France, and Spain. They may have been used as storage jars in the house, but most of those found have contained cremations.

—LB

For the chronology, date, and find-places of similar jars, see C. Isings, *Roman Glass from Dated Finds* (Gröningen, 1957), pp. 86–87, form 67; for a similar example, see J. Hayes, *Roman and Pre-Roman Glass in the Royal Ontario Museum* (Toronto, 1975), no. 618, pl. 39 (from Vaison-la-Romaine, southern France).

BOTTLE

Roman, c. A.D. 100–150
Glass, h. 10 ³/₈ in. (26.2 cm)
3262

The body of this large bottle forms a straight-sided cylinder. It has a flat shoulder and slightly concave base. The neck is straight and vertical, and the rim was probably wide and flat. It is chiefly remarkable for its brilliant iridescent sheen; the underlying color is basically greenish gray, but it is streaked and swirled with mother-of-pearl, peacock blue and green, mauve, orange, pale blue, turquoise, gold, and red, all manifesting themselves in turn and in different combinations as the vessel is looked at under differing light.

This bottle was made in the eastern Mediterranean, possibly Cyprus.

—LB

The beauty of this bottle's shape and color, and that of many other pieces in his collection, refutes Freud's demurral that he could not appreciate the formal qualities of art, but only its subject matter:

> I may say at once that I am no connoisseur in art, but simply a layman. I have often observed that the subject-matter of works of art has a stronger attraction for me than their formal and technical qualities, though to the artist their value lies first and foremost in these latter. I am unable rightly to appreciate many of the methods used and the effects obtained in art. (SE, 13, p. 211)

—FM

For this shape, see J. Hayes, *Roman and Pre-Roman Glass in the Royal Ontario Museum* (Toronto, 1975), no. 209.

OIL LAMP

Roman, c. A.D. 40–80
Terracotta, ⁷/₈ × 4 ¹/₈ × 3 ¹/₈ in. (2.2 × 10.3 × 7.9 cm)
4238

Erotic scenes, both heterosexual and homosexual, are commonly found on lamps in the Roman period. On the discus of this lamp is a relief of a pair of lovers on a couch. The man lies on his back with his head on a cushion, while the woman sits on top of him facing right with her hand on her hip. Both are naked, except for the crumpled drapery covering the man's right leg.

The clay is light brown, with a darker, unevenly applied brown slip. The lamp was made in two molds and joined at the shoulder. The nozzle, decorated with volutes, is rounded at the tip. The rounded shoulder is separated from the discus by three incised lines.

—LB

A lamp in the British Museum (Q 934) comes from a parallel mold; see D. M. Bailey, *A Catalogue of Roman Lamps in the British Museum*, vol. 2 (London, 1980), pl. 18.

SILVER RING WITH

BLUE GLASS INTAGLIO

Roman, 1st century B.C.–1st century A.D.,
setting: 20th century
Glass, 3/8 × 3/4 in. (1 × 1.8 cm)
5046

This intaglio is probably ancient and bears a pastoral scene of a shepherd with two goats lying in the shade of a tree, one on a pile of rocks. Such pastoral scenes are common on the engraved gems that most well-to-do Romans carried and used as seals; the subject probably appealed both to those who actually lived and worked in the country, and to those city-dwellers who liked to romanticize the joys of country life, the "caves and living lakes, sweet sleep below the tree" idealized by such poems as Virgil's Georgics.

—LB

Freud's practice of giving intaglio stones, which were set in rings, to his closest colleagues began in 1912, with the formation of the "Committee," a group that included Freud, Karl Abraham, Sándor Ferenczi, Ernest Jones, Otto Rank, and Hanns Sachs; in 1919 Max Eitingon was added. The group rallied to support Freud and the fundamental tenets of psychoanalysis in the face of defections by early followers, such as Adler and Jung, and criticism from outside the field. The idea of the support group, with the intriguing overtones of a secret society, was presented to Freud in a letter written by Ernest Jones. Freud responded:

> What took hold of my imagination immediately is your idea of a secret council composed of the best and most trustworthy among our men to take care of the further developments of psychoanalysis and defend the cause against personalities and accidents when I am no more.... I know there is a boyish and perhaps romantic element too in this conception, but perhaps it could be adapted to meet the necessities of reality. (Freud to Jones, August 1, 1912)

The first meeting of the Committee occurred on May 25, 1913, and Freud celebrated the event by presenting each member with an ancient intaglio. Freud himself wore an intaglio ring engraved with a head of Jupiter.

In later years, after the original Committee had dissolved, Freud continued the spirit of this first presentation by giving intaglios to other supporters, including Marie Bonaparte, Anna Freud, Lou Andreas-Salomé, Ernst Simmel, and Arnold Zweig. The ring shown here was given to the German psychoanalyst Simmel in 1928. In a letter accompanying the gift Freud wrote:

> Once upon a time these rings were a privilege and a mark distinguishing a group of men who were united in their devotion to psychoanalysis.... I renew the old custom with you.... Forms may pass away, but their meaning can survive them and seek to express themselves in other forms. So please don't be disturbed by the fact that this ring signifies a regression to something that no longer exists, and wear it for many years as a memory of your cordially devoted Freud. (Freud to Simmel, November 11, 1928)

—FM

For an account of Roman engraved gems, their subjects, techniques, and usage, see G. M. A. Richter, *The Engraved Gems of the Greeks, Etruscans and the Romans* (London, 1971), pt. 2; for the Roman attitude toward the country, see K. D. White, *Country Life in Classical Times* (London, 1977). On the formation of the Committee, see Ernest Jones, *The Life and Work of Sigmund Freud* (New York, 1955), II, chap. 6, pp. 152–67.

HEAD OF A BODHISATTVA

Chinese, Ming Dynasty, 15th–17th century
Cast iron, 9 ⁵/₈ × 6 ⁵/₈ × 5 ³/₄ in. (24.5 × 16.8 × 14.5 cm)
3151

This head probably comes from a standing figure of a Buddhist attendant, possibly a bodhisattva, a saintly and benevolent being who attends Buddha and, out of compassion, has chosen to forego nirvana until all others have attained it. The figure would have been placed in a Buddhist temple or monastery, possibly with another identical figure, the pair flanking a Buddha.

A serene expression adorns the bodhisattva's relaxed face, with its downcast eyes and high nose. Typical of Buddhist figures, the head has long ears draped with ribbons or scarves. The hair is parted in the middle and falls in waves around the forehead, while at the back of the head, it is combed straight up. The bodhisattva wears a typical hat that resembles the shape of an Indian stupa, a shrine containing a fragment of Buddhist scripture or a holy relic. (The profile of the Chinese pagoda resembles the stupa because it developed from this Indian shrine.) Four rectangular holes around the base of the hat may be attachment points for an elaborate crown of pendants.

This head was cast hollow; the casting seams can be seen down the back of the head and at the sides under the ears.

—JP

For two similar cast-iron attendant figures, see *Chinese, Korean, and Japanese Sculpture: The Avery Brundage Collection* (San Francisco, 1974), p. 306.

HEAD OF A GUARDIAN FIGURE

Chinese, Ming Dynasty, 15th–17th century
Bronze, 6 3/4 × 5 7/8 × 6 1/8 in. (17 × 15 × 15.5 cm)
3444

This guardian figure stares out at us with piercing eyes from beneath a knit and muscular brow. His teeth are bared; his face is framed with flamelike hair. Depicted in the style of the earlier Tang period, he has a single topknot and a three-pointed helmet ornament on his forehead. Evil spirits approaching the entrance to a sacred tomb or temple would be frightened away by this terrifying guardian.

This figure is possibly a *dvarapala*, a kind of Buddhist guardian always found in pairs protecting entrances. These Buddhist guardians are typically represented in a dramatic fashion, with fierce expressions, contorted limbs, and exaggerated musculature, in contrast to the calm, serene portrayals of Buddhas and bodhisattvas.
—JP

See Sotheby's New York auction catalogue, March 16, 1984, lot 112, for a comparable example.

126

CAMEL

Chinese, early Tang style, 20th century forgery
Terracotta, 13 ³/₄ × 9 × 3 ¹/₂ in. (35 × 23 × 9 cm)
4392

During the late seventh to early eighth century A.D., unglazed figures (*mingqi*) were placed in Chinese tombs to indicate the status and wealth of the deceased. Larger figures were formed in two-part molds, fired, and then covered in a whitish slip and overpainted with unfired polychrome colors. Bright and colorful figures of servants, officials, dancing girls, musicians, animals, grooms, and foreigners combined to present a picture of the cosmopolitan lifestyle of Sian, the Tang capital, at the time one of the most civilized and sophisticated cities in the world. Camels and horses were considered auspicious signs of material comfort, since they represented a connection with the Silk Route and all the luxuries and exotic goods that it implied.

Although this imposing terracotta figurine of a Bactrian two-humped camel is in the early Tang style of the early eighth century, and can be compared with an excavated piece dated A.D. 711 from the tomb of Yang Futing, it is in fact a modern forgery. During the 1920s and 1930s, many Tang tomb figures were dug up from the areas of the ancient Tang capitals of Sian and Loyang. They became very popular with Western residents in China and consequently were manufactured to meet an increasing demand. The chaotic political situation in the decades following the Chinese revolution of 1912 made it difficult to enforce checks on authenticity or export. Large numbers of these figures were produced and exported, to be bought by nonspecialist Western collectors such as Freud. An expert can tell this is a forgery by the applied paint, which flakes off easily and is an unconvincing imitation of the unfired colors of Tang figures.

—JP

On the piece excavated from the tomb of Yang Futing, see *Kaogu*, 1964, p. 6, pl. 1X, no. 3.

127

TABLE SCREEN

Chinese, Qing Dynasty, 19th century
Wood and jade; screen (without stand): 7 $^5/_8$ × 5 × 1 in.
(19.5 × 12.6 × 2.5 cm)
3001

This screen and its stand are carved from a reddish wood in an openwork decoration of leaf scrolls. The figure of a scholar carved in white jade is inset into the center of the screen.

Intended to create an atmosphere conducive to contemplation, such table screens found their place on the desk of a scholar, along with brush holders, ink stones, water droppers, brush rests, and other decorative objects associated with writing. Screens were carved with designs of trees, vines, and hillsides, encouraging the scholar to escape, in his thoughts, to an imaginary vista. Landscape screens had a connection with Daoism and the idea of transcending the realm of official duties for the simplicity of the natural world. The scholar's desk was often placed by a window looking over a traditional Chinese garden, which like the screens, reproduced the natural world in miniature form.
—JP

For examples of comparable table screens, see Sotheby's London auction catalogue, July 24, 1987, lots 240–49.

BUDDHIST LION PAPERWEIGHT

Chinese, Qing Dynasty, 18th–19th century
Jade, 2 3/8 × 1 5/8 × 1 1/4 in. (6 × 4 × 3.2 cm)
4001

Jade has been carved in China from the Neolithic Period (fifth millennium to eighteenth century B.C.), and the Chinese have traditionally treasured jade even more than Westerners have valued gold. The carving of jade is a slow and difficult process requiring even harder abrasives, such as quartz sand or crushed garnet. Originally reserved for ritual objects, jade came to be used for decorative items, especially those that adorned a scholar's desk, such as this green jade lion paperweight.

In Chinese depictions of lions, the male usually plays with a ball and the female fondles a lion cub. This paperweight is unusual in that the lion combines both male and female characteristics; the semirecumbent lion has a ball with tassels in its mouth and plays with four cubs, which climb over it.

Lions are not native to China but came from India as part of the iconographic vocabulary introduced with Buddhism in the third century A.D. Early Chinese representations depict lions realistically as terrifying beasts. From the fifth century A.D. onward, fearsome guardian lions are found flanking the Buddha in carvings in cave temple complexes, such as Yungang in northern China.

In the Ming and Qing Dynasties (1368–1911), Buddhist lions had assumed a domesticated form, the so-called dogs of *fo* (*fo* = Buddhism). They are presented as frolicsome creatures wearing collars and bells, more pets than guardians, which may be why these lions came to be referred to as dogs; indeed, the Chinese especially bred the Pekingese dog to resemble these dogs of *fo*. Throughout the Ming and Qing Dynasties, large carved stone statues of these playful lions appeared in pairs outside houses, temples, and even outside the Forbidden City, the walled area in central Beijing containing the imperial palaces of the Chinese empire.

—JP

NETSUKE IN THE FORM OF A SHISHI

Japanese, Edo Period, 18th–19th century
Ivory, 2 × 1 ³/₈ × 1 in. (5 × 3.5 × 2.5 cm)
4028

Japanese men in the Edo period wore a loose-fitting garment tied with a sash at the waist, and carried a variety of items hanging from the sash by a cord—tobacco pouches, pipes in cases, *inrō* (seal cases), *yatate* (a writing brush and inkwell combination). The toggle at the end of the cord, which kept it from slipping, was called a netsuke. At first these toggles were probably simple objects such as a piece of wood (netsuke means rootfix), but gradually complicated carvings in ivory, wood, and lacquer were made.

This netsuke is in the shape of a *shishi*, the Japanese version of a Buddhist lion-dog and a favorite subject because of its association with the Chinese scholar. In this ivory *shishi*, the details of a raised bushy tail and a long curly mane down its back are brought out by staining. The ball in the *shishi*'s mouth indicates that this is a male lion-dog and is a sign of the Edo craftsman's virtuosity: this loose piece of ivory was carved within the completed netsuke.

—JP

For further reading, see Richard Barker and Lawrence Smith, *Netsuke, The Miniature Sculpture of Japan* (London, 1976).

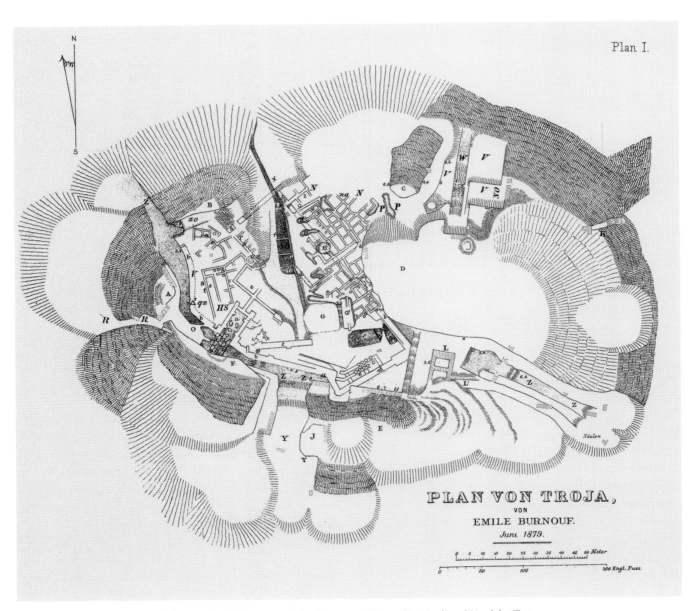

Plan of Troy, from Heinrich Schliemann's 1881 account of the discovery of Troy, *Ilios, Stadt und Land der Trojaner.*

A MIGHTY METAPHOR: THE ANALOGY OF ARCHAEOLOGY AND PSYCHOANALYSIS

DONALD KUSPIT

The archaeological metaphor, as it has been called, is pervasive in Freud's vision of psychoanalysis. The metaphor makes a prominent appearance in two major essays, the "Fragment of an Analysis of a Case of Hysteria" (1905 [1901]), otherwise known as the Dora case, and "Constructions in Analysis" (1937), an important statement of psychoanalytic method. It thus effectively informs, and perhaps dominates, Freud's sense of psychoanalysis from the earliest days of its development to the end of his life. To understand the archaeological metaphor is to understand the thrust, if not the detail, of psychoanalytic thinking, its general orientation, if not its particular procedures and concepts. It is not simply a dramatic device to enliven and adorn the discourse of psychoanalysis—a way of disseminating and even popularizing its approach to the psyche—but the major instrument of its self-understanding.

In fact, the archaeological metaphor sustains its momentum in Freud's thought because of its contradictory connotations. Freud seems to have seriously thought of psychoanalysis as a kind of archaeology, in goal as well as method, although, as Philip Rieff has pointed out, their goals only partly coincide and in fact differ in a crucial way.[1] At the least, Freud used archaeological language to structure his conception of the psyche, especially in the case of the topographical model. At the same time, his allusion to archaeology was probably a way of broadening the appeal of psychoanalysis, making it accessible to the nonmedical, if educated, public. The analogy of psychoanalysis to archaeology can even be understood as a theatrical pitch to the public at large—the unintellectual crowd. The analogy associated an unpopular, suspect enterprise with a popular, respectable one, for Heinrich Schliemann's discovery of Troy—his demonstration of the reality of its heroes, the facts that informed the legend—gave archaeology a special celebrity, an honored social place: it was an adventure that produced concrete results, a means of showing the truthfulness of literary fantasy. As Peter Gay has said, Freud "probably envied [Schliemann] more than any other" man, not only, I suspect, "because in discovering 'Priam's treasure' he had found true happiness" but because of Schliemann's social success. "There is happiness" not "only as fulfillment of a child's wish" but of an adult's ambition.[2]

Freud's appeal to archaeology can be regarded as an effort to ingratiate psychoanalysis with society—to win its approval and trust, to gain an influential place in it—and even to have some of the heroic quality associated with archaeology rub off on psychoanalysis. In Freud's eyes, psychoanalysis, like archaeology, was a heroic investigation of legendary reality. Both uncover lost reality, ancient worlds that have become legendary with time. There were Atlantises sunken in the psyche as well as in the ocean. Freud directly compared the discoveries of psychoanalysis with those of archaeology: the primitive aspects of the psyche, at least in their gross features, resembled primitive worlds, and vice versa. Their dialectical reciprocity was greater than expected: just as archaeology reminded us of the continuing influence in our civilization of past modes of social organization and outlook (most noteworthily for Freud in religion), so psychoanalysis reminds us of the continuing influence on our intimate lives of primitive psychic forms of experience and points of view. Both deal with the unexpected presence and power of the past. Both are means of remembering it. Both tend to absolutize the archaic. For Freud, archaeology and psychoanalysis announce the same fundamental paradox: each is a way of engaging and articulating what remains alive—in effect immortal—and continues to determine our humanness, yet seems dead and buried and lost forever, permanently forgotten. The past even seems forgettable, because antiquated or obsolete, maladaptive in the real world of the present, and thus trivial.

Freud probably shared Europe's imperialist belief in its civilization's relative superiority. In a sense, archaeology served this belief by presenting examples of "inferior" earlier civilizations. Of course, the content of this superiority and inferiority were not crystal clear; but what did seem unquestionable to Freud was that "inferiority" was attached to the infantile, while "superiority" meant being adult. Primitive, earlier civilizations were more childlike than adult, and as such only nominally describable as civilized.[3] For Freud, the ultimate sense of adulthood was conveyed by science,[4] which meant having the ego strength to sustain the reality principle: to not flinch in the face of reality, and to observe and analyze it rigorously, working at it conscientiously rather than fantasizing about—spontaneously overestimating—it, which is a way of loving it blindly. Freud, of course, came to doubt the "civilized" character of Europe, as well as the stability of adulthood,[5] but he apparently never gave up the notion of the childlikeness of early civilizations.

His thinking on this was essentially Comtean. Much as there was a cognitive development from religion through metaphysics to positivistic science, so there was a correlative psychosocial development from the prehistoric through the ancient (partially historical) to the modern world. Just as in the one there was a clarification of the principles of thinking, so in the other there was an expansion of consciousness (and finally a growth of self-consciousness), inseparable from the willingness—which increased the ability—to remember. The progressive development of civilization also involves what in *The Interpretation of Dreams* Freud called, in discussing "the changed treatment of the same [oedipal] material" in Shakespeare's *Hamlet* and Sophocles' *Oedipus Rex*, "the secular advance of repression in the emotional life of mankind" (SE, 4, p. 164).

Part of childlikeness is the reluctance to face reality directly, an inability to sustain orientation to reality, to develop a scientific approach to it. The more ancient the civilization, the more it was inclined to mask and embroider facts with collective fantasy—to mythologize them. Sophocles did not (and probably could not) tell the story of a child's tangled relationship with its mother and father straightforwardly (it is unlikely that he even thought of studying the relationship in careful detail), but had to symbolize and bury it in a dramatic fable, giving its rough edges and obscure aspects narrative smoothness and clarity. He gave a generalization about life's artistic substance rather than breaking it down to emotional and behavioral particulars.

Insofar as it is a social strategy, Freud's appeal to archaeology is no doubt a logical fallacy on the order of the appeal to authority, an attempt to prejudice people in psychoanalysis's favor by associating it with the special authority and appeal of archaeology, which seemed capable of extraordinary revelation. But the appeal to archaeological authority also suggestively communicates authoritative core distinctions in psychoanalysis: that between surface and depth, manifest and latent, adult and infantile, civilized and uncivilized, historic and prehistoric (or rather, the historic obscured by the partial amnesia of the legendary, the half-forgetfulness of the mythopoetic), fact and fantasy. These distinctions seem at once vertically (hierarchically) and horizontally structured. One term subordinates the other, but they are inextricably in conflict. Perhaps they are comparable to Hegel's master and slave. The one is superior to the other, yet neither exists without the other; but they achieve mutuality through essential conflict. Transcendence of conflict changes both, but Freud studies such positive transcendence—in contrast to the "negative transcendence" of repression—less than Hegel does. Thus, the terms of Freud's distinctions are value-tinged as well as descriptive. Freud studies the terms in their psychological necessity, but he sometimes seems to approve of what the higher one signifies, although he never forgets the ironical character of the relationship between "higher" and "lower." Freud explicated some distinctions more than others and sometimes seems to subsume all in one—the manifest/latent distinction is primary, and informs the sense of dream analysis as an archaeological enterprise[6]—but he uses all of them to structure his discourse. Much of it is casually encoded in archaeological language.

In any case, the archaeological metaphor is as demystifying as it is mystifying: as much a way of suggesting psychoanalysis's power to reveal the plain truth hidden in the mysterious fiction as to idealize the facts so that they seem fabulous. For Freud, archaeology was as much a mode of enchantment, a romanticizing of inquiry and understanding, as a symbol of the patient, steady analytic work of uncovering and reconstructing the unremembered past. Archaeology was at once the model for early psychoanalysis and a way of mythologizing its import, not unrelated to Plato's use, in the last book of the *Republic*, of the myth of the underworld to communicate in a narrative, intuitive way a treacherous psycho-logic that is otherwise difficult to comprehend and accept.[7] One might better speak of the archaeological myth than of metaphor to convey both the comprehensiveness of the archaeological idea in Freud's psychoanalytic thinking and its various roles as intellectual buttress, protective fortification, and cosmetic camouflage for psychoanalytic theory.[8] Freud was taken with archaeology not only because of the unusual findings it promised, which psychoanalysis also promised, but because the psyche itself seemed archaeological in character, that is, a realm of relics and ruins.

As I have suggested, Freud never eliminated the archaeological metaphor. While it has been said that he never completely gave up any idea he had once accepted, but continued to use it suggestively as the occasion warranted, his attachment to the archaeological metaphor was especially intense, for it embodied the working assumptions of psychoanalysis, or more precisely, its basic attitude to the life-world: its scepticism. This becomes clear when we compare the early allusion to archaeology in the Dora case history, where Freud uncritically compares himself to an archaeologist—not simply correlating psychoanalysis and archaeology, but in effect declaring psychoanalysis to be a kind of archaeology—with the later allusion in "Constructions in Analysis" (SE, 23), where he sharply differentiates the two. Even as he worked his way through the analogy, freeing psychoanalysis from its dependence on archaeology, he continued to use it to propel himself into psychoanalytic conceptual space, and in a sense as the vindication of psychoanalysis.

Freud's fixation on the archaeological metaphor and its practical persistence as a springboard, however much it came to be theoretically questionable, was not simply a bad conceptual habit of thinking, or worse yet, a linguistic tic or atavistic image, a sort of involuntary regression inhibiting the progressive clarification of psychoanalytic concepts, detrimental to the health of psychoanalysis, the way Freud's habit of smoking cigars was detrimental to his health. The archaeological metaphor was not Freud's fantasy formulation of psychoanalysis, his hallucination of the field, the crutch of its youthful self-consciousness, but was in fact emblematic of the psychoanalytic approach as such, indeed, an assertion of what seems most critical in it. For Freud, the archaeological orientation of psychoanalysis was inseparable from its deflationary power: its role as "a disturber of man's narcissism,"[9] of his "*naive* self-love" and "megalomania" (SE, 16, pp. 284–85). Archaeology symbolizes psychoanalysis at its most debunking and revolutionary. For psychoanalysis, the life given in the clinical situation is not to be taken at face value but as a site of past life to be dug up in order to discover its true constitution. Psychoanalysis's consistent refusal to accept the present as given leads straight to its sense of archaeological purpose. Moreover, the process of psycho-archaeological investigation is the beginning of the process of psychic change. For archaeological probing is in effect a preliminary act of intervention, affording preliminary insight. It is a kind of partial interpretation, or pre-interpretation, or propaedeutic broadly hinting at the need for change. It is the uncomfortable awakening necessary for sharp-eyed full consciousness. The act of uncovering the past necessarily brings the psychic present into question, promising transformation.

If nothing else, the archaeological metaphor signals psychoanalysis's ironical attitude to everyday appearances. Psychoanalysis is a mode of doubt to the extent that it refuses to accept the face—the self-estimate—that people put on themselves. In refusing to let the world save face, as it were, psychoanalysis in effect undermines acceptance of the conventional surface of society or at least encourages reservations about everyday appearance. The shift from the naive to the psychoanalytic attitude—from nonarchaeological (surface) awareness to archaeological (depth) awareness—it proposes is not unlike Husserl's shift from the "natural" to the phenomenological attitude. The psychoanalytic and phenomenological attitudes are different versions of the same critical consciousness. Both are deliberate and fundamental changes of orientation—revolutionary reorientations—opening up the possibility of an unconventional, alternate vision of the lifeworld. Both position one to find new meanings in the lifeworld, to discover the unexpected ways one has invested meaning in it. Indeed, they teach one to expect it to have unexpected meaning, "opening one's eyes" to the novelty of its reality.

In general, psychoanalysis's postulation of archaeologically indirect meanings and its tendency to take everyday life as a psycho-archaeological text—its use of both "metaphor hermeneutics" and "text-world hermeneutics," as Don Ihde calls them[10]—makes it threatening and unsettling. Psychoanalysis is inseparable from the "hermeneutics of suspicion," which is an archaeological hermeneutics, for it denies the seemingly self-evident and insists upon alternative meanings fraught with uncanny necessity. Archaeology is the perfect symbol of disruptive psychoanalytic suspicion, for all archaeological findings exist in a hermeneutic condition of uncertain meaning—no doubt encouraging speculative attribution of meaning, affording food for imaginative thought—which they never quite escape. The archaeological metaphor conveys psychoanalysis's uncompromising curiosity and its interpretive propensity, which is why Freud never disclaimed it. It encapsulates the insistent questioning and questing consciousness inseparable from psychoanalytic understanding.

In the "Prefatory Remarks" to the Dora case Freud wrote:

> In the face of the incompleteness of my analytic results, I had no choice but to follow the example of those discoverers whose good fortune it is to bring to the light of day after their long burial the priceless though mutilated relics of antiquity. I have restored what is missing, taking the best models known to me from other analyses; but, like a conscientious archaeologist, I have not omitted to mention in each case where the authentic parts end and my constructions begin. (SE, 7, p. 12)

In "Constructions in Analysis," after noting that "what we are in search of is a picture of the patient's forgotten years that shall be alike trustworthy and in all essential respects complete" (SE, 23, p. 258), Freud states that this picture is, in effect:

> [a product of the analytic] work of construction, or, if it is preferred, of reconstruction, [which] resembles to a great extent an archaeologist's

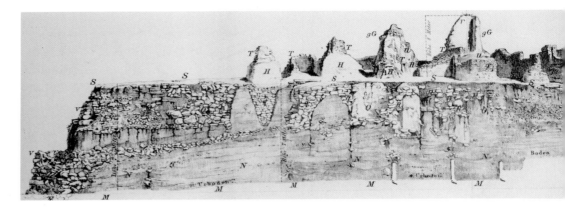

excavation of some dwelling-place that has been destroyed and buried or of some ancient edifice. The two processes are in fact identical, except that the analyst works under better conditions and has more material at his command to assist him, since what he is dealing with is not something destroyed but something that is still alive—and perhaps for another reason as well. But just as the archaeologist builds up the walls of a building from the foundations that have remained standing, determines the number and position of the columns from depressions in the floor, and reconstructs the mural decorations and paintings from the remains found in the debris, so does the analyst proceed when he draws his inferences from fragments of memories, from the associations and from the behaviour of the subject of the analysis. Both of them have an undisputed right to reconstruct by means of supplementing and combining the surviving remains. Both of them, moreover, are subject to many of the same difficulties and sources of error. One of the most ticklish problems that confronts the archaeologist is notoriously the determination of the relative age of his finds; and if an object makes its appearance in some particular level, it often remains to be decided whether it belongs to that level or whether it was carried down to that level owing to some subsequent disturbance. It is easy to imagine the corresponding doubts that arise in the case of analytic constructions.

The analyst, as we have said, works under more favourable conditions than the archaeologist since he has at his disposal material which can have no counterpart in excavations, such as the repetitions of reactions dating from infancy and all that is indicated by the transference in connection with these repetitions. But in addition to this, it must be borne in mind that the excavator is dealing with destroyed objects of which large and important portions have quite certainly been lost, by mechanical violence, by fire and by plundering. No amount of effort can result in their discovery and lead to their being united with the surviving remains. The one and only course open is that of reconstruction, which for this reason can often reach only a certain degree of probability. But it is different with the psychical object whose early history the analyst is seeking to recover. Here we are regularly met by a situation which with the archaeological object occurs only in such rare circumstances as those of Pompeii or of the tomb of Tutankhamun. All

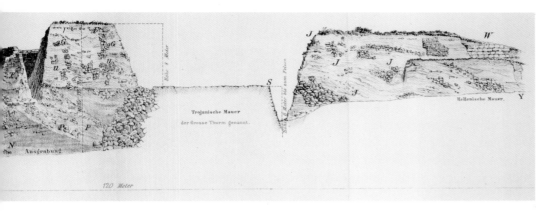

Cross-section of the central excavation trench at Troy, as published in Heinrich Schliemann's *Ilios*.

of the essentials are preserved; even things that seem completely forgotten are present somehow and somewhere, and have merely been buried and made inaccessible to the subject. Indeed, it may, as we know, be doubted whether any psychical structure can really be the victim of total destruction. It depends only upon analytic technique whether we shall succeed in bringing what is concealed completely to light. There are only two other facts that weigh against the extraordinary advantage which is thus enjoyed by the work of analysis: namely, that psychical objects are incomparably more complicated than the excavator's material ones and that we have insufficient knowledge of what we may expect to find, since their finer structure contains so much that is still mysterious. But our comparison between the two forms of work can go no further than this; for the main difference between them lies in the fact that for the archaeologist the reconstruction is the aim and end of his endeavours while for analysis the construction is only a preliminary labour. (SE, 23, pp. 259–60)

There is a crucial difference between these statements. In the one from the Dora case, the archaeologist and psychoanalyst are matter-of-factly equated. In the one from "Constructions in Analysis," the psychoanalyst is given an important advantage over the archaeologist: the psychic structures the psychoanalyst uncovers are intact, none the worse for wear, while the physical structures the archaeologist uncovers are usually in irreparably poor condition. They can never be entirely reconstructed, while in a sense the psychoanalyst has nothing to construct or reconstruct: he has only to discover. The archaeologist is in a more impossible, or at least less secure, position than the psychoanalyst, who can, as it were, have the object of his psychological inquiry and analytically eat it too. There is something smugly triumphant in Freud's assertion of psychoanalysis's advantage over archaeology, as though at last he had reached a long sought-for goal — his science finally besting the science with which it was most competitive (at least as much as with medicine). But is it true that psychical structures, while no doubt "incomparably more complicated" than the archaeologist's material ones, are unequivocally preserved in all their essentials? Can they be separated from their fantasy coating? Are they not in some way as mutilated and eroded — destroyed by, lost to — fantasy as the archaeologist's material structures are lost to mechanical violence, fire, and plundering? Is fantasy not a kind of violence done to the psychical structure, a plundering of it? Can psychic fantasy ever really be fully separated from psychic fact?

In any case, for Freud the psychoanalyst's uncertainty comes from the subtlety of the psychic structure itself, while the archaeologist's uncertainty comes from the conditions under which he or she necessarily works. Archaeologists must learn to live with it — learn to live with ignorance, learn like Tantalus to live with the object of their intellectual desire permanently out of reach — but psychoanalysts can sooner or later see their objects whole and clear, and hold them fast. Freud privileges psychoanalysis with true knowledge: this is when it leaves archaeology behind.

Nonetheless, Freud repeatedly locates his psychoanalytic inquiry in an archaeological context; it seems indispensable. It finally seems to come apart, but only after it leads psychoanalysis, in the person of Freud, to self-understanding, self-clarification. Is this overestimating the importance and persuasive power of the archaeological context for Freud? Is it unreasonable to extend the archaeological metaphor to speak of the archaeological context of psychoanalysis? Do I dare dispute Freud's own sense of his use of analogy, as in his assertion that "analogies ... are only intended to assist us in our attempt to make the complications of mental functioning intelligible by dissecting the function and assigning its different constituents to different component parts of the apparatus" (SE, 5, p. 536)? Is it the case that Freud prosaically realized, through clinical labor, that no psychical structure could be completely destroyed, that it survived intact through historical time, and then poetically stated this fact through the archaeological metaphor in order to persuade us of it? If it were only that simple. The question of what can or cannot survive burial, what is or is not recoverable, and in what state it is recovered, cannot be asked without archaeological awareness. It grows out of this awareness spontaneously; it is inseparable from archaeo-logic. Every formulation of early psychoanalysis, whether technical or theoretical, implies archaeological awareness, because psychoanalysis at its inception was more or less an inquiry into memory.

On December 6, 1896, Freud wrote to Fliess:

> [I am] working on the assumption that our psychical mechanism has come into being by a process of stratification: the material present in the form of memory-traces being subjected from time to time to a *re-arrangement* in accordance with fresh circumstances — to a re-*transcription*. Thus what is essentially new about my theory is the thesis that memory is present not once but several times over, that it is laid down in various species of indications. ... I should like to emphasize the fact that the successive registrations represent the psychical achievement of successive epochs of life.[11]

Commenting on this statement, Ole Andkjaer Olsen and Simo Koppe remark:

> Freud thus believed that the psychic apparatus was composed of separate memory systems whose spatial relationship corresponded to their temporal deposits, similar to the way archaeological findings and geological deposits

were older the deeper one dug. Freud did not determine how many systems existed, but in time only two genuine memory systems remained: the unconscious and the preconscious. The unconscious was the older of the two systems.[12]

The archaeological metaphor is inseparable from Freud's sense of the importance of memory in psychic disturbances and in the creation of psychic structures in general. The house of psyche is not simply built on a foundation of memories, but it is a mansion composed of many rooms of memory, each built at a different time and often on the ruins of other memory-rooms, exactly the way Rome has been built and rebuilt many times, with some of the past visibly surviving in the present but most of it lost, as Freud tells us in another (and lovingly, almost extravagantly, extended) archaeological metaphor in *Civilization and Its Discontents* (SE, 21, pp. 69–70). As Freud and Breuer emphasized in a famous statement in the *Studies on Hysteria*: "Hysterics suffer mainly from reminiscences" (SE, 2, p. 7).

The archaeological metaphor, then, is inseparable from Freud's idea of the stratified character of psychic structure, especially if far from exclusively evident in *The Interpretation of Dreams*. Not only memories but the meanings of dreams are stratified:

> Dreams frequently seem to have more than one meaning. Not only, as our examples have shown, may they include several wish-fulfillments one alongside the other; but a succession of meanings or wish-fulfillments may be superimposed on one another, the bottom one being the fulfillment of a wish dating from earliest childhood. (SE, 4, p. 219)

In a footnote added in 1914, Freud not only notes "the fact that the meanings of dreams are arranged in superimposed layers" but calls attention to Otto Rank's study of "the fairly regular stratification of symbols in dreams provoked by pressure of the bladder" (SE, 4, p. 219). Superimposition or stratification of dream meanings and dream symbols follows the model of the process of stratification of memories. Indeed, for Freud every dream meaning and dream symbol has a memory-trace at its core. Freud's conception of a process of stratification is basic to his conception of development as well as the dream, which is archaeological in import: "Every dream was linked in its manifest content with recent experiences and in its latent content with the most ancient experiences" (SE, 4, p. 218).

Freud uses the terms "ancient" and "prehistoric" more or less interchangeably, as in his allusion to his "prehistoric old nurse" reincarnated as a maid-servant in one of his dreams (SE, 4, p. 248). Commenting on Gottfried Keller's use, in *Der Grüne Heinrich*, of the Nausicaa story from Homer's *Odyssey*, Freud writes:

> The deepest and eternal nature of man, upon whose evocation in his hearers the poet is accustomed to rely, lies in those impulses of the mind which have their roots in a childhood that has since become prehistoric. Suppressed and forbidden wishes from childhood break through in the dream. (SE, 4, p. 247)

Thus, psycho-archaeological excavation uncovers the ancient or prehistoric memories of childhood, memories constituted by wishes—wishes in disguise. At its most fundamental, the psyche is constituted by ancient wishes: its foundation is a compacted structure of stratified wishes. Indeed, one can say that the columns of consciousness in the psyche stand in the foundational depressions made by the memory-traces of wishes. For Freud, the dream is an obvious archaeological site, a natural place to begin digging for wishes and the memory of wishes. It is a kind of tumulus—tumor?—of consciousness, a strange bulge announcing something hidden, buried within it. Dream analysis involves digging for and dissecting its tissue of memory-traces. For Freud, the dream was especially ripe for excavation—a site of consciousness begging for excavation—but as we know he regarded other, if less obvious, phenomena, such as parapraxes, as psycho-archaeological sites.

At one point Freud, describing the relationship of the component "agencies" or "systems" of "the mental apparatus" to one another, writes:

> These systems may perhaps stand in a regular spatial relation to one another, in the same way in which the various systems of lenses in a telescope are arranged behind one another. Strictly speaking, there is no need for the hypothesis that the psychical systems are actually arranged in a *spatial* order. It would be sufficient if a fixed order were established by the fact that in a given psychical process the excitation passes through the system in a particular *temporal* sequence. (SE, 5, p. 537)

The archaeological metaphor, embodiment of the process of stratification, articulates spatial and temporal stratification simultaneously. It permits Freud to talk of the psyche in spatial and temporal terms, that is, as a structure and a process at once. Archaeologically speaking, they are in principle one and the same.

Apart from the primary usage of the archaeological metaphor to signal what is most fundamental in psychoanalytic thinking, from its developmental conception of the psyche to its understanding of dreams, Freud makes numerous references to archaeological matters. Perhaps the most important one is his mention of Johann Winckelmann, the founder of classical archaeology (SE, 5, p. 196). Winckelmann's decision to visit Rome changed his life; Freud alludes to him in the course of his analysis of a number of dreams expressing his own wish to visit Rome. Rome, of course, is a living archaeological site, a space of major stratification in which many ancient memories are materially preserved in fragments. Freud's comparison of the psyche to Rome in *Civilization and Its Discontents*, illustrative of the "general problem of preservation in the mind," has already been noted. Gay links the analogy to Freud's obsessive collecting of antiquities, part of his general "addictive partiality for the prehistoric ... second in intensity only to his nicotine addiction."[13] For Freud they literally were preserved pieces of the mind, petrified parts of the psyche. Surrounding himself with them, he symbolically immersed himself in the psyche.

In describing a dream of his mother being carried, as though dead, by "people with birds' beaks," Freud remarks, "The strangely draped and unnaturally tall figures with birds' beaks were derived from the illustrations to Philippson's Bible. I fancy that they must have been gods with falcons' heads from an ancient Egyp-

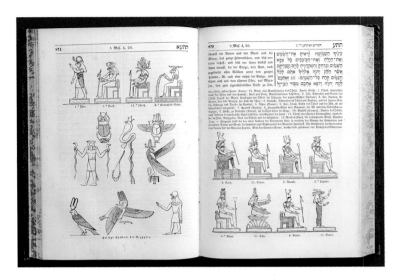

Pages from the Freud family Bible, *Die israelitische Bibel*, edited by Ludwig Philippson. (Photo: Freud Museum)

tian funerary relief" (SE, 5, p. 583). The birds' beaks, of course, remind us of the dream which Freud made so much of in his study of Leonardo da Vinci. Another archaeological occurrence in a dream, the appearance of "an Etruscan cinerary urn," out of which his wife was giving him a drink of water (SE, 4, p. 124), also suggests the evocative power of the archaeological metaphor, especially its implication of death, more precisely, its connection with the dead, or rather, the ghosts of unconscious wishes. Archaeology is, after all, a search for the remains of the dead and a demonstration of how uncannily alive they still are. Indeed, death is the primary meaning associated with archaeology, as the Italian Futurist painter Umberto Boccioni indicates when, in desperate pursuit of new stylistic life—a new future for art—he shouts, in contempt of traditional artists obsessed with old narratives and old modes of representation, "Out with you, archaeologists infected with chronic necrophilia!"[14] Was Freud a chronic necrophiliac? Certainly the psyche is, retentive as it is of dead but emotionally immortal objects. It sometimes seems like nothing but a cemetery in which it is not clear how many bodies are buried, nor how many of them have been truly laid to rest.

Archaeological associations and associations to antiquity, which are inseparable for Freud, are generally connected with parental figures—imagos—by him. In explaining his funerary dream, Freud remarks that "the introduction of the cinerary urn was probably yet another wish-fulfillment. I was sorry that the vase was no longer in my possession." (He had given it away.) In fact, the telling detail is that the water "tasted so salty (evidently because of the ashes in the urn)." Did the dream recall a childhood memory of his mother giving him a drink of water when he awoke in the middle of the night? Did the salt water represent the tears he shed at not being able to sleep with her? Did he wish her dead to distance himself from her—to deny the wish to sleep with her? Were these the tears of his unhappiness? Or was it water of life made undrinkable by the presence of death in it? Did the simple salt water encapsulate the struggle between the life and death forces? No doubt this is all too speculative, but so is a dream. Even the most innocuous-looking dream has uncanny permutations. As Freud himself noted, its implications spread endlessly; it leads us down unexpected paths, paths we didn't even know existed in the psyche. We hold to the thread of psycho-archaeology to find our way through this labyrinth of meaning.

Perhaps the most telling of Freud's archaeological associations are those which directly evoke classical antiquity in support of his ideas. Indeed, analogy for him is a security prop, and the association of psychoanalysis with classical antiquity was an especially secure staff for it to lean on. Sometimes one thinks of Freud, for all his fluency, as a stuttering Moses—his style in fact has the quirkiness of *parole* rather than the solemnity of *langue*—who had to rely on classical antiquity as an Aaron who would give him a silvery tongue, who would honeycoat his aggressive scientific intentions. Thus, he compares indestructible unconscious wishes to "the ghosts in the underworld of the Odyssey—ghosts which awoke to new life as soon as they tasted blood" (SE, 5, p. 553). They form the "store of infantile memories" that are "a *sine qua non* of repression" (SE, 5, p. 604). The famous line (SE, 5, p. 608) from Virgil's *Aeneid* (VII.312)— "Flectere si nequeo superos, Acheronta movebo" (If I cannot bend the Higher Powers, I will move the Infernal Regions)—wittily summarizes the archaeological intentionality of Freud's psychoanalysis. Just as Freud's eldest son, when he was eight years old, was excited by "the legends of Greece" (SE, 4, p. 129), so Freud was excited by them, throughout his whole life.

Jung testified to the importance of the archaeological metaphor in Freud's thinking when he appropriated it to begin his own *Psychology of the Unconscious*. There he compares the universal "Incest Fantasy ... the essential root of that powerful ancient dramatic material, the Oedipus legend," which "Freud calls to mind" as the basis of "individual psychologic conflict," with

> the impression made by ... that wholly peculiar feeling which arises in us if, for example, in the noise and tumult of a modern street we should come across an ancient relic—the Corinthian capital of a walled-in column, or a fragment of inscription. Just a moment ago we were given over to the noisy ephemeral life of the present, when something very far away and strange appears to us, which turns our attention to things of another order; a glimpse away from the incoherent multiplicity of the present to a higher coherence in history. [15]

The archaeological metaphor also has great explanatory power for Jung. It points the way to an understanding of the psyche. He yearns for it to be true:

> It would be significant enough if only the far-reaching analogy between the psychologic structure of the historical relics and the structure of the recent individual psychologic products alone were demonstrated. (p. 6)

As with Freud, for Jung psychoanalysis involves a necessary excavation of the archaic strata of the psyche, which are as much collective as individual for him, as they ultimately are for Freud. Archaeology signifies the convergence of collective and individual psychology, and of the phylogenetic and ontogenetic in the psyche:

Through buried strata of the individual soul we come indirectly into possession of the living mind of the ancient culture, and, just precisely through
that, do we win that stable point of view outside our own culture, from
which, for the first time, an objective understanding of their mechanisms
would be possible. (p. 5)

For Jung analogy is an intimation, even anticipation, of a truth. Analogical
thinking is a kind of "dream or phantasy thinking" (p. 22), which he believes, in
agreement with Freud, is pervasive among "ancient people" (p. 25). It is at the
root of myth formation, which sharply differentiates it from "directed thinking"
(p. 30) — scientific thinking. There is little to separate Jung and Freud, at least at
this stage in their thinking (1914), in their attitude to archaeology and antiquity.
While Jung tends to reify the archaic as primary meaning, Freud tends to qualify
it as primary wish. Neither denies that it is primary memory. Neither denies its
universality and primordiality, nor their fascination with it and the antiquity that
represents it.

It is in the name of genuine scientific thinking that Donald P. Spence attacks the
archaeological metaphor. It derives, he claims, from Freud's sense of "the ambiguity of everyday life, the fact that things are almost never what they seem, that
surface is always deceptive, and that true understanding must always go beneath
the surface."[16] That is, the archaeological metaphor is a sign of the hermeneutics
of suspicion. Spence says:

> We may be overly impressed by the metaphor of going below the surface. To
> the extent that the unconscious is "deeper" and to the extent that a
> dynamic explanation invokes "depth" psychology, we may fool ourselves
> into thinking that we have made contact with more fundamental issues and
> have come closer to the "true" explanation. (p. 31)

In other words, the archaeological metaphor leads down a primrose path of false
explanation (and expectation) to a dead end. For Spence the archaeological metaphor is inseparable from the notion of depth; to eliminate one is to undermine
the other. Like other postmodernist psychoanalytic thinkers eager to make
psychoanalysis operational in linguistic terms, Spence vigorously applies
Occam's razor to Freud's preconception of depth. Spence's basic point seems to be
that an analogy is not an explanation, and that depth is a hypothesis not justified
by surface appearances. The archaeological metaphor is likely to be self-decep-
tive: it creates the illusion that one can understand visible, concrete phenomena
by regarding them as indicators of an abstract, invisible — numinous — depth,
where the truth really exists. The archaeological metaphor is more speculative
than analytic in import.

Noting "the enormous appeal of the archaeological metaphor in all branches of
psychoanalytic work" (p. 76), Spence accepts the view of it as "one of Freud's
master plots" (Brooks), "one of [Freud's] more convincing story lines" (Schafer)
(p. 78). He categorically states "that there are no clinical specimens which con-
vincingly support the archaeological metaphor" (pp. 78–79):

Clinical vignettes which seem to support the archaeological metaphor . . . are not true data for at least two reasons: With only a few exceptions—and the exceptions are usually the more trivial observations—the so-called data are significantly incomplete—anecdotal rather than archival; even if reasonably complete, they tend to be either theory-laden or context-laden. What is more, we have no grammar of early development, no clearly defined system by which early experience is transformed into later behavior.

Finally, Spence remarks:

The belief in an archaeology of the mind or of the session carries with it the idea that the pieces of the past remain intact and can be recovered unchanged. [As Freud asserted in the citation from "Constructions in Analysis."—D.K.] The metaphor encourages us to look for tracings of the past, variously disguised but somehow recoverable, which could be used to validate the theory—both within the patient and within the session. But such a belief entails a kind of positivism which simply does not apply to the clinical material. The search for historical truth fails once we realize that the observer is always part of what is observed. The search for data within the session to confirm this or that interpretation also rests on the assumptions that the clinical material exists independently of the observer, and that what was compelling or transparent for him will necessarily be the same for an outside judge. (pp. 111–12)

In fact, it is not archaeology but Freudian psychoanalysis that claims to be able to recover historical truth, as Freud himself acknowledged. Archaeology is much more tentative; also, it is much more hermeneutically sophisticated: it recognizes that without their meaning, the historical objects it recovers are incomplete. The objects exist relative to their meanings, not in themselves—not in their simple materiality. To put it another way, the historical truth is not simply a matter of memories, but the meanings these memories have for those who have them, and the meaning the remembered experiences had when they occurred.

Moreover, archaeology recognizes that the recovery of meaning is fraught with problems: it is possible to know the letter of the meaning, but not its spirit; the recovered meanings are rarely straightforward, especially the socially more complex ones; and we can never know what it was like to live these meanings, for they are no longer ours. Freud refuses the partial ignorance and epistemological problems that archaeology accepts as its lot. In his enthusiasm and self-belief, his trust in his own powers of mastery, he sees inarticulateness, uncertainty, and unconsciousness at the beginning of the psychoanalytic process, and articulateness, certainty, and consciousness at its end. For him archaeology signals not only the will to make what is unconscious conscious, and thus bring it under control, but the success of the effort, whatever its difficulty. For him, the psycho-archaeologically discovered truth frees one of superstition about the unconscious past. A believer in enlightenment, Freud never quite realized its equivocal character. Like a good Cartesian, he thinks he can be uncompromisingly clear and distinct. Finally, in Spence's words, he believes he can be a detached "outside judge" and participant-observer at once, disentangling the roles of theorist and technician. From Spence's point of view, this is no doubt exceptional grandiosity.

What Spence finally seems to want to do is to collapse the surface/depth, present/past, manifest/latent distinctions implicit in the archaeological metaphor. They predetermine the reading of the psychological data, in effect absolutizing one reading. This reifies and dogmatizes psychoanalysis. Spence wants to recreate it as an open discourse rather than as a statement of absolute phenomena. He also wants it to be much more than a reconstruction and reliving of the past:

> In arguing for an accumulation of commentaries rather than the excavation of a session (or a person's mind), we are saying goodbye to the archaeological metaphor and substituting something much closer to an open conversation. We are suggesting that wisdom does not emerge by searching for historical truth, continually frustrated ... by a lack of clear specimens and context-free data; rather, wisdom emerges from the gradual accumulation of differing readings of the same situation and the accumulating overlay of new contexts. Notice how the metaphor has changed. No meaning attaches to any one piece which is buried in the past, in the unconscious, or in the clinician's incomplete records; no excavation is necessary. Instead, the meanings are constantly in flux, seen each time against a different context which provides a change of emphasis; figure and ground are constantly in motion. (p. 180)

What Spence should say is that the meanings are constantly in flux because they exist in the present, and imply a future, whatever their relation to the past. In any case, Spence's "new brand of tough-minded hermeneutics," which "assumes that not everything has a pattern, or more specifically, it assumes that no pattern exists until it is discovered," a "null position" which he equates with the "null hypothesis in statistics" (pp. 210–11), is commensurate with archaeological thinking, which, as I have suggested, accepts tentativeness and readiness to re-contextualize—reconceive—its data. Spence, I believe, is attacking archaeologism, which knows in advance the patterns it will find, or at least is on the lookout for certain patterns, which it tends to find everywhere and overgeneralize.

Should we, then, with Spence, say goodbye to the archaeological metaphor? Certainly he convinces us that we must say goodbye to the archaeologistic metaphor. But the archaeological metaphor can continue to have value, provided it is reconceived. I began to do so when I compared the psychoanalytic attitude with the phenomenological attitude, arguing that the archaeological attitude had the same critical import as they did. If the psychoanalytic attitude is an epoche[17]—reduction—positioning us to conceive phenomena as intelligible and meaningful in psychological terms, then the archaeological attitude is a reduction within the psychoanalytic reduction: an epoche positioning us to conceive psychological data as intelligible and meaningful specifically in terms of the past. (To convert phenomena to data means to qualify them in terms of some cognitive task.) That is, the archaeological reduction posits that the data reference the past; more specifically, it interprets or makes the data intelligible as signifiers of past meanings (not literal past experiences). To put this another way, where the psychoanalytic attitude reduces phenomena to psychological intelligibility and meaningfulness, the archaeological attitude reduces the psychoanalytically available data to mnemonic intelligibility and meaningfulness. That the archaeologized data will eventually be discovered to constitute a circular system of signifiers called "the past" is secondary to the archaeological reduction itself, which can be conceived as a necessary epistemological fiction.[18]

Thus archaeology is not simply a means to end amnesia, but an assertion that there is none: the past lives all around us, it is sedimented in the present, we are surrounded by it, but in the symbolic form of memory; more precisely, we unwittingly live memories. The larger point of the archaeological attitude is that we must decode the present to reveal it as the memorable, lived past. The past exists in suspended form in the present; archaeology precipitates it out of the solution of presentness and shows why certain things are experienced as having more presence than others. Archaeology suggests that the present is specious, tilting us toward the past from which it emerges.

Within the archaeological attitude, progressive and regressive tendencies must be sharply differentiated. In a sense, Spence does this for us when he distinguishes between psychoanalysis as a "hermeneutic adventure" and as "a staid, pseudoscientific account" (p. 151). He advocates the former and opposes the latter. The adventure, with its implication that "the context of discovery will very likely have the appearance of a disconnected series of insights, strung together by time" (p. 153), is progressive in import. The account, with its preconception of the psychoanalytic goal to be reached—the discovery of "the hidden message," as Spence says—and the method of reaching it—recovery of the historical past (usually conceived in an all too unsubtle, one-dimensional way)—is regressive. For Spence, the crucial difference between the adventure and the account is that the latter does not take into consideration the psychoanalyst's self-awareness. Spence means something more than awareness of countertransference. He quotes with approval Gray's idea "that perhaps the most important element in the study of technique 'lies in identifying, *in more than usual detail*, the manner or choice of the analyst's *forms of attention* during the conduct of the analysis' " (the first italics are Spence's; p. 151) and Gray's call for knowledge "of those functions of the ego that potentially enable it to observe itself" (p. 152).

The progressive psychoanalyst would be the self-observant one, aware of his or her archaeological attitude and its effect on interpretation—the character of the insight offered. The regressive psychoanalyst is not aware of his or her archaeological attitude, or rather, takes it for granted as the natural psychoanalytic attitude, not realizing that it is simply one form of psychoanalytic attention. To be aware of one's form of attention is to be potentially able to change it, as the need arises. There is no reason why psychoanalysis should not be an archaeology of the present and the future, able to move freely between past, present, and future as intersecting objects of inquiry, converging in the patient's life. The psychoanalyst should be prepared to archaeologically dig into the patient's life as it is temporally presented and uncover the meanings implicit in the presentation.

(Presentation is always temporally grounded, which is another implication of the archaeological metaphor.) Temporal presentation may be as much in terms of worry about the future as about disturbance by the past (or present). Patients may suffer from anticipations as well as reminiscences. They may experience a loss of possibility as well as be overwhelmed by actuality. Perhaps psychoanalysis's most important task is to defend against meaninglessness and lack of intelligibility, by discovering the meanings of the patient's past, present, and future, thus making them intelligible. The archaeological attitude implies the general meaningfulness and intelligibility of temporal events, however uncertain we may be about particular meanings and however equivocal intelligibility always is. What is at stake in the archaeological metaphor is not historical truth, as Spence thinks, and as Freud did, but the intelligibility and meaningfulness of history.

Spence implies that the form of attention, and the psychoanalyst's attention to his or her forms of attention, seriously condition the field of discovery. The archaeological reduction is a form of attention that gives discovered data the form of the past, that is, conceives it as a disguised or surrogate past. If the psychoanalyst is unaware of operating with an archaeological form of attention, he or she is likely to foreclose on the field of discovery, that is, not find any further implications or meanings in the discovered data. Spence is arguing in effect that there is more than one way of making the field of discovery intelligible. Indeed, I would argue that no way has priority over any other, except in terms of a specific therapeutic task. However, I would also argue that archaeological attention to the past—which, as I have suggested, is not the only form of archaeological attention—is one possible way of making the field of discovery intelligible and the discovered data meaningful. Intelligibility and meaningfulness are achieved by regarding the field of discovery as the scene of memory. One therapeutic task is to remember; perhaps not the first task, as Freud seemed to think, but certainly one possible if not absolutely necessary task, and one rarely carried out completely. Indeed, it is probably impossible to do so.

"To remember," Merleau-Ponty writes, "is not to bring into the focus of consciousness a self-subsistent picture of the past; it is to thrust deeply into the horizon of the past and take apart step by step the interlocking perspectives until the experiences which it epitomizes are as if relived in their temporal setting."[19] Freud certainly seemed to advocate this reliving, but perhaps his error was to think it possible to create a self-subsistent picture of the past. That is, his error was to have a foundationalist sense of the past that was not necessary to his edifying therapeutic—reeducative—purpose.[20] However, he is probably correct in thinking that some sense of the past is necessary for any and every therapeutic task to be successful, since such a task invariably implies a reevaluation of the present and the projection of a new future: the existential realization of a new sense of possibility and choice in life.

Indeed, Freud was right in thinking that past meanings—past forms of intelligibility—spontaneously emerge in the course of the psychoanalytic process: recognition of the past is inseparable from it. This is why it can be called a psycho-archaeological process. In a sense, in the very act of showing us that the past is still alive, archaeology makes clear that it is unmistakably past: pastness is not presentness, and the influence of the past on the future can be restricted. Perhaps the true import of the archaeological metaphor is not the theory of the process of stratification of memories, but Freud's assertion that when the past is spontaneously relived, the psychoanalyst must grab it fast and discover what kind of life it is. Failure to do so means that the psychoanalyst is not properly reflective, and thus not properly responsible to the patient, who must be made reflective in order to change his or her life. As Merleau-Ponty writes, "Reflection is truly reflection only if it is not carried outside itself, only if it knows itself as reflection-on-an-unreflective-experience, and consequently as a change in the structure of our existence."[21] The psychoanalyst must participate in the patient's past with his or her reflections on (interpretations of) it, in order to generate the patient's reflection. The psychoanalyst must become a truly participant observer; must catalyze the patient's own psycho-archaeological awareness. If the psychoanalyst does not relive the past with the patient and does not offer reflection on it— reflecting as if inside the patient rather than as an "outside judge," to recall Spence's term—"it would be just as though, after summoning up a spirit from the underworld by cunning spells, one were to send him down again without having asked him a single question" (SE, 12, p. 164).

Freud used his antiquities to summon up the spirits of his own underworld and to reflect on them, to question them about himself. They were, in effect, inside him: instruments of self-analysis. They were transference objects, in which he could read his own prehistory. They also reminded him of the inescapability and pull of the collective past, that is, of the fact that we all exist, phe-nomenologically speaking, in already sedimented life.

NOTES

1. Philip Rieff, *Freud: The Mind of the Moralist* (Garden City, N.Y.: Doubleday, 1961), p. 45. Rieff writes: "To have a repressed past is to be sick of it, to be healthy is to live more fully in the present. It is in this sense that analytic effort differs from the labors of the archaeologist, to which it is often compared. The archaeologist is neither for nor against what he digs up, but the analyst is necessarily arrayed against the patient's past, since he sees it as an incubus on the present."

2. Peter Gay, *Freud: A Life for Our Time* (New York: Norton, 1988), p. 172. Gay discusses Freud's interest in antiquity, in conjunction with his collecting of antiquities, on pp. 170–73.

3. A good example of this belief is Freud's assertion, at the beginning of *Totem and Taboo*:

Prehistoric man, in the various stages of his development, is known to us through the inani-mate monuments and implements which he has left behind, through the information about his art, his religion and his attitude towards life which has come down to us either directly or by way of tradition handed down in legends, myths and fairy tales, and through the relics of his mode of thought which survive in our own manners and customs. But apart from this, in a certain sense he is still our contemporary. There are men still living who, as we believe, stand very near to primitive man, far nearer than we do, and whom we therefore regard as his direct heirs and representatives. Such is our view of those whom we describe as savages or half-savages; and their mental life must have a peculiar interest for us if we are right in seeing in it a well-preserved picture of an early stage of our own development. (SE, 13, p. 1)

4. This is, I think, apparent from "The Question of a Weltanschauung," the final lecture in the *New Introductory Lectures on Psycho-Analysis* (SE, 22).

5. "Why War?" (1932) testifies to the one and "Analysis Terminable and Interminable" (1937) testifies to the other. In a sense, the one is about the failure of civilization to lead to self-control, and the other about the failure of psychoanalysis to lead to it. In the former Freud notes that "the attempt to replace actual force by the force of ideas seems at present doomed to failure" (SE, 22, p.

208). In the latter, which also deals with "the instinct of destruction," Freud remarks that "even to exert a psychical influence upon a simple case of masochism is a severe strain on our powers" (SE, 23, p. 243).

6. Sarah Kofman writes in *The Childhood of Art, An Interpretation of Freud's Aesthetics* (New York: Columbia University Press, 1988), p. 30: "The grammar and logic of dreams are not those of consciousness, which, as Derrida has shown, are linked to the *logos* and the *phonē*. The logic of dreams is archeo-logic that makes use of primary processes that govern the unconscious system."

7. For a discussion of Plato's use of myth, see Paul Friedländer, *Plato* (New York: Harper and Row, 1964), chap. 9. Friedländer's remark (p. 210) that "Plato escapes the danger of a metaphysical dogmatism, just as the artistic form of the dialogue avoids the fixity of the written word, and irony the danger of dogmatic seriousness" seems particularly to the point of Freud's avoidance of psychological dogmatism, scriptural fixity (among other things, his use of analogy counteracts it, as does his dialogic tendencies, most in evidence in *The Problem of Lay Analysis*) and a seriousness which presumes to know all the problems and have all the answers, which some have claimed for him.

8. The archaeological metaphor is quite popular in modern thought. Michel Foucault in *The Archaeology of Knowledge and the Discourse on Language* (New York: Pantheon Books, 1982), pp. 138–40, offers a useful statement of the working principles of archaeology.

9. Edwin R. Wallace IV, *Freud and Anthropology, A History and Reappraisal* (New York: International Universities Press, 1983), p. 9. See also Gay, *Freud: A Life*, p. 449. In chap. 1, on the "Prehistory of Freud's Anthropology," Wallace offers a first-rate examination of Freud's "infatuation with archaeology" (p. 5). It is worth noting that it was the famous French archaeologist Alfred Maury who coined the term *"illusions hypnogogiques"* to refer to phenomena witnessed in the impressionable state between waking and sleeping. Freud made a number of allusions to Maury, who interpreted thousands of his own dreams. See Eugene Taylor, *William James on Exceptional Mental States* (Amherst: University of Massachusetts Press, 1984), pp. 27-28.

10. Don Ihde, *Consequences of Phenomenology* (Albany, N.Y.: State University of New York Press, 1986), p. 173. The conception of psychoanalysis as a species of hermeneutics has been attacked by Adolf Grünbaum, *The Foundations of Psychoanalysis, A Philosophical Critique* (Berkeley: University of California Press, 1985), in the "Introduction: Critique of the Hermeneutic Conception of Psychoanalytic Theory and Therapy." Perhaps the most extreme formulation of psychoanalysis as hermeneutics is Harold Bloom's fleeting, tantalizing association of it with kabbalistic interpretation in *A Map of Misreading* (New York: Oxford University Press, 1980), pp. 4–5; see also p. 85.

11. *The Complete Letters of Sigmund Freud to Wilhelm Fliess, 1887–1904*, ed. and trans. Jeffrey M. Masson (Cambridge: Harvard University Press, 1985), pp. 233–35.

12. Ole Andkjaer Olsen and Simo Koppe, *Freud's Theory of Psychoanalysis* (New York: New York University Press, 1988), p. 124.

13. Gay, *Freud: A Life*, pp. 172–73 (as in n. 2).

14. Quoted in Ester Coen, *Umberto Boccioni* (New York: Metropolitan Museum of Art, 1988; exhib. cat.), p. xiv.

15. C. G. Jung, *Psychology of the Unconscious* (New York: Dodd, Mead, 1944), p. 3. Subsequent references to this work appear in the text.

16. Donald P. Spence, *The Freudian Metaphor, Toward Paradigm Change in Psychoanalysis* (New York: Norton, 1987), p. 27. Subsequent references to this work appear in the text.

17. For a discussion of the epoche or phenomenological reduction, see my article "Parmenidean Tendencies in the Epoche," *Review of Metaphysics* 18 (June 1965), 739–70.

18. For a discussion of necessary fiction, see my article "Fiction and Phenomenology," *Philosophy and Phenomenological Research* 19 (Sept. 1968), 16–33.

19. M. Merleau-Ponty, *Phenomenology of Perception* (London: Routledge and Kegan Paul, 1962), p. 22.

20. I am using Richard Rorty's distinction between foundational and "edifying" philosophies. The latter involves the "project of finding new, better, more interesting, more fruitful ways of speaking," and may include moral and educative concerns as well as "the hermeneutic activity of making connections ... between our own discipline and another which seems to pursue in commensurable aims"; in his *Philosophy and the Mirror of Nature* (Princeton: Princeton University Press, 1979), p. 360. This implies horizontalization, or "that there are no privileged language games, no disciplines, no privileged activities" (Ihde, *Consequences*, pp. 185–86; as in n. 10).

21. Merleau-Ponty, *Phenomenology of Perception*, p. 62.

Sigmund Freud at his desk, etching by Max Pollack, 1914.

PSYCHOANALYSIS AND THE LEGACIES OF ANTIQUITY

ELLEN HANDLER SPITZ

But what if both of us have strayed on to a wrong path? ... What if we have shared the fate of so many interpreters who have thought they saw quite clearly things which the artist did not intend either consciously or unconsciously?
—Sigmund Freud, 1914

The scrims through which each era stages and views its past inevitably wear and fade. They must be patched, repainted, and rehung. Taking Freud's collection of antiquities as emblematic of a first staging of what may be viewed as an ongoing drama between the ancient world and psychoanalysis, this interpretive essay has two aims. First it attempts to show that, symbolically, Freud's choice of ancient Egyptian, Greek, and Roman cultures constituted, for him, a conflicted legacy in which feelings about his Judaic birth and heritage were deeply implicated. Second, it seeks to demonstrate that antiquity, as represented by this group of objects, continues to count as a major and underexplored legacy for contemporary psychoanalysis and the other mental health professions. Recent contributions to classical scholarship have suggested interpretive possibilities that supplement those of Freud and reopen the rich treasure trove of antiquity for fascinating new borrowings by present-day explorers of the psyche.

Unlike symptoms, which, it is hoped, succumb to the power of good interpretation, great myths thrive on rereadings and thereby gain an added significance and longevity.[1] Moreover, to critique old ties or urge the forging of new bonds between psychoanalysis and antiquity is but to follow a deep and turbulent current in Freud's ever-changing thought. To reinterpret the cultures of antiquity and rethink their relevance for modern clinical practice is to support Freud's belief, as attested by his classical collection, that antiquity provides an inexhaustible well of understanding vis-à-vis the human condition.

Freud's cherished antiquities reflect his profound indebtedness to a past that inspired him to make dazzling theoretical and interpretive leaps. Gazing at the assembled objects, we are moved to reflect on the curious fact that this Viennese neurologist, man of medicine and science, so clearly wished to be thus indebted and to elect his antecedents in the realms of mythology, art, and literature. We may interpret this desired legacy as symbolizing for him perhaps a permanence, an authority, an acceptability, a wreath of ancient glory and legitimization in the face of an initial and ongoing spurning of his intellectual enterprises.[2] Such speculation is irresistible to wanderers in the maze of Freud's voluminous writings and encircling scholarship. Both his oeuvre and the collection of antiquities betray the tangled skeins of signification and emotion by means of which life and work are, as he himself taught, inextricably knotted.

Each part of this essay takes a specific object in the collection as a starting point. First, with the statue of Amon-Re from Freud's desktop in mind, I shall address some of the complexities and ambiguities latent in Freud's desire for an ancient legacy. Second, turning to a small terracotta piece that might easily escape notice, a head of Demeter, I shall argue that certain ancient myths and practices, passed over by Freud, might nevertheless serve as fertile ground for the expansion of metaphor and meaning in present-day analytic work. I shall probe one such myth, illustrated by this piece, in some depth, but clearly the scope of such an endeavor must be partial and fragmentary. Its modest aim is to provide a background for contemplating the collection and an impetus to further study.

Central to the theme of the collection is the powerful awareness forced on its viewers that Freud, ever seeking clues to the riddles of psychic life, chose to peer into the murky reservoirs of ancient mythology and art. In so doing, he marked out a direction and a territory that mental health professionals today, intently gazing into the sterilized test tubes of the laboratory or examining orderly tabulations of statistical data, have tended increasingly to ignore. To these modern explorers of the mind, preoccupied with information systems, data processing, quantification, and so-called hard facts, Freud's forays, his retrospection and borrowings from past cultures, may seem merely quaint. Yet, as we gaze at his antique objects and conjure the cluttered study that housed them, we cannot fail to acknowledge the indelible impact upon us of his fascination with all this—at the impact of his deeply mythical cast of mind and his relentless pursuit of fantasy, dream, and desire.

Despite an interest in antiquity that originated in his childhood, Freud began actively collecting antiquities only after his father's death and during the period of his self-analysis; from that point, however, he continued to do so avidly throughout his lifetime.[3] Intimately present in his visual field on a daily basis and physically proximate, close enough to touch, these objects—statuettes, busts, vases, reliefs, tablets, receptacles—ever growing in number, formed, in the company of books and pictures, a thickly textured stage-set against which his patients' narratives and his interpretations of them were played out. Seated in his consulting room, listening hour by hour, penning the theories that were to transform our self-understanding, Freud shared physical space and visual field with these carved, limned, and modeled objects; he worked, as it were, under their gaze.[4]

A naive project, therefore, might be to plot manifest relations between them and the Freudian texts—direct references to myths illustrated by specific antiquities. No overall pattern emerges, however, since many pieces cannot be directly tied to written allusions. Yet, despite a dearth of superficial one-to-one correspondence, it is clear that deep currents bind the artifacts to the written texts. Adapting J. W. N. Sullivan's sensitive account of the genius of Beethoven, we can regard Freud's passion for antiquity as a theme with a life of its own that combined with other elements to form ever more complex synthetic wholes in the unfolding of his life's work.[5] Or, if this seems excessively poetic, we might invoke a highly original insight of Didier Anzieu and apply it to the collection.[6]

In a discussion of Freud's so-called Rome dreams (reported in chapter 5, *The Interpretation of Dreams*, SE, 4, pp. 193–98),[7] Anzieu begins with the supposition that Freud began to collect antiquities the summer before having these particular dreams. He suggests an interpretation of Freud's method of working that, I propose, sheds light on the way he "worked" with his collection, or, more precisely, on the way his collection may have "worked on" him.[8]

On the basis of the vivid imagery in the Rome dreams, Anzieu speculates that Freud's genius was capable of moving directly from vision to writing. Freud's creativity, he claims, was predicated on a hypercathexis of sight and writing; thus, Freud was able to transliterate directly what he saw or intuitively grasped without the intermediary of the spoken word, "to leap without transition from the body to the code."[9] This formulation is highly suggestive as we imagine Freud surrounded by visual art and attempt to grasp its impact on him as he listened and wrote.

We also gain insight into the depth of feeling associated with these objects when we learn that Freud had the habit of occasionally bringing a newly acquired purchase, such as a statuette, to the dinner table and placing it in front of him as he ate, then returning it later to his desk.[10] Our intuitive understanding of the phenomenon is further advanced by perceiving links between the antiquities and Freud's ineffable feelings about his Jewishness and his own characterization of them as enigmatic, mysterious, and unanalyzable.[11] In tracing the subtle ties here between art and allusion, I have found that the subject of Freud's Jewishness returns: the thickets of reference and association, never simple or straightforward, lead, as he himself has shown, in surprising and unforeseeable directions.[12]

The bronze figurine of Amon-Re that adorned Freud's desk serves as our point of departure.[13] This image ties directly with the first essay of *Moses and Monotheism* (SE, 23, pp. 1–137), where Amun figures in the opening pages as a displaced god. Here Freud, in his late seventies, argues, in a highly problematical text, that Moses was an Egyptian nobleman who transmitted to the Jewish people a stern monotheism based on the cult of Aten (which Pharaoh Amenhotep IV, Akhenaten, inaugurated, thereby temporarily suppressing the time-honored worship of Amun, god of Thebes), and that the Jews murdered Moses. Standing as a major document in the evidence for Freud's complex relations with Judaism,[14] this manuscript caused considerable turmoil both for its author (he spoke of it as tormenting him like an unlaid ghost, SE, 23, p. 103) and for others. It was considerably, even agonizingly, worked over and its publication delayed.[15] The antiquities are connected here as well, in that suggestions have been made that, in some richly overdetermined way, Freud's very passion for them can be traced to his ambivalent awareness of an ancestry that originated in the lands of the Orient and the Mediterranean.[16]

Amon-Re, Egyptian, 716–332 B.C., bronze.
(Photo: Freud Museum)

This supposition is bolstered by the fact that Freud's initial collecting of antiquities immediately postdated the death of his father, Jacob,[17] who, although in practice a liberal and nonobservant Jew, represented for Freud a major link with his Jewishness.[18] We are told that Jacob "was fond of reading the Torah"[19] and that he introduced Freud at age seven to the family's illustrated Philippson Bible.[20] A further link in the chain that binds Freud, Egypt, Moses, Jacob, and Judaism is the biblical figure of Joseph, favorite son of Jacob, interpreter of dreams and viceroy in Egypt, with whom Freud identified in complex ways.[21]

The most dramatic (and painful) association of Jacob Freud with Judaism is poignantly conveyed through the impact made on his son by an incident he relates in *The Interpretation of Dreams*. Freud was told as a child by Jacob that the

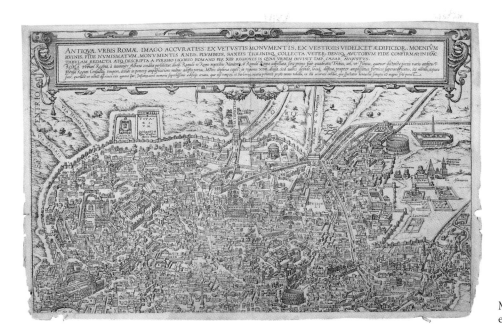

Map of ancient Rome, a sixteenth-century etching owned by Freud. (Photo: Freud Museum)

latter was insulted and humiliated in the street merely because he was recognized as being a Jew. Freud's youthful reaction on hearing this anecdote was to fantasize a scene from Roman history in which he, in the role of the child Hannibal, swore to avenge his father by marching against Rome (SE, 4, p. 197). This memory arose out of his associations to the fourth Rome dream, which, as noted above, dates from the period just following Jacob's death and the time of Freud's initial forays into collecting (SE, 4, pp. 196–98).[22]

Thus, Rome, like Egypt the origin of a sizable number of Freud's antiquities, is linked both with his father and with Judaism. In a penetrating analysis of each of the four Rome dreams, Anzieu sorts out the threads in their tangled web of linkages.[23] He makes a point that bears directly on Freud's collection, even though he does not say so straight out. Remarking that Rome (i.e., the Greco-Roman heritage) is a culture that Freud chose, as opposed to the Judaic one into which he was born, Anzieu comes just short of interpreting that, in giving the former priority over the latter, Freud was symbolically denying his father and claiming a different origin. He was, as it were, enacting his own version of a "family romance" (SE, 9, p. 237).[24]

Linked with Egypt and scion of Greece, it is Rome, mingled with the others, that becomes another element in the heritage of Freud's conflicted choice. Bolstering this interpretation, Anzieu draws a parallel between the two heroes Moses and Aeneas, pairing them as conquerors of unknown lands and founders of new laws.[25] In seeing them thus, however, we cannot neglect the agonistic underside of the equation: Rome (which Freud longed to visit for years before actually making the trip) figures for him not only as desired goal but as opponent and oppressor. Anzieu, following the content and timing of the dreams, reads Freud's upsurge of ambivalent longings for "Roma" (which, spelled backwards as in the dream mechanism of reversal into its opposite, becomes "Amor")[26] as symbolizing in part an infantile yearning for the body[27] of the oedipal mother rekindled in fantasy now by the death of the father. It is apropos that Freud throughout his lifetime acknowledged and theorized only the positive side of what he saw as the privileged primary relationship between a mother and son. This partial view on his part cannot be independent of the fact that this aspect of his longing for Rome remained unaddressed. The point is underscored by his seeming obliviousness, in quoting Virgil's lines, "Flectere si nequeo superos, Acheronta movebo," as his epigraph for *The Interpretation of Dreams*, that these words are uttered not by the hero Aeneas but rather by the enraged and scheming goddess Juno.[28]

In emphasizing that Freud elected for himself an intellectual heritage different from that of his ancestors, it seems hardly necessary to point out that none of his cherished ancient objects is in any sense Jewish and that Jewish rituals and observance were anathema to him.[29] Thus, to return to Amun and the treatise *Moses and Monotheism*, written in the last years of his life, when travel had become impossible and the collected antiquities were his only tangible link with their sites of origin, we may speculate on a subliminal agenda for the entire project. In redefining Moses as Egyptian (and, implicitly, as *not* Jewish), was Freud not also unconsciously redefining the relations between himself and the legacy represented by this very collection of antiquities?[30] Was he not compelling these objects, as it were, to assume a more intimate relation with him? Was he not, in essence, coercing them into a heritage of birth rather than of mere choice? By acknowledging in the opening sentence of the text of *Moses and Monotheism* the implicit aggression against his fellow Jews, was he not betraying and masking a deeper and more personal level of aggression?[31] If so, his early mention of the dethroning of Amun (and the commanding presence of this statue on his desk) assumes, as I have suggested, a paradigmatic significance.

My point—if Moses could be considered Egyptian, then so, in fantasy, might Freud—is supported by Freud's lifelong fascination with the figure of Moses.[32] In his 1914 essay "The Moses of Michelangelo," for example, he speaks of the patriarch in this representation as making a profound impression on him. Splitting the identifications, he fantasizes here that he is a member of the mob upon whom Moses gazes and glares (SE, 13, p. 213). But who is this "mob?" Bearing in mind Freud's association of his father with Judaism and recognizing this fantasied mob to whom Freud feels momentarily attached as none other than the "children of Israel," we cannot avoid emphasizing what it is they have just done: they have at that very moment been caught in an act of arrant rebellion, a breach of trust, a rejection of God, above all, a reversion to idolatry (SE, 13, p. 213).[33] Mapping Freud's ambivalences onto this image while picturing his growing collection of statues, we can glimpse what is at stake here in the doubling of identifications and the screening function of the "inscrutability" (SE, 13, p. 213) he attributed to the statue.

Relevant here also are the disparaging comments Freud permitted himself about his father in his essay "A Disturbance of Memory on the Acropolis" (SE, 22, p. 239ff). Here, to explain a sudden dysphoria he suffered on realizing his childhood dream of reaching Athens—another cherished site of antiquity— Freud remarks on his father's inferior education and lack of interest in the classics; he points out the disparity between his own feelings at this important moment and those his father might have been expected to have had under similar circum-stances. He interprets his own love of antiquity as an advance over his benighted father and attributes the momentary dysphoria to conflicts aroused by the enjoy-ment of that which his father could not possibly have appreciated. One feels the confluence of shame, guilt, and triumph: the shame of the small son whose inad-equate father did not retaliate when insulted and who was likewise too edu-cated to admire pagan antiquity; the guilt of the grown son who perceives himself suddenly as having surpassed, triumphed over, that father.

All of this has taken us far from the bronze statuette of Amun. But perhaps this is only an illusion, for, circling round him all the while, we have taken him as a figure for other displaced gods and overthrown idols. Our discussion points to the complexity of Freud's investment in his antiquities and to the multiple agendas met by his collecting as well as by the interpretive choices he made with respect to antiquity in his theoretical usage of it.[34] Bitterly disdainful of Jewish self-hatred in others, his own unresolved conflicts in this area seem to have created something of a scotoma in his self-understanding.[35] To conjure him surrounded in his study by miniature figures of gods and goddesses (Aphrodite, Athena, Dionysos, Artemis, Amun, Hathor, Osiris, and others) is to recall the second command-ment of the Torah (Exodus 20), which expressly prohibits sculptured images on account of their association with polytheism and idolatry.

If we invoke the dream mechanism of representation by reversal into its opposite, this image of Freud in his study produces a striking inversion of a well-known midrash or rabbinic commentary.[36] Here, in order to explain why Abraham was chosen to be the father of the Jewish people, the story is told that Abraham, the son of an idol maker named Terah, one day in his father's absence went into the workplace and smashed the idols there. Freud, in the absence of his own father, Jacob, surrounded himself with idols which, assuredly, he did not worship but which afforded him, apparently, an extraordinary and not unambiguous pleasure.

If such issues matter in Freud's passion for antiquity, we may conclude that the myths and artifacts of ancient Egypt, Greece, and Rome functioned for him not only, as others have intimated, to connect him with a past but also to separate him from a past. If so, his passionate "addiction" to collecting may also have served unconscious repetitive efforts at mastery and integration as well as the enactment of an ongoing family romance. As with other aspects of his oeuvre when viewed from the perspective of his life, this one may be seen as a heroic attempt to create (and coerce) an elusive harmony between culture, family, and individual.

Beyond the figure of Amun, other pieces in the collection relate more overtly to Freud's psychoanalytic oeuvre. I wish to point out only a few. Two vases depicting Oedipus and the Sphinx as well as additional sphinx images may be taken as sym-bolizing Freud's fascination with its riddle and his idealized self-image as a solver of riddles.

Moving accounts describe Freud's well-known pallor and agitation on receiv-ing, at age fifty, the famous medallion inscribed with the line from the end of

Sophocles' *Oedipus Rex*:[37] "Who knew the famous riddle and was a man most mighty." His reaction was caused by the sudden revival of his youthful fantasy that one day his own bust inscribed with these very words would adorn the courtyard of the University of Vienna (an unlikely honor for a Jew, but one that eventually came to him sixteen years after his death). This episode reveals not only the intensity but the longevity of Freud's identification with Oedipus, an identification that substantially preceded his discovery of the Oedipus complex and the creation of psychoanalysis—a point that underscores the circularities inherent in his interpretive strategies vis-à-vis antiquity.[38]

On this topic, namely, Freud's deep identification with Oedipus and his use of this particular myth as a cornerstone of theory, it is worthwhile noting points of convergence in the stories of Moses and Oedipus and the fact that the structure of Freud's own family mirrored that of Oedipus.[39] In all three cases, there are distancings of the boy child from his father of birth as well as scenes that place questions of origins at the forefront; in the Oedipus myth and in the structure of Freud's own family, an overlapping of generations produced conflations and confusions—riddles—over issues of origin and destiny (a powerful motive for the continuing investment in a family romance).

Both yoked to and disjoined from his personal past, antique references were used by Freud in ways that occasionally verged on the preemptive (as, for example, his passing allusion to the *Oresteia* as a support for equating intellectuality with father and sensuality with mother; SE, 23, p. 114).[40] Rather than confront the ancient world as "other," as an eccentric locus from which to behold contemporary practices, his approach was appropriative and idealizing—an attitude, however, by no means discordant in fin-de-siècle Vienna, where classicism continued to be revered in the midst of a welter of countercultures.[41] Freud saw antiquity as embodying universal human themes and as a felicitous anticipation and confirmation of his own theoretical formulations.[42] Thus, characterized by processes of circular infusion and reinfusion, his borrowings have occasionally attracted the criticism of contemporary classicists, who express dismay at what they consider his Procrustean tendencies.[43]

But like Freud we, too, inhabit an inexorable afterlife of antiquity, particularly with regard to the Greeks, whose myths and metaphors have played a major role in molding our (psychoanalytic) culture. To reinterpret these within the framework of our own time, with its stringencies and ideologies, is inescapably to become prey, with him, in the nets of hermeneutic entanglement.

Shifting scenes now, I should like to turn to a small terracotta head, identified as Demeter,[44] and consider an area where Freud's work, especially since his death, has come under some criticism both by scholars and by clinicians, namely, his construction of gender. Despite his bold intellectual iconoclasm, Freud's construction of gender was markedly conservative. Dominated by the symbol of the phallus and the polarity between having and lacking the biological organ for which it stands, his theory offered only this metaphor, present or absent, for sexual difference.[45] Female reproductive organs, female development, and feminine psychology were repeatedly interpreted as a variant on, complementary to,

Head of Demeter, Greek, 6th century B.C., terracotta. (Photo: Freud Museum)

opposite of, or inferior to the male model as norm. It is important to state, however, that Freud was never fully satisfied with his formulations of female sexuality and development and continued to revise them throughout his lifetime. Furthermore, his basic position has been considerably modified in the clinical literature, especially during the last twenty-five years, as it was even during his lifetime.[46] Although the implicit misogyny of the original formulations is traceable directly to antiquity (as Freud knew), the extant corpus of ancient myth, art, and social practice lends itself to supplementary readings that may yet have much to offer modern psychoanalysis in this area of contemporary concern.

Powerful persuasive readings backed by precedent, such as Freud's of *Oedipus*, tend to preempt the stage and occlude plausible alternatives. However, as Sophocles' drama teaches, interpretation itself can create permanent blind spots.[47] Thus Freud, in colonizing antiquity for his purposes, closed as well as opened the territory. My aim is to suggest perspectives that might supplement his usage and stimulate an expanded dialogue between psychoanalysis and antiquity.

I have chosen this head of Demeter because of the fascinating myth to which it refers. Freud, having read Ovid, clearly knew the story of Demeter and Persephone, at least in this version. Yet, although in all its forms it addresses the theme of mother-daughter relations, which Freud eventually came to recognize as central to female development, he never chose to interrogate this exemplary myth in terms of his own important question: "What does the little girl require of her mother?" (SE, 21, p. 235). His scattered references to it curiously bypass its central motif. He refers to Demeter only with regard to an incident that occurs in her daughter's absence (SE, 14, p. 338) and to Persephone as a chthonic figure with no mention of her relationship to her mother (SE, 12, p. 299). These omissions suggest that Freud may have addressed himself with less depth and sensitivity to the range and complexities of feminine psychology than to comparable masculine issues. Taking this small figure of Demeter as a point of departure, I wish to urge her story as a source of rich material for psychoanalysts confronting these issues anew.

Giving priority to the role of the mother, the myth can be summarized as follows:[48] Demeter, goddess of fertility and the harvest, has a beautiful daughter Persephone (Kore) who, while gathering flowers with other young girls one day in an idyllic setting, plucks a fateful narcissus.[49] This flower was placed before her as a lure by her father, Zeus, on behalf of his brother Hades, god of the underworld, who had seen the girl and developed a passion for her. As Persephone plucks the flower, a rift opens in the earth, and Hades suddenly appears in a horse-drawn chariot; he surprises, terrifies, and abducts her. Zeus, meanwhile, remains throughout the myth a distant, shadowy figure who, by staging his daughter's violation, enacts by proxy his incestuous wishes toward her. He is never portrayed as having any direct contact with her, and her entire filiation is bound up with her mother.[50]

Demeter's response to the loss of Persephone is, by turns, sorrowful, depressed, and then bitterly indignant. Wandering the earth in an effort to discover what has become of her beloved child and to regain her, she enacts a sequence that seems uncannily to prefigure the stages of melancholia as outlined by Freud in 1917 (SE, 14).[51] Turning aggression inward against herself, she tears the covering on her hair, refuses food and drink, ceases to bathe. Upon learning that Zeus abetted the rape, her grief reaches fever pitch. Cutting herself off from all company of the gods, disfiguring herself, she assumes the appearance of an aged woman whose childbearing years are over.

Shortly after this, in the course of her subsequent wanderings, Demeter "adopts," as it were, another woman's child; she "becomes" a mother again as a means of undoing her loss and of symbolically recovering Persephone. Yet the child, in this case, is a boy, and the incident has disturbing overtones: Demeter seeks, by breathing on him, clasping him to her bosom, and placing him each night in a fire in order to turn him into a god, to utterly possess him—thus separating him irrevocably from his own mother. In this way, under the guise of beneficence, she turns passive into active; she relives her trauma by inflicting it on another through identification with the aggressor.[52] By displacement, this incident reveals multiple levels of Demeter's unacknowledged ambivalence toward Persephone—jealousy toward her as the (incestuously) preferred object of the father and envy for her burgeoning fertility, symbolically represented by the boy child taken in fantasy as Persephone's future child, a child who also represents the dangerous and unfaithful male world which has betrayed her.[53]

The intensity of Demeter's mingled sexuality and aggression toward this "new child" is spied out by the boy's real mother, and a confrontation between the two women ensues. At this point in the myth Demeter reveals herself in all her glory as a mighty goddess and, rejecting the substitute child, throws off her melancholy disguise. Vehemently now, she turns her aggression outward. Withholding her own fertility, she punishes Zeus, and by causing a cruel famine to spread across the land, she coerces him into returning Persephone to her. Persephone, in the underworld, pining for her mother, is elated when Hermes, at the bidding of Zeus, comes to rescue her. Hades, however, slips a pomegranate seed into her mouth (symbolic of heterosexual union with its many seeds and blood-red juice); thus, secretly, he binds her to him and secures her return.

This myth ends with a compromise solution that leaves the modern mind perhaps slightly less easy than the ancient. Persephone is partially restored to Demeter. By tasting the pomegranate in the underworld, however, she is bound forever to her husband, with whom her mother can, henceforth, only share her. According to different versions of the myth, she spends one-third or one-half of the year with him and the other half or two-thirds with Demeter. When mother and daughter are united, they are portrayed as radiantly happy, and the earth is fertile; when Persephone returns to Hades, however, Demeter is melancholy and dejected. Interestingly, in the Homeric Hymn to Demeter, the final reconciliation between daughter, mother, and Olympian Zeus comes about through the agency of Rhea, a goddess who represents the fertility of the previous generation, she being the grandmother of Persephone and mother of Demeter. [54]

As with all great myths, alternate versions present fascinating details that call for lengthy treatment, and psychologically valid readings may logically contradict one another. What follows is a modest opening of the question: how might this material illuminate Freud's own query as to what a little girl requires of her mother (and vice versa)? Does the myth represent normal or disturbed relations between a mother and daughter, or some layering and combination of these? In celebrating the enduring power of the mother-daughter bond at the expense of joyful heterosexuality, does the myth endorse its own solution or express wishes and fears—fears of wishes and denial of fears? And precisely what wishes and fears are at stake here? What developmental levels of fantasy are addressed—the infantile, the adult, or some combination? Does the myth correspond to male or female fantasies, or to both? (The aggressive bridegroom, for example, appears clinically in adult fantasies of both genders. [55]) Superficially dyadic in form, the myth marginalizes its male characters, but in my telling here, I have tried to reintroduce triadic determinants into the narrative. Its cyclical content and solution brilliantly evoke the female reproductive system as well as the seasons of the year and convey that, because a girl shares her mother's biology, their object relations are deeply structured by this sameness. And the questions posed by the myth may likewise seem to flow in circles.

Dramatizing in its initial episode an abrupt and bewildering moment of schism that occurs in mother-daughter relations shortly after puberty, the myth returns us to a time when, in ancient Greece, girls who still played with dolls and toys were abruptly taken from their childhood homes and married to men considerably older than themselves. [56] Under altered social conditions today, puberty and marriage are separated by a decade or two, and menarche often triggers not only a resurgence of early ambivalence in the mother-daughter dyad but a special renewal of closeness. However, when separation does become a dominant theme, mutual adoration can turn overnight into antagonism, caring be suddenly construed as criticism, and closeness widen out into a chasm.[57]

The Demeter-Persephone myth portrays such rupture in dyadic terms as a warding-off of anticipated loss by its precipitation, a turning (on both sides) of passive into active. Thus, distance (psychological/spatial) functions to defend the mother-daughter pair against their unspoken knowledge that the daughter's flowering beauty, her newly acquired reproductive capacity, can result in a heterosexual relationship that threatens to disrupt and supersede the ties that bind them to one another. On this reading, the myth enacts both a fantasy (of violent male intrusion) that precipitates unbearable emotional distance (in the female dyad) and a fantasied rapprochement between the members of this dyad (exclusive of the male). What the myth strikingly avoids, in so doing, is any direct representation of aggression between mother and daughter. This primary dyad remains intact throughout, and aggression is projected outward on to the male(s).[58]

Dreading her loss (of self? of object?), a mother goes in search of a daughter she needs to keep. What does it mean for Demeter to regain Persephone, to "save" her? At what price is Persephone rescued from Hades and returned to earth? One possible reading casts Demeter as the omnipotent pre-oedipal mother, more powerful than all males. A related interpretation casts her as the narcissistic mother who, under the pretext of salvation, sacrifices her child in order to preserve herself—Persephone representing to her an indispensable element of her own body, self, fertility.[59] Thus, Persephone, reverting to her mother to gratify the latter's need, is forever barred from achieving loving heterosexual relations. In this reading, Demeter only superficially rescues a cherished and victimized child; on the contrary, she herself plays the role of victimizer, using her daughter for her own ends.[60] To say this, however, is to interpret against the grain both of the manifest content and of the overall tone of the myth. Not only does it bracket the fact that Persephone's initiation into heterosexuality comes via weakly disguised incest and rape, but it denies the mood and language of the myth, which clearly exalts and idealizes the mother-daughter dyad—its symmetry, mutuality, and tenderness. Yet this very idealization could be interpreted as a defense against underlying and disavowed pathology: the unconflicted love serving as a rationalization for a tragic inability of both mother and daughter to separate.

Taking another tack, that of historicizing the myth, classicist Marilyn Arthur has suggested that under extreme forms of patriarchy women need ongoing contact with one another in order to achieve and sustain self-definition—hence, the desperation of Demeter's search and the idealization (at the beginning and end of the myth) of the mother-daughter pair and of exclusively female bonding.[61] However, even under present social conditions of increased political and economic freedom and articulate presence for (some) women, deeply felt needs for maintaining the ties rendered in this myth have not been significantly mitigated. Clinical evidence reveals that despite external changes, women require not only stable maternal introjects but ongoing contact with one another and with primary maternal objects,[62] especially at moments associated with fertility—menarche, marriage, pregnancy, birth, and the nurturance of children. The myth, which tells its story (manifestly) from the mother's side, stresses Demeter's desire to be available as an ongoing presence in Persephone's life, to play an active role and foster identifications between her daughter and herself. Women who lose mothers before childbirth mourn them at this time, and both mothers and daughters who reestablish relations after the painful disharmonies of adolescence derive mutual benefits from their reunion and discover more fully their own unique capacities for nurturance, a point underscored in the myth by the presence, in the end, of the figure of the grandmother.

While associating youthful innocence in an enclosed female space with playfulness and freedom from care, the myth, by contrast, equates marriage, in the form of Hades, with brutality and death. For Persephone, the joys of marriage and heterosexual love are absent.[63] In spite of being restored to her mother (or perhaps because of it), her sacrifice continues. She neither establishes a satisfying marriage nor is it clear that she ever becomes a mother herself.

This dark parallelism (nuptials and death) evokes the recent work of classicist Nicole Loraux on congruities between marriage, death, and virgin sacrifice in Greek tragedy.[64] Antigone, led to her death, is expected to "marry somebody in Hades," and Euripides' Agamemnon, referring to his doomed daughter Iphigenia, laments that Hades will marry her before long.[65] The status of virgin, however protected and pleasurable to a young girl while it lasted, was untenable after childhood in Greek culture. In one way or another, it, and she, had to be sacrificed. Clearly, shards of such notions of necessary sacrifice persist in fantasies that continue to deform the feminine psyche. Fed by pervasive visual and literary tropes,[66] they need to be more widely addressed by contemporary clinical writings on female (genital) anxieties and conflicts.[67]

Reading Loraux against the background of Arthur, we see Demeter's loss of Persephone replayed in Hecuba's tragic loss of Polyxena, and in Clytemnestra's loss of Iphigenia. The latter case is of interest because it marks a contrast between Clytemnestra's two daughters. One, Iphigenia, is, like Persephone, taken away by males to be sacrificed, an act that precipitates maternal melancholy, rage, revenge (and, finally, in the case of Demeter, reparation). The other, Electra, is (in Aeschylus' version) not separated from the mother, and thus a different tragic outcome is plotted for her: she grows resentful, hostile, and precipitates an act of violence against her mother (inciting her brother Orestes to murder).[68]

In the first case, male aggression from without splits the female dyad with the ultimate result of reuniting it, at least in fantasy;[69] in the second case, however, the female dyad, not disrupted by a male from without, imports male aggression and uses it to rend the relationship asunder. Both are tragic paths. With Clytemnestra and Electra, we have no initial image of closeness, as is intimated in the Demeter-Persephone myth. Thus, Electra's rage, like Orestes', can be interpreted in part as a response to maternal deprivation, as dyadic envy as well as triadic jealousy.

Freud evinced scant interest in these complexities. Despite the multifaceted nature of his collection of antiquities, his theoretical attention remained riveted on the towering figure of Oedipus, whose tale, he seemed to believe, could stand alone as a paradigm to which all others, even when the protagonists were female, could be referred, if not reduced.[70]

In tracing the specific regions of a woman's body that figure in her sacrifice in Greek tragedy, Loraux focuses on the throat, the scene also of major symptoms both in Freud's "Studies on Hysteria" (SE, 2) and in the Dora case (SE, 7). This detail raises the question as to whether antiquity actually offers metaphors for the female body other than its lacking or "being" a phallus.[71] The image of Demeter, mythical mother, symbol of harvest, wandering the earth in search of her daughter, suggests a possible answer.

Metaphors of the female body in ancient Greek culture have recently been traced by classicist Page duBois, who proposes allegories of representation that may supplement constructions of gender based entirely on models of deficiency.[72] A full, closed surface, the fertile earth gives rise spontaneously to plants, fruits, and wildflowers. This first metaphor, cited by duBois, is derived from Hesiod, where Gaea, Earth, gives birth parthenogenetically to Uranus, her husband.[73] Earth, analogous with the female body, is thus experienced in the dawn of Greek culture as an unsown meadow, spontaneously generative.

Later, this fertility, appropriated for agriculture, becomes linked in myth and metaphor with sexual reproduction. As man ploughs the earth and sows seeds in the furrows he has made, the female body comes to be compared also with empty ovens that can cook up babies when filled with grain, with earthenware vessels into which wine and grain can be poured, and with stone tablets[74] upon which man can write with his stylus/phallus.[75] In duBois's construction of this trajectory, the male is seen as colonizing the female body and as gradually appropriating her generative powers while, incrementally, nature is transformed into an ever more complex culture.[76] Rather than woman as parthenogenic source of life (as in Hesiod), woman becomes the nurse, the nurturer of male seed (as in Aeschylus' *Eumenides*).[77] Yet, fundamentally for the Greeks, earth is mother, Demeter is female, and, even unploughed, uncultivated, she produces food. The plough increases but does not cause her fertility.[78] Utterly dependent on the earth for their sustenance, the ancients must have experienced an overwhelming ambivalence toward her, an ambivalence extended as well to the human mother who has, like the earth, the capacity to withhold nourishment from children, and, in addition, the power to withhold children from men (as, for example, in Euripides' *Medea*).

Pondering the myth of Demeter-Persephone against this background is to grasp its significance, longevity, and power, qualities attested to, among others, by classicist Walter Burkert, who refers to it as the "crystallization of Greek mythology."[79] In bypassing it, Freud lost an opportunity, perhaps, for theoretical elaboration of feminine psychology. Here, for example, we see how a mother may try in desperation to keep a daughter from a father by threatening him (not the daughter) and by withholding her own fertility—a pattern not equivalent to (threatened) castration of the boy child by the father as a means of preventing access to the mother. Yet much remains uncanny and elusive. When Burkert speaks of the myth as encompassing a circularity, a self-containedness that excludes man, he means mankind as opposed to the gods—but the meaning of gender works as well. Being doubles, mother and maiden, Demeter and Persephone each contains the other within herself. Descending and retreating, the tale moves within a closed system, like the generative earth, with man ploughing and playing in it a crucial but marginal role. Neglected by Freud, it stands enigmatically as a testament to the rich legacy of antiquity that remains to be explored by contemporary psychoanalysis.

NOTES
I would like to express my appreciation to the many colleagues and friends who generously gave time to discuss aspects of this interdisciplinary essay with me, shared their specialized knowledge, and led me to sources I might otherwise have missed; I wish also to apologize to colleagues whose relevant works and ideas could not be mentioned in this brief essay. I owe special thanks to Cantor Edward Graham; Rabbi H. Leonard Poller; Rabbi Jeffrey Sirkman; Prof. Marilyn Arthur, Wesleyan University; Prof. Milad Doueihi, Johns Hopkins University; Prof. Yael S. Feldman, New York University; Muriel Gold Morris, M.D.; Ruth F. Lax, Ph.D.; Helen Abramowicz, M.D.; Joanna B. Strauss, M.S.W.; Harlan Spitz, M.D.; Nathaniel Geoffrey Lew, and, above all, my coparticipants in this project, Prof. Donald Kuspit, Prof. Peter Gay, Dr. Martin Bergmann, and, especially, Lynn Gamwell—whose sparkle and indomitable spirit illuminated these efforts from start to finish. I am grateful also to the Fund for Psychoanalytic Research of the American Psychoanalytic Association, which supported research that found its way into these pages. My greatest debt, of course, is to the monumental legacy of Sigmund Freud, who bequeathed to us all the powerful lenses through which we are now both privileged and compelled to see. —E.H.S.

1. Ellen Handler Spitz, "The Inescapability of Tragedy," *Bulletin of the Menninger Clinic* 52 (1988), 377–82.

2. Among the many remarks one could cite here, see Freud's autobiographical study of 1925: "When, in 1873, I first joined the University, I experienced some appreciable disappointments. Above all, I found that I was expected to feel myself inferior and an alien because I was a Jew" (SE, 20, p. 9).

3. See Suzanne Cassirer Bernfeld, "Freud and Archaeology," *American Imago* 8:2 (1951), 107–28.

4. See Lynn Gamwell, above, pp. 27–28, for a description of the way in which Freud actually placed the objects to face him while he worked.

5. See J. W. N. Sullivan, *Beethoven: His Spiritual Development* (New York: Mentor Books, 1927).

6. See Didier Anzieu, *Freud's Self-Analysis*, trans. Peter Graham (Madison, Ct.: International Universities Press, 1986).

7. Freud describes a series of dreams based, as he says, on a longstanding yearning to visit Rome. In the first of these, he dreams he is on a train and sees the Tiber and the Ponte Sant' Angelo through the window. In the second, he is led to a hilltop and sees Rome shrouded in a mist. In the third, he finally arrives in Rome but finds the scenery disappointing, a pastiche of associations that he traces in some detail. In the fourth, he is in Rome but, oddly, sees a profusion of German posters tacked up on a street corner; in part, he interprets this as expressing his wish to meet his colleague Fliess in Rome rather than Prague which, as he had written the day before, he thought might not be an agreeable place for Germans to walk about (see also SE, 4, pp. 323–24). Didier Anzieu, in his fascinating *Freud's Self-Analysis*, comments at length on these dreams (pp. 182–212).

I wish to offer a thought made explicit neither by Freud nor by Anzieu with respect to the second dream. The image of Freud led to a hilltop and shown the city of Rome shrouded in mist strongly suggests that of Moses in Deuteronomy 34:1–4, and lends added weight to the profound and not fully conscious identifications between Freud and Moses.

8. Anzieu, *Freud's Self-Analysis*, pp. 207–209. For a discussion of the role of the artistic image in structuring psychic experience, see Ellen Handler Spitz, "The Artistic Image and the Inward Gaze," *The Psychoanalytic Review* 75 (1988), 111–28.

9. Anzieu, *Freud's Self-Analysis*, p. 209.

10. See Ernest Jones, *The Life and Work of Sigmund Freud*, vol. 2 (New York: Basic Books, 1955), p. 393.

11. See Peter Gay, *Freud: A Life for Our Time* (New York: Norton, 1988), p. 602; see also, Gay, *A Godless Jew* (New Haven: Yale University Press, 1987), pp. 132–34.

12. For a study of Freud's unacknowledged indebtedness, for example, to the interpretative traditions of rabbinical Judaism, see Susan A. Handelman, *The Slayers of Moses* (Albany: State University of New York Press, 1982).

13. See Joan Raphael-Leff, "If Freud Was an Egyptian: Freud and Egyptology," forthcoming, *Proceedings of the International Conference on Psychiatry*, held in Cairo, Egypt, March, 1988, for an analysis of Freud's interest in Egyptology. Raphael-Leff argues that despite the many references to Egypt in his texts and the numerous Egyptian artifacts in his collection, only the Greco-Roman material was developed theoretically by Freud because it served a defensive function for him vis-à-vis unanalyzed pre-oedipal material that the Egyptian imagery and mythology convey—imagery represented in his collection principally by the statue of Isis and Horus.

14. See Peter Gay, *Freud, Jews, and Other Germans* (Oxford: Oxford University Press, 1978); *A Godless Jew*; and *Freud: A Life*.

15. See Gay, *Freud: A Life*, pp. 604–11, 632–37; and *A Godless Jew*, pp. 44, 148–52.

16. Gay, *Freud: A Life*, pp. 601–602.

17. See Gamwell, above, pp. 23ff.

18. It is poignant to note that in the year before his death, painfully ill, hounded out of Vienna by the Nazis, and awaiting a permit to leave for England, Freud spoke of himself as an "old Jacob" about to be taken by his children to Egypt (letter to Ernst Freud, May 12, 1938).

19. See Jones, *Life and Work*, vol. 3 (1957), p. 350 (as in n. 10). Jones here describes the Torah as "a book of Jewish philosophy rather than of religion," a misleading error.

20. See Raphael-Leff, "If Freud Was an Egyptian" (as in n. 13). For a fine discussion of the possible enduring influence on Freud of his early exposure to the Philippson Bible, see William G. Niederland, "Freud's Fascination with Archaeology and Its Connection with the Philippson Bible," unpublished manuscript read to the New York Psychoanalytic Society, February 9, 1988.

21. For a discussion of Freud's identification with Joseph, see Leonard Shengold, "Freud and Joseph," in *Freud and His Self-Analysis* (New York: Jason Aronson, 1979).

22. See also Anzieu, *Freud's Self-Analysis*, p. 183 (as in n. 6).

23. Ibid., pp. 182–212.

24. Thus there is, among the latent meanings of the collection, that of parricide, a theme notably absent from Judaism; see Yael S. Feldman, "Recurrence and Sublimation: Toward a Psychoanalytic Approach to Biblical Narrative," in Barry N. Olshen and Yael S. Feldman, eds., *Approaches to Teaching the Hebrew Bible as Literature* (New York: MLA Publications, 1989), pp. 78–82.

25. See Anzieu, *Freud's Self-Analysis*, pp. 177, 457.

26. Ibid., p. 194.

27. Ibid., pp. 182–212 passim.

28. This epigraph, "If I cannot bend the higher powers, I will move the infernal regions," is appropriate for a text that explores the ways in which what cannot be openly enacted in waking life is played out in the nocturnal and instinctual realm of dreams. For an excellent commentary, in addition to Anzieu, *Freud's Self-Analysis*, pp. 176–78 (as in n. 6), see Jean Starobinski, "Acheronta Movebo," *Critical Inquiry* 13:2 (1987), 394–407. Juno is, obviously, *not* the mother of Aeneas; yet, in her relentless persecution of him, she figures as a split-off bad mother (a maternal imago insufficiently recognized by Freud, because to have done so would have been to endow her with intolerable powers); she is a foil for the beautiful and adoring Venus, Aeneas' actual mother in Virgil's text.

29. "The effort to provide Freud with a Jewish intellectual ancestry is no more productive than the search for his Jewishness in his patients or his jokes" (Gay, *A Godless Jew*, p. 129; as in n. 11). In the same text, Gay makes the point that Freud prohibited his wife, Martha, from lighting Shabbat candles (for which behavior she called him "*Unmensch*," monster). In Gay's view, Martha Freud "retained a trace of indignation, perhaps of sadness, in the presence of the imperious atheist who had … swept her away from her family and, more painfully, from her faithfully practiced religious observances" (p. 153).

30. Ibid., p. 150.

31. Ibid., p. 152. For a penetrating analysis of relationships between Freud and Moses, psychoanalysis and rabbinical models of interpretation, see Handelman, *The Slayers of Moses*, especially chap. 5, pp. 132–37 (as in n. 12), where the analysis overlaps aspects of mine.

32. See Gay, *A Godless Jew*, p. 150 (as in n. 11). See also Harold P. Blum, "Freud and the Figure of Moses," *The Journal of the American Psychoanalytic Association*, forthcoming.

33. Each of the interpretations offered in my text is, however, contested in various ways in the rabbinical tradition. See, for example, *The Torah: A Modern Commentary*, ed. W. Gunther Plaut (New York: Union of American Hebrew Congregations, 1981), pp. 642–54.

34. See, for example, Feldman, "Recurrence and Sublimation" (as in n. 24), for a discussion related to Freud's theorizing on the basis of Greek rather than Judaic themes (cf. Oedipus versus Isaac).

35. See Gay, *Freud: A Life*, p. 605 (as in n. 11).

36 . *Midrash Rabbah*, trans. Rabbi Dr. H. Freedman and Maurice Simon (London: The Soncino Press, 1961), Genesis I, 38:13, pp. 310–11. For a slightly different version, see the Babylonian Talmud, Baba Kama 8.1, cited in Louis Ginzberg, *The Legends of the Jews* (Philadelphia: The Jewish Publication Society of America 5715–1955), vol. 1, pp. 197–98.

37. See Jones, *Life and Work of Sigmund Freud*, vol. 2, p. 14 (as in n. 10), and also Peter L. Rudnytsky, *Freud and Oedipus* (New York: Columbia University Press, 1987), p. 4.

38. This important point is made and emphasized by Rudnytsky, *Freud and Oedipus*, p. 5.

39. See Marthe Robert, *From Oedipus to Moses: Freud's Jewish Identity*, trans. Ralph Manheim (New York: Doubleday, 1976); see also, among the many sources elaborating on this point, the family tree depicted in Anzieu, *Freud's Self-Analysis*, p. 248 (as in n. 6).

40. For a variety of psychoanalytically relevant perspectives on the *Oresteia*, see Melanie Klein, "Some Reflections on The Oresteia," in *Envy and Gratitude and Other Works, 1946–1963* (Glencoe: Free Press, 1963); Marian Tolpin, "The Oresteia: A Cure in Fifth Century Athens," *Journal of the American Psychoanalytic Association* 17 (1969), 511–27; Froma Zeitlin, "The Dynamics of Misogyny: Myth and Mythmaking in the Oresteia," *Arethusa* 11 (1978), 149–84; Andre Green, *The Tragic Effect* (Cambridge: Cambridge University Press, 1979); Mary Lefkowitz, *Women in Greek Myth* (Baltimore: Johns Hopkins University Press, 1986); Bennett Simon, *Tragic Drama and the Family* (New Haven: Yale University Press, 1988).

41. For diverse general approaches to the intellectual background of Freud's endeavors, see Rudnytsky, *Freud and Oedipus* (as in n. 37); Allan Janik and Stephen Toulmin, *Wittgenstein's Vienna* (New York: Simon and Schuster, 1973); John E. Gedo and George H. Pollock, eds., *Freud: The Fusion of Science and Humanism, The Intellectual History of Psychoanalysis* (New York: International Universities Press, 1976); and for a feminist gloss on classical scholarship in general, see Eva C. Keuls, *The Reign of the Phallus* (New York: Harper and Row, 1985), pp. 9–11. For additional background reading on this topic, see the annotated bibliography in Gay, *Freud: A Life*, pp. 747–49 (as in n. 11).

42. For an interesting and speculative analysis of the possible defensive nature of this posture, see Raphael-Leff, "If Freud Was an Egyptian" (as in n. 13).

43. See, among others, Jean-Pierre Vernant, "Oedipus Without the Complex," in *Tragedy and Myth in Ancient Greece*, by J-P Vernant and Pierre Vidal-Naquet, trans. Janet Lloyd (Atlantic Highlands, N.J.: Humanities Press, 1981), p. 65; and Page duBois, *Sowing the Body: Psychoanalysis and Ancient Representations of Women* (Chicago: University of Chicago Press, 1988), pp. 1–36 passim.

44. Collection Inventory, Freud Museum.

45. For a Lacanian perspective, see Juliet Mitchell and Jacqueline Rose, eds., *Feminine Sexuality: Jacques Lacan and the école freudienne*, trans. Jacqueline Rose (New York: Norton, 1982).

46. In addition to the early contributions of such well-known psychoanalytic authors as Ernest Jones, Helene Deutsch, Melanie Klein, and Karen Horney, there is a voluminous post-Freudian psychoanalytic literature on female psychology. I have space to cite only a few key contributions: Judith Kestenberg, "On the Development of Maternal Feelings in Early Childhood," *The Psychoanalytic Study of the Child* 11 (1956), 275–91, and also her "Outside and Inside, Male and Female," *Journal of the American Psychoanalytic Association* 16 (1968), 457–520; *Female Psychology: Contemporary Views*, ed. Harold Blum (New York: International Universities Press, 1977); Janine Chasseguet-Smirgel, "Freud and Female Sexuality: The Consideration of Some Blind Spots in the Exploration of the 'Dark Continent,' " reprinted in *Sexuality and Mind* (New York: New York Universities Press, 1986; originally published in 1976); Nancy Chodorow, *The Reproduction of Mothering* (Berkeley: University of California Press, 1978); Carol Gilligan, *In a Different Voice* (Cambridge: Harvard University Press, 1982); Ethel S. Person, "The Influence of Values in Psychoanalysis: The Case of Female Psychology," in *Psychiatry Update*, ed. Lester Grinspoon (American Psychiatric Association, 1983); Robert Stoller, *Presentations of Gender* (New York: Yale University Press, 1985); and Doris Bernstein, "Female Genital Anxieties, Conflicts, and Typical Mastery Modes," *The International Journal of Psycho-Analysis*, in press.

47. See Spitz, "The Inescapability of Tragedy" (as in n. 1).

48. This retelling is both an abridgment and an amalgam; see *Hesiod, The Homeric Hymns and Homerica*, trans. H. G. Evelyn-White (Loeb Classical Library, Cambridge: Harvard University Press, 1924), and *The Metamorphoses of Ovid*, trans. Mary M. Innes (Harmondsworth, Middlesex, 1955). See also an interesting retelling in Robert May, *Sex and Fantasy: Patterns of Male and Female Development* (New York: Norton, 1980), pp. 7–13; and a fine psychoanalytically informed critical article by Marilyn Arthur, "Politics and Pomegranates: An Interpretation of the Homeric Hymn to

Demeter," *Arethusa* 10 (1977), 7–47. See also *The Homeric Hymn to Demeter*, ed. Helene P. Foley (Princeton: Princeton University Press, forthcoming).

49. The narcissus may be seen as emblematic of the girl's youthful self-involvement and delight in her own loveliness as well, perhaps, as her desire to add something to it. It is also of interest to compare the myths of Persephone and the youthful Narcissus.

50. See Claude Lévi-Strauss, *The Elementary Structures of Kinship*, trans. James Harle Bell, Richard von Sturmer, and Rodney Needham (Boston: Beacon Press, 1969), on kinship and women as a medium of exchange between men. It has been much remarked that Freud failed to perceive this dimension of the Dora case (SE, 7), and that in failing to recognize it, he colluded with it and became, as it were, one of the men among whom Dora was being passed.

Apropos the Demeter-Persephone myth, it is crucial for a psychological understanding that takes into account not just the dyadic but the implicit triadic nature of all mother-daughter relations (a perspective downplayed in the mythic narrative) that Persephone's initiation into heterosexual relations comes by means of trickery, surprise, physical violence, and betrayal by her father. This act is seen as betrayal, moreover, only from the women's point of view; in Ovid, the father protests Demeter's complaints of piracy and claims that, on the contrary, his brother's act of abduction should be seen as an act of love, and that the lord of the underworld is a fitting husband for their daughter (see Ovid, *Metamorphoses*, V, 522–30). Thus the father both rationalizes and reveals the incestuous pleasure he takes in colluding with the abduction, and we are reminded once again of Dora.

51. See Marilyn Arthur's sensitive analysis in "Politics and Pomegranates," pp. 15–17 (as in n. 48).

52. See Arthur's comments, ibid., pp. 22–26; see also the discussion in Robert May, *Sex and Fantasy*, pp. 11–13 (as in n. 48). See also, Nancy Felson Rubin and Harriet M. Deal, "Some Functions of the Demophon Episode in the Homeric Hymn to Demeter," *Quaderni Urbinati di Cultura Classica*, n.s. 5 (1980), 7–21, for a structuralist approach.

53. Arthur, "Politics and Pomegranates," p. 23 (as in n. 48).

54. Ibid., pp. 30–31.

55. Muriel G. Morris, M.D., personal communication.

56. See Xenophon, *Oeconomicus*, III.12–13 and VII.5–6 (Loeb Classical Library). It is interesting to note here that the narcissus flower which attracts Persephone in the myth is described as a toy; see Hymn to Demeter in *Hesiod, The Homeric Hymns and Homerica*, p. 289 (as in n. 48).

57. For a cataclysmic portrayal of this rift in contemporary American letters, from the daughter's viewpoint, see Jamaica Kincaid, *Annie John* (New York: New American Library, 1983).

58. It is fascinating, however, that the one moment of conflict between two women (Demeter and Metaneira, mother of the boy Demophon) that is portrayed in the myth proves catalytic to Demeter and empowers her to act on what she perceives as her own and her daughter's behalf.

59. See Alice Miller, *The Drama of the Gifted Child* (New York: Basic Books, 1981), for a venomous description of the narcissistic parent.

60. See John F. Makowski, "Persephone, Psyche, and the Mother-Maiden," *The Classical Outlook* (March/April 1985), 73–78, for several interesting readings of the myth.

61. See Arthur, "Politics and Pomegranates," p. 8 (as in n. 48).

62. Muriel Gold Morris, M.D., personal communication. Clinicians, for example, who treat adult women patients remark on the frequency in their discourse of references to mother (personal communication, Ruth F. Lax, Ph.D.).

This is a point Freud missed in his analysis of Dora; see Freud, "Fragment of an Analysis of a Case of Hysteria" (SE, 7). There is voluminous literature on this case; many commentators, however, have noted that Freud's implicit devaluation of the mother, and his failure to recognize the impact on Dora of her father's rejection of the mother, indicate an underestimation on his part of the importance of the young girl's need to identify with the parent of her own sex and her special vulnerability to the quality of the parental relationship.

63. This is true in the central narrative of Persephone and Demeter but not in the inserted incident, a point stressed by Arthur and central to her understanding of the psychological meaning of the myth as a whole (see "Politics and Pomegranates"; as in n. 48).

64. See Nicole Loraux, *Tragic Ways of Killing a Woman* (Cambridge: Harvard University Press, 1987).

65. Sophocles, *Antigone*, in *Sophocles I*, trans. Elizabeth Wyckoff (Chicago: University of Chicago Press, 1954), p. 177, line 654, and Euripides, *Iphigenia in Aulis*, in *Euripides IV*, trans. Charles R. Walker (Chicago: University of Chicago Press, 1958), p. 236, line 461.

66. A fascinating example of the conflation between bridal and burial in the life of a woman can be seen in the art historical dispute over a painting by Gustave Courbet (mid-1850s), *La Toilette de la morte, ou La Toilette de la mariée*, described by Linda Nochlin in Sarah Faunce and Linda Nochlin, eds., *Courbet Reconsidered* (New Haven: Yale University Press, 1988), pp. 126–28.

67. See Bernstein, "Female Genital Anxieties" (as in n. 46).

68. See Aeschylus, *The Libation Bearers*, in *Aeschylus I: Oresteia*, ed. and trans. Richard Lattimore (Chicago: University of Chicago Press, 1953).

69. This is exquisitely dramatized by a duet in the prologue of Martha Graham's ballet "Clytemnestra" (1958), where the mother fantasizes that her dying daughter is reaching out to her from across the stage.

70. Freud states: "I should like to insist that ... the beginnings of religion, morals, society and art converge in the Oedipus complex. This is in complete agreement with the psychoanalytic finding that the same complex constitutes the nucleus of all neuroses, so far as our present knowledge goes. It seems to me a most surprising discovery that the problems of social psychology, too, should prove soluble on the basis of one single concrete point—man's relation to his father" (*Totem and Taboo*; SE, 13, pp. 156–57).

71. For a comprehensive, scholarly overview of Greek attitudes toward the male and the female body, see Marilyn Arthur, "Sexuality and the Body in Ancient Greece," in *Trends in History*, forthcoming.

72. See duBois, *Sowing the Body* (as in n. 43).

73. See *Hesiod and Theogonis*, trans. Dorothea Wender (Harmondsworth, Middlesex: Penguin Books, 1973), p. 27.

74. See duBois, *Sowing the Body*, p. 28ff.

75. Just to indicate the incredible persistence through the centuries of this particular imagery, one might recall the lines of a song entitled "Sixteen Going on Seventeen," by Rodgers and Hammerstein from "The Sound of Music" (1959): "Your life, little girl, is an empty page, that men will want to write on."

76. The woman's body as nature is a trope discussed by Linda Nochlin with respect to the paintings of Courbet; see Faunce and Nochlin, eds., *Courbet Reconsidered*, 1988 (as in n. 66).

77. See Aeschylus, *The Eumenides*, in *Aeschylus I: Oresteia*, Lattimore, p. 158 (as in n. 68).

78. See duBois, *Sowing the Body*, p. 92.

79. See Walter Burkert, *Structure and History in Greek Mythology and Ritual* (Berkeley: University of California Press, 1979), chapter entitled "Mother and Daughter: The Crystallization of Greek Mythology," pp. 138–42. See also Robert May, *Sex and Fantasy* (as in n. 48).

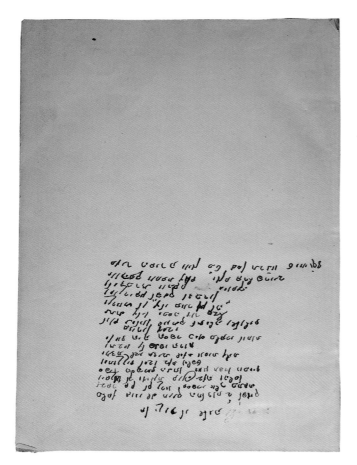

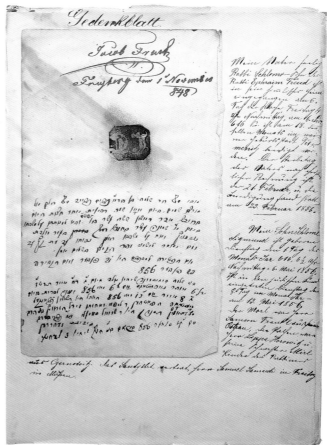

The Freud family Bible, bearing Jacob Freud's Hebrew inscriptions dedicating
the volume to Sigmund (left) and recording the date of his birth (right).

SCIENCE AND ART IN FREUD'S LIFE AND WORK

MARTIN S. BERGMANN

Freud taught us that every love is complex and multidetermined. His love for the classical past and archaeology is no exception. The aim of this essay is to illuminate the nature of this love and its relationship to Freud's lifework: psychoanalysis.

On Freud's thirty-fifth birthday, his father returned to him a German illustrated Bible, known as the Philippson Bible. Jacob Freud had added a Hebrew dedication (incidentally, a dedication that his son could not have deciphered).[1] The handwriting and the style are those of a man well versed in the Hebrew language, but not of a religious Jew. The language of this dedication marks Jacob Freud as a member of the Hebrew movement of enlightenment, a movement that sought to infuse secular knowledge into the Jewish ghettos of eastern Europe.[2] We know from Freud's *Interpretation of Dreams* that this Bible played a role in a number of his dreams (SE, 5, p. 583). From this dedication we learn that, unlike many Jews of his generation, Sigmund Freud did not have to wage war against the tyranny of Jewish orthodoxy.

The Philippson Bible, at first glance, seems to follow the pattern of many Jewish Bibles that contain Hebrew text, translation, and commentary. However, instead of the traditional commentary compiled by Jewish sages, Philippson gives a lesson in comparative mythology. The verses of Deuteronomy 4:19 read:

> And lest thou lift up thine eyes unto heaven, and when thou seest the sun, and the moon, and the stars, even all the host of heaven, shouldest be driven to worship them, and serve them, which the Lord thy God hath divided unto all nations under the whole heaven. (p. 870)

This verse gives Philippson the opportunity to launch an illustrated lecture combining astronomy with Egyptian and Greek mythologies. The influence of Max Müller's comparative mythology is evident.[3]

We also know that as a young man Freud was ambivalent about his Jewish heritage, and only relatively late in life did he find in Moses an object of identification (SE, 13; see also SE, 23). In 1867, when Freud was eleven years old, the Jews of Austria received full civil rights, and for a time hopes ran high that this nation's century-old anti-Semitism finally belonged to the past. Indeed, Freud thought of launching a political career. However, the rise of a new racial anti-

Semitism soon curtailed his hopes. Twice in his life Freud felt German patriotic emotions: once in 1870 when Bismarck unified Germany, and again during World War I when he was for a time swept up in the patriotic tide, as his correspondence with Karl Abraham indicates.[4] Apart from these short lapses, Freud was a humanist and a citizen of the world. Freud knew Victor Adler well, the future leader of Austrian social democracy.[5] However, socialism, which at that time appeared as a solution to the diseases of nationalism and anti-Semitism, never held an appeal for him.

In a letter written in July 1882 to his then-fiancée and future wife Martha Bernays, he said, "As for us, this is what I believe: even if the form wherein the old Jews were happy no longer offers us any shelter, something of the core, of the essence of this meaningful and life-affirming Judaism, will not be absent from our home."[6] A powerful feeling of belonging to the Jewish group never left Freud, but it was a sense of belonging empty of cultural content. Alienated from the Jewish past, constantly made aware of discrimination, Freud found refuge and a safe harbor in the classical past. The great men he admired, Goethe, Schiller, and Heine, were also smitten by the same love for Greece.

In a sensitive book entitled *The Tyranny of Greece over Germany*, E. M. Butler showed how Johann Winckelmann's (1717–68) discovery, or perhaps one should say creation, of a Greece consisting of "noble simplicity and serene greatness" was an essential ingredient in the development of German poetry in the eighteenth and nineteenth centuries.[7] From Goethe to Hölderlin, Heine, and Nietzsche, these Germans looked to Greece for spiritual renewal. In Butler's view, it was Heine, the German-Jewish poet (1797–1856), who delivered the coup de grâce to the idealized image of Greece.

Butler did not include Freud among those smitten by the Greek ideal, but Freud's relationship to the classical past deserves examination. Freud loved Italy but developed a prohibition against visiting Rome (SE, 4, pp. 193–98). Incidentally, he overcame this inhibition through his own self-analysis and mastered it in 1901.[8] After this mastery, Freud commented, "It only needs a little courage to fulfill wishes which till then have been regarded as unattainable" (SE, 4, p. 194n). In one of his dreams he transferred the Slaughter of the Innocents from Bethlehem to Rome. Rome had become to Freud the Promised Land which, like Moses, he felt he would never be permitted to enter. In 1901, Freud had come within fifty miles of Rome and was planning to bypass it again on a trip to Naples. Struggling with what he came to call his Rome inhibition, Freud was engaged in analyzing a dream when the following sentence came unbidden to his mind: "Which of the two, it may be debated, walked up and down his study with the greater impatience after he had formed his plan of going to Rome — Winckelmann, the Vice Principal, or Hannibal, the Commander-in-Chief?" (SE, 4, p. 196). To understand this enigmatic statement, we have to keep in mind that Hannibal, the Semitic general of Carthage who nearly conquered Rome, was one of Freud's childhood heroes. We might call Hannibal an emergency hero, called up to bolster Freud's sense of Jewish pride. Winckelmann, a convert to Catholicism, was in this case equated with Rome. The unbidden sentence can therefore be translated: "Should I actively conquer Rome, that is, my Rome inhibition, or should I bow to it?"

In 1907 Freud was asked by a publisher to name ten good books. Among others, he named Gomperz's *Greek Thinkers*,[9] which became a sourcebook for many of Freud's ideas. There he became acquainted with Empedocles, the pre-Socratic Greek philosopher whose writings foreshadowed Freud's dual instinct theory. Freud also was deeply influenced by Plato.[10] By all accounts, the most productive encounter between Freud and the Greek past took place when he read Sophocles' *Oedipus Rex*. Not many encounters in the realm of ideas have been so fruitful; this one made possible Freud's discovery of the Oedipus complex.

By a fortunate coincidence, we know that Freud read *Oedipus Rex* when he was seventeen years old and shortly after he first fell in love with Gisela Fluss, the subject of Freud's *Screen Memories*, published in 1899. One cannot claim that it was a propitious time for Freud, the young lover, to read this tragedy, but it left a profound impression on him. Freud discovered the Oedipus complex when, "a dim presentiment following," he exchanged hypnosis for free association. His theory was the product of his self-analysis and is dramatically told in his correspondence with Fliess.[11] To Sophocles, the fate of Oedipus was the fate of one man. To Freud, it became the fate of Everyman.

In place of the prophecy of the oracle, Freud put the unconscious wish. Before an oracle all are helpless, but before the unconscious we need not be helpless if we are willing to undertake psychoanalysis and make these unconscious wishes conscious. In many ways Freud misread *Oedipus Rex*, and a very productive misreading it turned out to be. Freud ignored the fact that Oedipus was mutilated and exposed to death by his father; therefore, Freud's Oedipus complex never had a chance to develop out of the inner psychological needs of an Oedipus. Even more telling, when Freud introduced the argument that Oedipus accepted the punishment even though his crime was committed unintentionally, Freud did so because he felt guilty over his oedipal wishes. Freud introduced the biblical concept of guilt into the Greek matrix. To the Greeks, Oedipus had polluted Thebes, and pollution was punishable whether it was committed knowingly or not. The discovery of the Oedipus complex Freud owed to the classical past, but the interpretation of guilt he gave it he had inherited from his Jewish past.

The same problem that created the Rome inhibition reappeared, although in a different form, when Freud visited the Acropolis in Athens in 1904, accompanied by his brother. It is difficult for modern travelers who have been to Greece a number of times to appreciate that this journey in Freud's time was still far from usual. Freud reported on it in an open letter that he published in honor of the French novelist Romain Rolland in 1936 (SE, 22). In that letter he stated that the experience surpassed anything he had ever seen or could have imagined. Nevertheless, he remembered how reluctant he was to go to Athens, and how he had to be persuaded to go there rather than to nearby Corfu. While on the Acropolis, Freud had an experience of derealization; he had to ask his brother if it were true that they were really there. In the essay written thirty-two years later Freud reported: "In my unconscious I had not believed in [the Acropolis], and ... I was

A nineteenth-century engraving of Athens, by H. Nestel, in Freud's print collection. (Photo: Freud Museum)

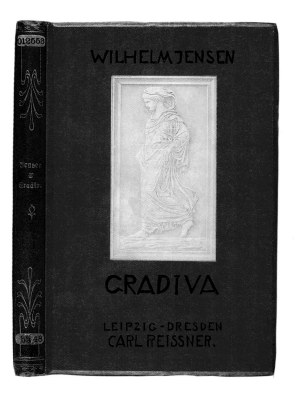

Freud's plaster reproduction of the classical relief
Gradiva (right), and the cover of Jensen's novella.
(Photos: Freud Museum; The British Library)

only now acquiring a conviction that 'reached down to the unconscious'" (SE, 22, p. 241). Further analysis showed that Freud had really doubted he would ever be so fortunate as to see the Acropolis. Going a step deeper in his self-analysis, Freud found that Athens could not have meant much to his father, for whom the Greek past was a closed book. To be on the Acropolis meant, to him, to have surpassed the father. This "oedipal victory" was denied in the derealization.

While Freud confessed a great deal in the letter to Rolland—perhaps more than other men would do—he did not tell everything. He did not explain why an event that took place in 1904 was still so alive that it required self-analysis in 1936. I offer an interpretation that Freud did not make: the visits to Rome and Athens, which would not have meant much to his father, were also symbols of disloyalty to his Jewish past, since both Greece and Rome were enemies of Israel at a certain period in history.

In 1907 Freud published an analysis of the novella *Gradiva* by Wilhelm Jensen.[12] Today this work of Freud (SE, 9) is seldom read and no longer quoted in the psychoanalytic literature. But there was a time when it ranked high in the estimation of psychoanalysts; it became customary to adorn the consultation room with a copy of the Vatican relief on which the story of Gradiva had been woven. The novella deals with the life of a young archaeologist who lost all his sexual wishes and concentrated entirely on his work. It so happened that he fell in love with a relief in the Vatican museum which showed a woman with her gown slightly raised and her ankle exposed. The archaeologist spins a whole fantasy around this woman and believes that she perished in Pompeii in the eruption of Vesuvius.

Drawn to Pompeii and there imagining that he meets Gradiva, he encounters a childhood sweetheart whose gait reminds him of the gait of the Roman woman. He gradually recovers from the delusion through the skillful therapy of his childhood beloved.

One can imagine how this novella appeared to Freud, for in it his theories were described. It also included dreams that Freud deciphered with a great deal of skill. In retrospect, however, this analysis represents a unique event in which Freud himself succumbed to the charm of the artist. He forgot that the childhood sweetheart was only a substitute for the mother with whom the adult cannot fall in love without evoking the dread of incest. The substitution of the childhood sweetheart enabled the artist to give his reader the fulfillment of a wishful fantasy without evoking the dread of an incestuous relationship. In addition, Freud thought that his archaeologist was cured, when in fact he only exchanged his previously repressed sexuality for a fetishistic fixation on the ankle.

Freud used the archaeological metaphor to illustrate the unconscious frequently and powerfully. He emphasized their similarities as well as their differences. In archaeology and in psychoanalysis, burial acts as preservation, but in archaeology every new layer is built on ruins. In the unconscious, it is as if all the many layers of Rome could coexist intact and simultaneously in the same space (SE, 21, p. 70). The central technical term that Freud introduced into psychoanalysis from archaeology was the concept of reconstruction (SE, 23, p. 259). For him, although not necessarily for all psychoanalysts, it was a central concept. It is related to the question whether psychoanalysis is primarily a science or an art.

I will now venture to state my interpretation of Freud's love for archaeology. Freud's derealization on the Acropolis was an attempt to deny that he was really in Athens, and on a deeper level that he was the oedipal victor over his father. He could easily analyze the same conflict in 1936 because by that time he was already old, unable to travel, and no longer compelled to experience himself as the oedipal victor. If we add the Athens experience to the equation archaeology = unconscious and assume that Freud, like every analysand at times under the pressure of resistances, lost his belief in the reality of the unconscious and in his own discovery of the Oedipus complex, his collection of archaeological statues would have a special value: their presence in his consulting room testified that the buried unconscious can indeed be resurrected and brought back to life. In the uncharted voyage into the unconscious, archaeology acted as a reassurance that he was not alone and was on the right path.

What was the impact of Freud's archaeological collection on his analysands? The Wolf Man described the effect on him:

> Here were all kinds of statuettes and other unusual objects, which even the layman recognized as archaeological finds from ancient Egypt. Here and there on the walls were stone plaques representing various scenes of long-vanished epochs. A few potted plants added life to the rooms, and the warm carpet and curtains gave them a homelike note. Everything here contributed to one's feeling of leaving the haste of modern life behind, of being

sheltered from one's daily cares. Freud himself explained his love for archaeology in that the psychoanalyst, like the archaeologist in his excavations,
must uncover layer after layer of the patient's psyche, before coming to the
deepest, most valuable treasures.[13]

The poet H.D. (Hilda Doolittle) left us a less stereotyped account. Between
1933 and 1934, at age forty-seven, she was a patient of Freud, then seventy-seven
years old. Clinically she suffered from a disturbance more severe than neurosis. In
such cases, psychoanalysts often employed methods different from the standard
psychoanalytic procedure. Her case may not be typical of Freud's analytic work,
but it is certainly interesting. Whatever the reason, Freud took H.D. to his private working room:

> I did not always know if the Professor's excursions with me into the other
> room were by way of distraction, actual social occasions, or part of his plan.
> Did he want to find out how I would react to certain ideas embodied in these
> little statues, or how deeply I felt the dynamic *idea* still implicit in spite of the
> fact that ages or aeons of time had flown over many of them? Or did he mean
> simply to imply that he wanted to share his treasures with me, those tangible
> shapes before us that yet suggested the intangible and vastly more fascinat-
> ing treasures of his own mind? Whatever his idea, I wanted then, as at other
> times, to meet him half-way; I wanted to return, in as unobtrusive a way as
> possible, the courtesy that was so subtly offered me. If it was a *game*, a sort of
> roundabout way of finding out something that perhaps my unconscious
> guard or censor was anxious to keep from him, well, I will do my best to play
> this game, this guessing game—or whatever it was.

H.D. reacted as many analysands would in her place—as if she had been given
a psychoanalytic examination, a kind of Rorschach test. Freud speaks:

> "*This* is my favorite," he said. He held the object toward me. I took it in my
> hand. It was a little bronze statue, helmeted, clothed to the foot in carved
> robe with the upper incised chiton or peplum. One hand was extended as if
> holding a staff or rod. "She is perfect," he said, "*only she has lost her spear.*" I
> did not say anything. He knew I loved Greece.[14]

"She is perfect only she has lost her spear." Pallas Athena is a goddess who owes
nothing to her mother; she sprang full-grown from her father's head. She therefore symbolizes a woman who denies her femininity. She also lends herself to the
fantasy that H.D. herself is reborn out of Freud's head. What Freud was doing was
called by Ekstein "interpreting within the metaphor."[15] In a symbolic language, a
language that his patients may be able to accept, Freud is telling her that in his
eyes she is perfect, even though she does not have a phallus. Stated in this way,
the interpretation is left up to the patient to accept or reject. It avoids a confrontation that could bring about a transference crisis and might be a source of danger
to the patient. It is, however, less effective than the straight interpretation,
namely, that H.D. had never overcome the fact that she did not have a penis.
Indeed, in a state of positive transference, not free from masochism however,

Freud's study, Vienna, 1938.
(Photo: © Edmund Engelman)

H.D. identifies herself with Alcestis (in Euripides' play), the Greek woman who volunteered to die instead of her husband. H.D. was thirty years younger than Freud; she would have liked to donate to him some of the years left to her.

However, even the interpretation within the metaphor can evoke, and in this case did evoke, a negative transference:

> "She is perfect," he said and he meant that the image was of the accepted classic period, Periclean or just pre-Periclean; he meant that there was no scratch or flaw, no dent in the surface or stain on the metal, no fold in the peplum worn down or eroded away. He was speaking as an ardent lover of art and as an art collector. He was speaking in a double sense, it is true, but he was speaking of value, the actual intrinsic value of the piece; like a Jew, he was assessing its worth; the blood of Abraham, Isaac and Jacob ran in his veins. He knew his material pound, his pound of flesh, if you will, but this pound of flesh was a pound of *spirit* between us, something tangible, to be weighed and measured, to be weighed in the balance and—pray God—not to be found wanting![16]

Anti-Semitic ideas surface, but they are immediately transformed: a Jew knows know to assess value in monetary terms. He demands his pound of flesh. Abraham, Isaac, and Jacob are named, but Shylock is only implied. His pound of flesh symbolizes the imaginary phallus he is asking her to give up. All too quickly for her own therapeutic goals, H.D. transformed the hostility of the pound of flesh into the covenant of a pound of spirit.

In his introductory lectures to psychoanalysis (SE, 16, p. 285), Freud enumerated three major blows that science inflicted on the self-esteem of man. The first one came from Copernicus, when he showed that the earth was not at the center of the universe. The second came from Darwin, when he proved that man descended from the animal kingdom. The third blow Freud assigned to himself, for he showed that man is not a master in his own house because he does not know his unconscious. In a state of health, the ego feels secure in its worthiness, in the trustworthiness of the reports it receives from the unconscious, and in its perceptions of the outside world. However, in neurosis, the ego feels uneasy. It comes up against the limits of its power, becoming confused and sometimes unable to even trust its own perceptions. It was in the company of Copernicus and Darwin that Freud wished to be remembered. History has not yet rendered its verdict; it is possible that he will be remembered in a different context, in a line that extends from Plato to Schopenhauer and Nietzsche.

Otto Fenichel, one of Freud's leading disciples, saw Freud's contribution to science to be that he taught us to look on mental life with the same objectivity with which physics, chemistry, and biology have viewed the phenomena of the external world.[17] Before Freud, the nineteenth century accepted a compromise: science could through medicine be applied to the body, but the mind had to remain an area reserved for philosophy and religion. Freud's contribution was to subjugate the mind to the laws of science, or, as Fenichel put it, "The object of psychoanalysis is the irrational, but its methods are rational."

In an encyclopedia article written in 1923 (SE, 18, p. 235), Freud defined psychoanalysis as first, a procedure for the investigation of mental processes; second, a method of treatment of neurotic diseases; and third, a collection of scientific information accumulating into a new scientific discipline. I have shown elsewhere that this tripartite division of psychoanalysis made comparisons with other sciences difficult; it tended to isolate psychoanalysis.[18]

In his open letter to Romain Rolland, Freud described his lifework somewhat differently:

> You know that the aim of my scientific work was to throw light upon unusual, abnormal, or pathological manifestations of the mind—that is to say, to trace them back to the psychical forces operating behind them and to indicate the mechanisms at work. I began by attempting this upon myself, and then went on to apply it to other people and finally, by a bold extension, to the human race as a whole. (SE, 22, p. 239)

This very wide scope of psychoanalysis raised the question as to who should practice it. In 1926 Theodore Reik, a prominent but nonmedical member of the Vienna Psychoanalytic Society who had made significant contributions to the psychoanalytic understanding of religion, was sued for the Austrian equivalent of malpractice. In his defense, and in the defense of other nonmedical psychoanalysts, Freud wrote the essay "On The Question of Lay Analysis." There he stated:

> In the mental life of children to-day we can still detect the same archaic factors which were once dominant generally in the primeval days of human civilization. In his mental development the child would be repeating the

history of his race in an abbreviated form, just as embryology long since recognized was the case with somatic development. (SE, 20, p. 212)

Freud goes on to describe that because the incestuous wishes are powerful in human heritage, they have never been fully overcome. Man therefore grants such wishes to his mythological gods. They can enjoy what mankind had to renounce. The connection between psychoanalysis and the history of civilization led Freud to believe that to confine psychoanalysis to medical education would deprive it of a source of vitality and new ideas:

> For we do not consider it at all desirable for psychoanalysis to be swallowed up by medicine and to find its last resting place in a textbook of psychiatry under the heading "Methods of Treatment," alongside of procedures such as hypnotic suggestion, autosuggestion, and persuasion.... As a "depth psychology," a theory of the mental unconscious, it can become indispensable to all the sciences which are concerned with the evolution of human civilization and its major institutions such as art, religion and the social order.... The use of analysis for the treatment of the neuroses is only one of its applications; the future will perhaps show that it is not the most important one. In any case it would be wrong to sacrifice all the other applications to this single one, just because it touches on the circle of medical interests. (SE, 20, p. 248)

Such observations lead directly to the question whether psychoanalysis is a scientific discipline to be practiced by people who are trained along professional lines, in the manner of lawyers or dentists, or whether it is a calling to be practiced by persons with a special empathetic capacity to understand other human beings. Strange as it may seem, psychoanalysis is a domain of both art and science.

When a psychoanalyst works with a patient, he works out of an internalized model of treatment, a model he has learned in his training. This model helps him to understand and organize his analysand's free associations, which, had he not possessed such a model, would otherwise remain inchoate. However, the model has its disadvantages, for the analyst might not hear what is beyond his model. Since Freud's death, other models have been developed by other psychoanalysts.

Freud's own model, probably under the influence of archaeology, consisted of three phases (SE, 18, p. 152). In the first, psychoanalysis procures from the patient the necessary information; the analyst listens and asks questions. During this phase, the psychoanalyst waits until the analysand's history coalesces into a gestalt in the analyst's mind. The general premises are the same for all patients, but every analysand carries within a unique variation on the general human theme. The variation includes the traumatic events in every patient's life, such as illnesses, premature separations, and the idiosyncrasies of the parents. It also includes the defense mechanisms each individual built up as a result of his or her past. These defenses, useful as they may have been during infancy, persist even though they no longer fulfill an essential function.

When the psychoanalyst has grasped these interconnections, the second phase of analysis begins. He offers to the analysand his own reconstruction, that is, his understanding of how the person became the kind of person he or she is. It is during this phase that the analyst is particularly active. The reconstruction evokes reactions: pressure, anger, and occasionally gratitude for the understanding that the analysand has received. The period of reconstruction is followed by the third period of "working through," when analyst and analysand go over the reconstruction to make it more accurate. In this last phase, analyst and analysand work as a team. The first two phases psychoanalysis shares with archaeology, but the third is unique to psychoanalysis.

The same can be said about psychoanalytic interpretations given by the analyst to his patients. No two psychoanalysts make the same interpretation. The data patients present as their histories, the dreams they report, the slips of the tongue they make, and the transference relationships they develop, are seldom, if ever, open to only one interpretation. Even after an exhaustive period of free association, room remains for many interpretations. Many of the analyst's interpretations come directly from the storehouse of accumulated psychoanalytic ideas, but the most important interpretations occur to the analyst through a cooperation he receives from his own unconscious. Every psychoanalysis is, to a lesser or greater extent, a voyage of discovery. It is here that no amount of training can take the place of psychoanalytic talent.

In a famous letter that Freud wrote on October 9, 1928, to Oskar Pfister, who was both a Protestant clergyman and a psychoanalyst, Freud asked: "Why have the religiously devout not discovered psychoanalysis? Why did one have to wait for a totally Godless Jew?"[19] The remark raises the question whether Freud discovered psychoanalysis or created it. Today the distinction between discovery and creation is less sharp than it was in Freud's day. In his generation, it was believed that the scientist discovered a secret of nature that hitherto was like a letter written in an ancient and undecipherable script. The idea is still prevalent that what one scientist overlooks or omits, even if he were misled by the data, a later scientist will complete. It is not so with artists. If Shakespeare had not written his plays and sonnets, or if Michelangelo had not painted the ceiling of the Sistine Chapel, no one for all time would have written those plays or painted that ceiling.

If Freud had not lived, would someone else have discovered psychoanalysis? The answer is difficult for psychoanalysis, as we have seen, and consists of many parts. It is conceivable that someone would have discovered infantile sexuality, and that someone else would have discovered transference, and perhaps another person would have hit on the idea that dreams can be used for therapeutic purposes. But it is not plausible that one man would have made all these discoveries in the exact sequence and order with which Freud made them. In other words, Freud's discoveries, like the work of the very great artist, would never have been duplicated. There was nothing inevitable in the discovery of psychoanalysis. The decision whether to rank Freud among the great scientists or the great artists must be left open.

NOTES

1. I had the privilege of reading the inscription at the opening of the Freud Museum in London and have commented on it in M. Bergmann, "Moses and the Evolution of Freud's Jewish Identity" (1971); reprinted in *Judaism and Psychoanalysis*, ed. M. Ostow (New York: Ktav Publishing House, 1982), pp. 115–42. It reads, in part:

> My dear Son,
>
> It was in the seventh year of your age that the spirit of God began to move you to learning. I would say the spirit of God speaketh to you: "Read in My book; there will be opened to thee sources of knowledge and of the intellect.". . . Since then I have preserved the same Bible. Now, on your thirty-fifth birthday I have brought it out from its retirement and I send it to you as a token of love from your old father.

2. The so-called Hebrew Enlightenment began in France after Napoleon, in the period after the 18 Brumaire coup d'état, offered the Jews of France a choice between returning to Israel or full citizenship in France. The "Sanhedrin" (the cultural/religious body that guided the affairs of Jewish life in France) voted for citizenship. The aim of the movement was to introduce the culturally and religiously isolated Jews into the mainstream of European life. See S. W. Baron, *A Social and Religious History of the Jews*, 2d ed., 18 vols. (New York: Columbia University Press, 1952–69).

3. Max Müller, the renowned German philologist and Orientalist, lived in Oxford much of his life. He developed the theory that myths originated from metaphors describing natural phenomena.

4. See *A Psychoanalytic Dialogue: The Letters of Sigmund Freud and Karl Abraham*, ed. H. Abraham and Ernst Freud (New York: Basic Books, 1965).

5. On Victor Adler and the Social Democratic movement in Austria, see William M. Johnson, *The Austrian Mind: An Intellectual and Social History, 1848–1938* (Berkeley: University of California Press, 1972).

6. Ernst Freud, ed., *The Letters of Sigmund Freud*, trans. Tania and James Stern (New York: Basic Books, 1960), p. 22.

7. E. M. Butler, *The Tyranny of Greece over Germany* (Cambridge: Cambridge University Press, 1935).

8. See Bergmann, "Moses and the Evolution," p. 123.

9. T. Gomperz, *Greek Thinkers*, 4 vols. (London: John Murray, 1901).

10. M. Bergmann, *Anatomy of Loving: Man's Quest to Know What Love Is* (New York: Columbia University Press, 1987).

11. See *The Complete Letters of Sigmund Freud to Wilhelm Fliess 1887–1904*, ed. and trans. Jeffrey M. Masson (Cambridge: Harvard University Press, 1987).

12. Wilhelm Jensen, *Gradiva: ein pompejanisches Phantasiestück* (Gradiva: A Pompeian fantasy) (Dresden: C. Reissner, 1903).

13. Muriel Gardiner, ed., *The Wolf-Man* (New York: Basic Books, 1971), p. 139.

14. Passages are from H.D. (Hilda Doolittle), *Tribute to Freud* (New York: Pantheon Books, 1956), pp. 102–104.

15. See R. Ekstein, *Choices of Interpretation in the Treatment of Borderline and Psychotic Children and Interpretation within the Metaphor* (New York: Appleton-Century-Croft, 1966), especially chaps. 7 and 8.

16. H.D., *Tribute to Freud*, p. 106.

17. Otto Fenichel, "Some Remarks on Freud's Place in the History of Science," *Psychoanalytic Quarterly* 15 (1946).

18. M. Bergmann, "What is Psychoanalysis?," *The Evolution of Psychoanalytic Technique*, ed. M. Bergmann and F. Hartmann (New York: Basic Books, 1976), pp. 2–18.

19. Freud originated this remark; see Peter Gay, *A Godless Jew* (New Haven: Yale University Press, 1987).

FREUD'S LIBRARY AND AN APPENDIX OF TEXTS RELATED TO ANTIQUITIES

WENDY BOTTING

J. KEITH DAVIES

"I have sacrificed a great deal for my collection of Greek, Roman and Egyptian antiquities, and actually have read more archaeology than psychology..." (letter to Stefan Zweig, February 7, 1931).[1] In this emphatic statement, the founder of psychoanalysis hoped to correct Zweig's unflattering opinion of his personality, but in doing so, Freud undoubtedly overstated the emphasis of his reading. As Peter Gay has commented (above, p. 16), this "very exaggeration testifies to the privileged place his antiquities held in Freud's mental economy." That Freud's fascination with antiquity extended to his reading is amply borne out by the contents of his library. His intellectual interest and grasp of the antique world had a depth and breadth complementary to his passion for collecting.

Europeans for centuries had been fascinated by the remains and monuments of classical antiquity which testified to the existence of past and seemingly superior societies. During the cultural upsurge of the Renaissance, the heritage of antiquity was taken as an ideal and a model.

The works of Johann Winkelmann (1717–68), who is considered to be the founder of classical archaeology, did much to spread and popularize a notion of an idealized classical culture, particularly in Germany, and had a great influence on Goethe. Winkelmann's declaration that "the only way for us to become great ... is to imitate the Greeks" became a manifesto for Germanic culture, and this objective came to dominate the educational systems of Germany and Austria. Greek and Latin were taught, and classical history, literature, law, and mythology came to provide a common frame of reference for the educated classes throughout Europe.

During the early decades of the nineteenth century, as a result of Napoleon's Egyptian campaign and the building of the Suez Canal, all things Egyptian became fashionable and antiquities flooded into Europe. A systematic and disciplined study of the ancient Egyptians was made possible by the eventual decipherment of hieroglyphic script by J.-F. Champollion in 1822. The study of the Egyptian language opened up to examination the entire culture of this vanished civilization—its customs, law, social practices, and, perhaps most important, its religion. Many scholars were also motivated to investigate historical and archaeological evidence for confirmation of biblical scripture.

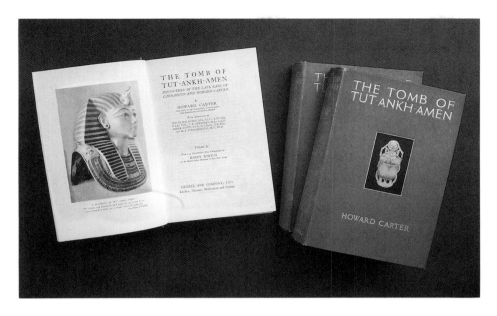

Freud's copy of Howard Carter's *The Tomb of Tut-Ankh-Amen*. (Photo: Freud Museum)

This was the intellectual environment in which Freud grew up and which reflected his own predisposition: "I am reading Burckhardt's *History of Greek Civilization*, which is providing me with unexpected parallels. My predilection for the prehistoric in all its human forms remains the same" (letter to W. Fliess, January 30, 1899). [2] Freud's researches were directed not only to the early childhood experiences of the individual but also to the origins of civilization and culture.

At the basis of Freud's library are detailed technical reports of numerous archaeological excavations. Archaeology had developed from mere antiquarianism or outright treasure hunting and looting into a methodical and disciplined study, and during Freud's lifetime it entered what might be seen as a golden age of exploration and discovery. The accounts of all the most famous practitioners found their place on Freud's shelves: Heinrich Schliemann's *Ilios*, *Mykenae*, and *Tiryns*; Wilhelm Dörpfeld's *Troja und Ilion*; Sir Arthur Evans's account of his work at Knossos, *The Palace of Minos*; and the world-famous discovery by Howard Carter, *The Tomb of Tut-Ankh-Amen*. The presence of more obscure reports, specialist periodicals, technical handbooks, and topographies testify to Freud's close interest in current developments in the field.

Other volumes deal with the whole range of artifacts being discovered in the course of excavation, examples of which Freud had in his own collection or which were to be found in the much larger collections of national museums. Freud's interest was eclectic, and this is reflected in his library. Topics include sculpture and figurines, ceramics, painting and frescoes, amulets, vases, glass, and jewelry, as well as the large-scale monuments and architecture of antiquity.

At an interpretive level, the library contains reconstructions of the past in the form of narrative histories, cultural histories, and speculative anthropologies. Freud cites the work of Darwin, Sir James Frazer's *Golden Bough* and *Totemism and Exogamy*, and William Robertson Smith's *Lectures on the Religion of the Semites* as sources on which he drew. Also represented are the works of Andrew Lang, James Breasted, Sir Ernest Wallis Budge, and Sir Gaston Maspéro.

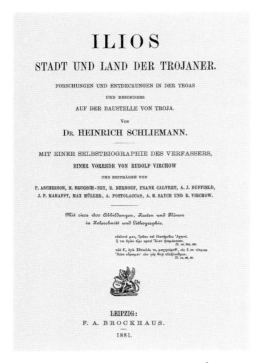

ILIOS
STADT UND LAND DER TROJANER.

FORSCHUNGEN UND ENTDECKUNGEN IN DER TROAS
UND BESONDERS
AUF DER BAUSTELLE VON TROJA.

Von
Dr. HEINRICH SCHLIEMANN.

MIT EINER SELBSTBIOGRAPHIE DES VERFASSERS,
EINER VORREDE VON RUDOLF VIRCHOW
UND BEITRÄGEN VON
P. ASCHERSON, H. BRUGSCH-BEY, E. BURNOUF, FRANK CALVERT, A. J. DUFFIELD,
J. P. MAHAFFY, MAX MÜLLER, A. POSTOLACCAS, A. H. SAYCE UND R. VIRCHOW.

Mit circa 1800 Abbildungen, Karten und Plänen
in Holzschnitt und Lithographie.

LEIPZIG:
F. A. BROCKHAUS.
1881.

The title page of Freud's volume of Heinrich
Schliemann's *Ilios*. (Photo: Freud Museum)

As Freud's interests changed and developed, so did his library. It appears that
he disposed of volumes as they became damaged or no longer held his interest. He
was also in the habit of giving away books to relatives, friends, and colleagues.
The library underwent a more radical sorting when it was divided and packed
while Freud waited to flee from Vienna in 1938. His biographer Ernest Jones
describes the act laconically: "There were many ways of killing the weary time of
waiting. Freud went through his books, selected those he wished to take to
London and disposed of the ones he no longer wanted."[3]

Estimates of the number of books in the collection in Vienna and the number
moved to London are necessarily approximate, but the contents of the Berggasse
19 library are thought to have numbered some 2,500 volumes in 1938. That
Freud elected to move his archaeology books is an indication of their importance
to him in the final period of his life.[4] In the end, about two thousand books,
almost the entire library, were moved to London, where they are now housed at
20 Maresfield Gardens, Freud's London address and today the Freud Museum.[5]

Other smaller collections of the books that remained from the Berggasse 19
library lie scattered today in several locations in Europe and the United States. A
number of essays have been written on the status of the books that Freud did not
move to London, studies generally concerned with authenticating them as once
having been part of his library, but further investigation into these collections is
necessary.[6]

Those books not kept by Freud were passed to a Viennese dealer, Paul
Sonnenfeld, who then sold most of them to antiquarian bookseller Heinrich
Hinterberger. (Sonnenfeld kept approximately seventy titles, which are now in
the Special Collections Division of the Library of Congress, Washington, D.C.)[7]
Hinterberger advertised the collection (along with hundreds of other books
not belonging to Freud) as that of "a famous Viennese scientific explorer."
Dr. Jacob Schatzky, librarian of the New York State Psychiatric Institute, recog-
nized this as a description of Freud, and he acquired the collection for the
Institute in 1939. These books are now in the Special Collections Division of the
Health Sciences Library at Columbia University in New York City.[8]

There is also a small group of books from Freud's personal library, gathered
from various sources, at the Sigmund Freud Haus at Berggasse 19, Vienna, now a
museum.[9]

An additional five titles, derived from a private collection, are lodged in the
Library of Congress,[10] and Anna Freud is known to have given a small number of
books to a family friend.[11]

NOTES

1. *Briefe 1873–1939*, ed. Ernst and Lucie Freud (Frankfurt am Main: S. Fischer, 1960; 2d enlarged ed., 1968) pp. 420–21.

2. *The Complete Letters of Sigmund Freud to Wilhelm Fliess 1887–1904*, ed. and trans. Jeffrey M. Masson (Cambridge: Harvard University Press, 1985), p. 342.

3. Ernest Jones, *The Life and Work of Sigmund Freud*, vol. 3 (New York: Basic Books, 1957), p. 224.

4. The first major study of the nonpsychoanalytic items in the Berggasse 19 library, including a listing, was by Harry Trosman and Roger Dennis Simmons, "The Freud Library," *Journal of the American Psychoanalytic Association* 21:3 (1973), 646–87. See also Edward Timms, "Freud's Library and His Private Reading," in Edward Timms and Naomi Segal, eds., *Freud in Exile: Psychoanalysis and Its Vicissitudes* (New Haven: Yale University Press, 1988), p. 66, where the author reiterates that the "non-scientific" books in the London library represent the "heart" of Freud's collection.

5. The current holdings in the museum consist of approximately 1,600 titles (over 2,000) volumes. Also held there is Freud's collection of his own works in various languages and editions, Freud's collection of offprints of his articles in various journals, complimentary copies of offprints of articles by other authors, and series of various psychoanalytic journals.

   Further complicating the problem of arriving at a total is Freud's propensity for lending books, and his daughter and coworker Anna's in-house borrowing. Between 1968 and 1982 an unpublished card catalogue of the London library was compiled by Gertrude Dann (former librarian of the Hampstead Child Therapy clinic, now the Anna Freud Centre), with the help of Sophie Dann. Comparison with this listing reveals that over one hundred volumes now appear to be missing.

   To date, the only article on the history of the collection at the Freud Museum is an unpublished manuscript by Dorothea Hecken and Steve Neufield, "Reassembling Freud's Library—A Report and Recommendations," Freud Museum, London, April 1986. The Freud Museum is currently preparing a catalogue of the library for publication.

6. See David Bakan, "The Authenticity of the Freud Memorial Collection," *Journal of the Meeting of the Behavioral Sciences* 11:4 (Oct. 1975), 365–67; K. R. Eissler, "Bericht über die sich in den Vereinigten Staaten befindenden Bucher aus S. Freuds Bibliothek," *Jahrbuch der Psychoanalyse* 11 (1975), 10–50; Nolan Lewis and Carney Landis, "Freud's Library," *The Psychoanalytic Review* 44 (1957), 327–54; Hans Lobner, "Some Additional Remarks on Freud's Library," *Sigmund Freud Haus Bulletin* 1:1 (1975), 18–29.

7. See Eissler, "Freuds Bibliothek."

8. The proportion of this collection that can be definitively authenticated as having belonged to Freud has been much disputed. See Bakan, "The Authenticity of the Freud Memorial Collection"; Lewis and Landis, "Freud's Library"; and Eissler, "Freuds Bibliothek."

9. See Hans Lobner, "Some Additional Remarks on Freud's Library," *Sigmund Freud Haus Bulletin* 1:1 (1975), 18–29.

10. Eissler, "Freuds Bibliothek."

11. Personal communication to Freud Museum.

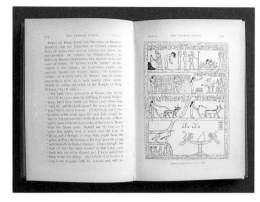

The Book of the Dead, edited and translated by Sir Ernest Wallis Budge. (Photo: Freud Museum)

Following is a list of books on archaeology and related areas that are preserved in Freud's last study and consultation room in the Freud Museum, London. This inventory includes specific topics in the arts and crafts of ancient societies, histories of antiquity, including ancient languages and religions, descriptive works on various archaeological sites, and classical art history. Freud owned and read many books concerning anthropology, history, or religion in general, but such titles have not been included in this appendix.

Ahrem, Maximilian. *Das Weib in der antiken Kunst* (Woman in the art of antiquity). Illus. Jena: E. Diederichs, 1914.

Altmann, Walter. *Die römischen Grabaltäre der Kaiserzeit* (Funerary altars of imperial Rome). Illus. Berlin: Weidmann, 1905.

Angkor. Paris: Tel, n.d.
Portfolio of 42 plates of the archaeological site.

Die Antike: Zeitschrift für Kunst und Kultur des klassischen Altertums (Antiquity: journal for the art and culture of classical antiquity). Ed. Werner Jaeger. Vols. 5–14. Berlin: W. de Gruyter, 1925.

Bachhofer, Ludwig. *Chinesische Kunst* (Chinese art). Illus. Breslau: F. Hirt, 1923.

Bigot, Paul Marie. *Notice sur le relief de Rome impériale* (Notes on the reliefs of imperial Rome). Illus. Rome: Romana, 1911.
Booklet; plans and view maps in envelope.

Boetticher, Adolf. *Die Akropolis von Athen: nach den Berichten der Alten und den neusten Erforschungen* (The Acropolis of Athens, according to reports from the ancients and from the most recent research). Illus. Berlin: J. Springer, 1888.

——————. *Olympia, das Fest und seine Stätte: nach den Berichten der Alten und den Ergebnissen der deutschen Ausgrabungen* (Olympia, the festival and its sites, according to reports from the ancients and the results of the German excavations). 2d ed. Illus. Berlin: J. Springer, 1886.

Borsari, Luigi. *The Roman Forum in the Light of Recent Discoveries.* 2d ed. Rome: Officina poligrafica romana, 1901.

Bossert, Helmuth. *Alt Kreta: Kunst und Kunstgewerbe im ägäischen Kulturkreise* (Ancient Crete: art and handicrafts in Aegean culture). Illus. Berlin: E. Wasmuth, 1921.

Bourguet, Emile. *Les Ruines de Delphes* (The ruins of Delphi). Illus. Paris: Fontemoing, 1914.

Brauchitsch, Georg von. *Die panathenäischen Preisamphoren* (Trophy amphora of the Panathenaeic games). Illus. Berlin: B. G. Teubner, 1910.

Breasted, James H. *A History of Egypt from the Earliest Times to the Persian Conquest.* Illus. London: Hodder and Stoughton, 1906.
Several marginal markings and underlinings.

British Museum. *Coins of Syracuse, Set 24.* London: British Museum, n.d.
Fifteen pictorial postcards in envelope.

——————. *A Guide to the Babylonian and Assyrian Antiquities.* Illus. London: British Museum, 1900.

——————. *A Guide to the First and Second Egyptian Rooms.* 2d ed. Illus. London: British Museum, 1904.

——————. *A Guide to the Third and Fourth Egyptian Rooms.* Illus. London: British Museum, 1904.

Brugsch, Heinrich. *Die Ägyptologie: Abriss der Entzifferungen und Forschungen auf dem Gebiete der ägyptischen Schrift; Sprache und Alterthumskunde* (Egyptology: a short survey on the deciphering and research concerning Egyptian writing, language, and archaeology). Leipzig: A. Heitz, 1897.
Several marginal markings and underlinings.

Buberl, Paul. *Die griechisch-ägyptischen Mumienbildnisse der Sammlung Th. Graf* (The Greco-Egyptian mummy-portraits from the collection of Th. Graf). Illus. Vienna: Kyrstall, 1922.

Budge, Sir Ernest Wallis. *Easy Lessons in Egyptian Hieroglyphics, With Sign List.* London: Kegan Paul, Trench, Trubner, 1902.

——————. *Egyptian Ideas of the Future Life.* 2d ed. Illus. London: Kegan Paul, Trench, Trubner, 1900.

——————. *Egyptian Magic.* Illus. London: Kegan Paul, Trench, Trubner, 1901.

——————. *An Egyptian Reading Book for Beginners.* London: Kegan Paul, Trench, Trubner, 1896.
Bookplate; several underlinings; translations section uncut.

——————. *First Steps in Egyptian: A Book for Beginners.* London: Kegan Paul, Trench, Trubner, 1895.
Bookplate.

——————. *A History of Egypt from the End of the Neolithic Period to the Death of Cleopatra VII,* B.C. 30. 8 vols. Illus. London: Kegan Paul, Trench, Trubner, 1902.

——————. *Osiris and the Egyptian Resurrection.* 2 vols. Illus. London: P. L. Warner, 1911.

——————, ed. and trans. *The Book of the Dead: An English Translation of the Chapters; Hymns of the Theban Recension.* 3 vols. Illus. London: Kegan Paul, Trench, Trubner, 1901.

Burckhardt, Jakob. *Die Cicerone: eine Anleitung zum Genuss der Kunstwerke Italiens* (The Cicerone: a guide to the appreciation of Italian art). 2 vols. 6th ed. Leipzig: E. A. Seemann, 1893.
Some marginal annotations.

——————. *Griechische Kulturgeschichte* (The history of Greek civilization). 4 vols. Berlin: W. Spemann, n.d.
Some marginal markings, vol. 3 only.

Burrows, Ronald. *The Discoveries in Crete and Their Bearing on the History of Ancient Civilisation.* 2d ed., Illus. London: J. Murray, 1908.
Some markings.

Buttles, Janet R. *The Queens of Egypt.* Illus. London: A. Constable, 1908.

Capart, Jean. *Abydos: le temple de Séti 1er, étude générale* (Abydos: the temple of Seti I, a general study). Illus. Brussels: Rossignol and Van den Bril, 1912.

———. *L'Art égyptien: choix de documents accompagnés d'indications bibliographiques* (Egyptian art: selected documents with bibliographic annotations). Illus. Brussels: Vroumant, 1909.

———. *Les Débuts de l'art en Égypte* (Primitive art in Egypt). Illus. Brussels: Vroumant, 1904.

Carter, Howard, and Arthur Mace. *The Tomb of Tut-Ankh-Amen: Discovered by the Late Earl of Carnarvon and Howard Carter.* 3 vols. Illus. London: Cassell, 1923–1933.

Cesnola, Louis Palma di. *Cypern: seine alten Städte, Gräber und Tempel—Bericht über zehnjährige Forschungen und Ausgrabungen auf der Insel* (Cyprus: its ancient cities, tombs, and temples—report on a decade of research and excavations on the island). Trans. Ludwig Stern. Illus. Jena: H. Costenoble, 1879.

Collignon, Maxime. *Handbuch der griechischen Archäologie* (A manual of Greek archaeology). Illus. Leipzig: P. Friesenhahn, n.d.

Conze, Alexander. *Die Kleinfunde aus Pergamon* (The small treasures of Pergamum). Illus. Berlin: Königliche Akademie der Wissenschaften, 1903.

Cybulski, Stephan. *Die Kultur der Griechen und Römer: dargestellt an der Hand ihrer Gebrauchgegenstände und Bauten* (The culture of the Greeks and Romans, seen in their utensils and buildings). Illus. Leipzig: K. F. Köhler, 1905.

Diez, Ernst. *Die Kunst der islamischen Völker* (The art of the Islamic peoples). Illus. Berlin: Athenaion, 1915.

Dörpfeld, Wilhelm. *Troja und Ilion: Ergebnisse der Ausgrabungen in den vorhistorischen und historischen Schichten von Ilion 1870–1894* (Troy and Ilium: results of excavations on the prehistoric and historic strata of Ilium 1870–1894). 2 vols. Illus. Athens: Beck and Barth, 1902.

Dussaud, René. *Les Civilisations préhélleniques dans le bassin de la mer Égée* (Prehellenic civilizations in the Aegean basin). 2d ed. Illus. Paris: P. Geuthner, 1914.
Signed: Freud, December 8, 1914.

Erman, Adolf. *Ägyptisches Glossar: die häufigeren Worte der ägyptischen Sprache* (Egyptian glossary: the more frequent words in the Egyptian language). Berlin: Reuther and Reichard, 1904.

———. *Die Hieroglyphen* (Hieroglyphs). Illus. Berlin: G. J. Göschen, 1912.
Marginal marking, p. 21.

Erman, Adolf, and Fritz Krebs. *Aus den Papyrus der Königlichen Museen zu Berlin* (Selections from the papyri of the Royal Museums in Berlin). Illus. Berlin: W. Spemann, 1899.

Evans, Sir Arthur John. *The Palace of Minos: A Comparative Account of the Successive Stages of the Early Cretan Civilization as Illustrated by the Discoveries at Knossos.* 4 vols. in 7. Illus. London: Macmillan, 1921–36.

Fechheimer, Hedwig. *Kleinplastik der Ägypter* (Small sculpture of the Egyptians). Illus. Berlin: B. Cassirer, 1921.

———. *Die Plastik der Ägypter* (Egyptian sculpture). Illus. Berlin: B. Cassirer, 1923.

Friedrich, Johannes. *Ras Schamra: ein überblick über Funde und Forschungen* (Ras Schamra: a survey of the finds and research). Illus. Leipzig: J. C. Hinrichs, 1933.

Furtwängler, Adolf, and H. L. Urlichs. *Denkmäler griechischer und römischer Skulptur* (Monuments of Greek and Roman sculpture). 2d ed. Illus. Munich: F. Bruckmann, 1904.

Gesellschaft für antike Kultur: Bericht (Society for the culture of antiquity: reports). Berlin: Gesellschaft für antike Kultur, 1924–28.

Grosse, Ernst. *Die Anfänge der Kunst* (The beginnings of art). Illus. Freiberg: J. C. B. Mohr, 1894.
Many marginal markings and underlinings.

Halbherr, F., and P. Orsi. *Àntichità dell'antro di Zeus ideo in Creta* (Antiquities from the cave of the Idean Zeus in Crete). Illus. Florence: E. Loescher, 1888.

Handcock, Percy. *Mesopotamian Archaeology: An Introduction to the Archaeology of Babylonia and Assyria.* Illus. London: Macmillan, 1912.

Haugwitz, Eberhard. *Der Palatin: seine Geschichte und seine Ruinen* (The Palatine: its history and ruins). Illus. Rome: Loescher, 1901.

Hausenstein, Wilhelm. *Die Bildnerei der Etrusker* (Etruscan sculpture). Illus. Munich: R. Piper, 1922.

Hirn, Yrjo. *Der Ursprung der Kunst: eine Untersuchung ihrer psychischen und sozialen Ursachen* (The origins of art: a psychological and sociological inquiry). Trans. M. Barth. Leipzig: J. A. Barth, 1904.

Hoeber, Fritz. *Griechische Vasen* (Greek vases). Illus. Munich: R. Piper, 1909.

Hoernes, Moritz. *Urgeschichte der bildenden Kunst in Europa von den Anfängen bis um 500 vor Chr.* (The prehistory of visual art in Europe from the beginnings to 500 B.C.). Illus. Vienna: A. Holzhausen, 1898.

Holtzinger, Heinrich, and Walther Amelung. *Die Ruinen Roms, und, Die Antiken-Sammlung* (The ruins of Rome, and, The collection of antiquities). Stuttgart: Union Deutscher Verlagsgesellschaft, n.d.

Huelsen, Christian. *Das Forum romanum: seine Geschichte und seine Denkmäler* (The Roman forum: its history and its monuments). Illus. Rome: E. Loescher, 1904; 2d ed. 1905. Signed: Dr. Freud, September 18, 1907.

—————. *I più recenti scavi nel foro romano* (The most recent excavations in the Roman Forum). Illus. Rome: E. Loescher, 1910.

Imhoof-Blumer, Friedrich. *Porträtköpfe auf antiken Münzen hellenischer und hellenisierter Völker: mit Zeittafeln der Dynastien des Altertums nach ihren Münzen* (Portrait heads on ancient coins of Hellenic and Hellenicized peoples: including chronologies of the dynasties of antiquity, based on their coins). Illus. Leipzig: B. G. Teubner, 1885.

—————. *Porträtköpfe auf römischen Münzen der Republik und der Kaiserzeit* (Portrait heads on Roman coins of the republic and imperial Rome). Illus. Leipzig: B. G. Teubner, 1879.

Jones, Sir Henry Stuart. *Classical Rome.* Illus. London: G. Richards, n.d.

—————. *Companion to Roman History.* Illus. Oxford: Clarendon, 1912.

Jung, Julius. *Grundriss der Geographie von Italien und den Orbis romanus* (A geographic compendium of Italy and the Roman world). 2d ed. Munich: C. H. Beck, 1897.

Kaemmel, Otto. *Rom und die Campagna* (Rome and the Campagna region). Illus. Bielefeld: Velhagen and Klasing, 1902.

Kaufmann, Carl Maria. *Handbuch der christlichen Archäologie* (Handbook of Christian archaeology). Illus. Paderborn: F. Schöningh, 1905.

Kaulen, Franz Philipp. *Assyrien und Babylonien nach den neuesten Entdeckungen* (Assyria and Babylonia according to the latest discoveries). 5th ed. Illus. Freiburg: Herder, 1899.

King, Leonard William. *Assyrian Language: Easy Lessons in the Cuneiform Inscriptions.* London: Kegan Paul, Trench, Trubner, 1901. Some marginal markings; signed: Dr. Freud, January 22, 1902.

Kisa, Anton Carel. *Das Glas im Altertume* (Glass in antiquity). 3 vols. Illus. Leipzig: K. W. Hiersemann, 1908.

Koldewey, Robert. *Das wieder erstehende Babylon: die bisherigen Ergebnisse der deutschen Ausgrabungen* (Babylon resurrected: the results of the German excavations to date). 3d ed. Illus. Leipzig: J. C. Hinrichs, 1914.

Lanciani, Rodolfo. *The Destruction of Ancient Rome: A Sketch of the History of the Monuments.* Illus. London: Macmillan, 1901.

Lange, Ludwig. *Römische Alterthümer* (Roman antiquities). 3 vols. Berlin: Weidmann, 1856–71.

Layard, Sir Henry Austen. *Discoveries in the Ruins of Nineveh and Babylon, with Travels in Armenia, Kurdistan and the Desert: Being the Result of a Second Expedition Undertaken for the British Museum.* 2 vols. Illus. London: J. Murray, 1853.

—————. *Nineveh and Its Remains.* 6th ed. 2 vols. Illus. London: J. Murray, 1854. Some marginal markings.

Leoni, Umberto. *The Palatine.* Illus. Rome: Frank, n.d.

Leoni, Umberto, and Giovanni Staderini. *On the Appian Way: A Walk from Rome to Albano.* Illus. Rome: R. Bemporad, 1907.

Löwy, Emanuel. *Der Beginn der rotfigurigen Vasenmalerei* (The origin of red-figure vase painting). Illus. Vienna: Hölder, Pichler, Tempsky, 1938.

—————. *Die griechische Plastik* (Greek sculpture). 2d ed. 2 vols. Illus. Leipzig: Klinkhardt and Biermann, 1916.

—————. *Lysipp und seine Stellung in der griechischen Plastik* (Lysippus and his place in Greek sculpture). Illus. Hamburg: Verlaganstalt and Druckerei, 1891. Signed: Dr. Freud, n.d.; dedicated by author, n.d.

—————. *Die Naturwiedergabe in der älteren griechischen Kunst* (The rendering of nature in early Greek art). Illus. Rome: E. Loescher, 1900. Dedicated by author, n.d.

—————. *Neuattische Kunst* (Neo-attic art). Illus. Leipzig: E. A. Seemann, 1922. Dedicated by author, n.d.

—————. *Polygnot: ein Buch von griechischer Malerei* (Polygonotus: a book of Greek painting). 2 vols. Illus. Vienna: A. Schroll, 1929. Dedicated by author, n.d.

—————. *Stein und Erz in der statuarischen Kunst* (Stone and bronze in statues). Illus. Innsbruck: Wagner, 1915. Dedicated by author, n.d.

—————. *Ursprünge der bildenden Kunst* (Origins of fine art). Vienna: Hölder, Pichler, Tempsky, 1930. Dedicated by author, n.d.

Luckenbach, Hermann. *Die Akropolis von Athen* (The Acropolis of Athens). 2d ed. Illus. Munich: R. Oldenbourg, 1905. Signed: Dr. Freud, October 24, 1905.

Martha, Jules. *L'Art étrusque* (Etruscan art). Illus. Paris: Firmin-Didot, 1889.

Marucchi, Orazio. *Gli obelischi egiziani di Roma* (The Egyptian obelisks in Rome). Illus. Rome: E. Loescher, 1898.

Maspéro, Sir Gaston. *Égypte* (Egypt). Illus. Paris: Hachette, 1912.

—————. *Ruines et paysages d'Égypte* (Ruins and landscapes of Egypt). Paris: E. Guilmoto, c. 1910.

Mau, August. *Pompeji in Leben und Kunst* (Pompeii in life and art). Illus. Leipzig: W. Engelmann, 1900.

Meissner, Bruno. *Grundzüge der babylonisch-assyrischen Plastik* (Fundamentals of Babylonian-Assyrian sculpture). Illus. Leipzig: J. C. Hinrichs, 1915.

Meyer, Eduard. *Ägypten zur Zeit der Pyramidenerbauer* (Egypt during the era of the pyramid-builders). Illus. Leipzig: J. C. Hinrichs, 1908.

Michaelis, Adolf. *Die archäologischen Entdeckungen des neunzehnten Jahrhunderts* (The archaeological discoveries of the 19th century). Leipzig: E. A. Seemann, 1906.

Mommsen, Theodor. *Römische Geschichte (Bd. 5, achtes Buch): die Provinzen von Caesar bis Diocletion* (History of Rome [vol. 5, book 8]: the provinces, from Caesar to Diocletian). Illus. Berlin: Weidmann, 1885.

Moortgat, Anton. *Frühe Bildkunst in Sumer* (Early Sumerian pictorial art). Illus. Leipzig: J. C. Hinrichs, 1935.

Moret, Alexandre. *Le Nil et la civilisation égyptienne* (The Nile and Egyptian civilization). Paris: A. Michel, 1937.

Müller, Iwan Phillip Eduard von, ed. *Handbuch der klassischen Altertums-Wissenschaft: Atlas zur Archäologie der Kunst* (Handbook of the history of classical antiquity: atlas of the archaeology of art). Illus. Munich: C. H. Beck, 1897.

Müller, Valentin Kurt. *Frühe Plastik in Griechenland und Vorderasien: ihre Typenbildung von der neolithischen bis in die griechischarchaische Zeit (rund 3000 bis 600 v. Chr.)* (Early sculpture in Greece and Asia Minor: typological development from neolithic times up to the archaic Greek era [c. 3000–600 B.C.]). Illus. Augsburg: B. Filser, 1929.

Müller, Walter August. *Nacktheit und Entblössung in der altorientalischen und älteren griechischen Kunst* (Nudity and disrobement in ancient Oriental and older Greek art). Illus. Leipzig: B. G. Teubner, 1906.

Myer, Isaac. *Scarabs: The History, Manufacture, and Religious Symbolism of the Scarabaeus in Ancient Egypt, Phoenicia, Sardinia, Etruria, etc.* London: D. Nutt, 1894.

National Museum, Naples. *Handbuch des National Museums zu Neapel und hauptsächliche illustrierten Monumente* (Handbook of the national museum in Naples and its major illustrated monuments). Illus. Naples: National Museum, n.d.

Neugebauer, Karl Anton. *Antike Bronzestatuetten* (Classical bronze statuettes). Illus. Berlin: Schoetz and Parrhysius, 1921.

Noack, Ferdinand. *Homerische Paläste: eine Studie zu den Denkmälern und zum Epos* (Homeric palaces: a study on monuments and on epic poetry). Illus. Leipzig: B. G. Teubner, 1903.

Ohnefalsch-Richter, Max. *Kypros, Die Bibel und Homer: Beiträge zue Cultur-, Kunst- und Religionsgeschichte des Orients im Alterthume* (Cyprus, the Bible and Homer: oriental civilization, art, and religion in ancient times). 2 vols. Illus. Berlin: A. Asher, 1893.

Overbeck, Johannes. *Pompeji in seinen Gebäuden, Alterthümern und Kunstwerken dargestellt* (Pompeii, as seen in its buildings, antiquities, and art). 4th ed. Illus. Leipzig: W. Engelmann, 1884.

Perrot, Georges, and Charles Chipiez. *Histoire de l'art dans l'antiquité* (History of art in antiquity). 10 vols. Illus. Paris: Hachette, 1882–1914.
Some marginal markings.

Petersen, Eugen Adolf Hermann. *Ara pacis Augustae* (The Ara pacis of Augustus). Illus. George Niemann. 2 vols. Vienna: A. Hölder, 1902.

—————. *Vom alten Rom* (Ancient Rome). Illus. Leipzig: E. A. Seemann, 1898.

Petrie, Sir William Flinders. *Amulets: Illustrated by the Egyptian Collection in the University College, London.* Illus. London: Constable, 1914.

—————. *Les Arts et métiers de l'ancienne Égypte* (Arts and crafts of ancient Egypt). Trans. Jean Capart. Illus. Brussels: Vroumant, 1912.

—————, ed. A *History of Egypt: From the Earliest Times to the XVIth Dynasty.* 4th ed. 6 vols. Illus. London: Methuen, 1899–1905.

Pfuhl, Ernst. *Malerei und Zeichnung der Griechen* (Greek painting and drawing). 3 vols. Illus. Munich: F. Bruckmann, 1923.

Picard, Charles, and P. De la Coste-Messelière. *Sculptures grecques de Delphes* (Greek sculpture at Delphi). Illus. Paris: E. de Boccard, 1927.

Reinisch, Simon Leo. *Die ägyptischen Denkmäler in Miramar* (The Egyptian monuments in Miramar). Illus. Vienna: W. Braumüller, 1865.
Marginal markings, p. 5.

Richter, Otto Ludwig. *Topographie der Stadt Rom* (Topography of the city of Rome). 2d ed. Illus. Munich: C. H. Beck, 1901.

Ripostelli, Giuseppe. *The Roman Forum.* Illus. Rome: C. Serena, n.d.

Rodenwaldt, Gerhardt. *Die Kunst der Antike (Hellas und Rom)* (The art of antiquity [Greece and Rome]). 2d. ed. Illus. Berlin: Propyläen, 1927.

Rücklin, Rudolf. *Das Schmuckbuch* (The book of ornaments). 2 vols. Illus. Leipzig: E. A. Seemann, 1901.

Sallet, Alfred. *Münzen und Medaillen* (Coins and medallions). Illus. Berlin: W. Spemann, 1898.
Signed: Dr. Freud, February 4, 1899.

Saloman, Geskel. *Erklärungen antiker Kunstwerke* (Interpretations of classical art). Illus. Stockholm: n.p., 1902.

Schäfer, Heinrich. *Amarna in Religion und Kunst* (Amarna in religion and art). Illus. Leipzig: J. C. Hinrichs, 1931.
Some marginal markings.

————. *Von ägyptischer Kunst: eine Grundlage* (Egyptian art: a foundation). 3d ed. Illus. Leipzig: J. C. Hinrichs, 1930.

Schäfer, Heinrich, and Walter Andrae. *Die Kunst des alten Orients* (Art of the ancient Orient). Illus. Berlin: Propyläen, 1925.

Schliemann, Heinrich. *Ilios, Stadt und Land der Trojaner: Forsuchungen und Entdeckungen in der Troas und besonders auf der Baustelle von Troja* (Ilios, the city and country of the Trojans: the results of researches and discoveries on the site of Troy and in the Troad). Illus. Leipzig: F. A. Brockhaus, 1881.

————. *Mykenae: Bericht über meine Forschungen und Entdeckungen in Mykenae und Tiryns* (Mycenae: a narrative of researches and discoveries at Mycenae and Tiryns). Illus. Leipzig: F. A. Brockhaus, 1878.
Signed: Dr. Freud, September 13, [?]; bookplate.

————. *Tiryns: der prähistorische Palast der Könige von Tiryns, Ergebnisse der neuesten Ausgrabungen* (Tiryns: the prehistoric palace of the kings of Tiryns, the results of the latest excavations). Illus. Leipzig: F. A. Brockhaus, 1886.

Schmidt, Robert Rudolf. *Die Kunst der Eiszeit* (Art of the Ice Age). Augsburg: B. Filser, n.d.
Thirty-two mounted plates in folder.

Schottmüller, Frida. *Bronze-Statuetten und Geräte* (Bronze statuettes and implements). Illus. Berlin: R. C. Schmidt, 1918.

Schrader, Hans. *Phidias*. Illus. Frankfurt am Main: Frankfurter Verlags-Anstalt, 1924.

Schubart, Wilhelm. *Das Buch bei den Griechen und Römern: eine Studie aus der Berliner Papyrussammlung* (A study of the book in Greece and Rome: from the Berlin papyrus collection). Illus. Berlin: G. Reimer, 1907.

Sellin, Ernst. *Tell Ta'annek*. Illus. Vienna: C. Gerold, 1904.

Sittl, Karl. *Archäologie der Kunst* (The archaeology of art). Illus. Munich: C. H. Beck, 1895.
Marginal markings, pp. 303 and 310.

Spiegelberg, Wilhelm. *Geschichte der ägyptischen Kunst bis zum Hellenismus* (History of Egyptian art until Hellenic times). Illus. Leipzig: J. C. Hinrichs, 1903.

Steindorff, Georg. *Die Blütezeit des Pharaonenreichs* (The golden age of the pharaohs). Illus. Bielefeld: Velhagen and Klasing, 1900.

————. *Die Kunst der Ägypter: Bauten, Plastik, Kunstgewerbe* (The art of the Egyptians: building, sculpture, arts, and crafts). Illus. Leipzig: Insel, 1928.

Sydow, Eckart von. *Primitive Kunst und Psychoanalyse: eine Studie über die sexuelle Grundlage der bildenden Künste der Naturvölker* (Primitive art and psychoanalysis: a study on the sexual basis for visual arts of primitive peoples). Illus. Leipzig: Internationaler Psychoanalytischer Verlag, 1927.

Thomsen, Peter. *Palästina und seine Kultur in fünf Jahrtausenden: nach den neusten Ausgrabungen und Forschungen dargestellt* (Palestine and its culture through five thousand years: according to the most recent excavations and research). 3d ed. Illus. Leipzig: J. C. Hinrichs, 1931.

Urlichs, Ludwig von. *Einleitende und Hilfs-Diziplinen* (Introductory and complementary disciplines). Munich: C. H. Beck, 1892.
Vol. 1 of a series on archaeological practice.

Watzinger, Carl. *Denkmäler Palästinas: eine Einführung in die Archäologie des Heiligen Landes* (Palestine's monuments: an introduction to the archaeology of the Holy Land). 2 vols. Illus. Leipzig: J. C. Hinrichs, 1933–35.
Vol. 2 cut to p. 89 only.

Weber, Otto. *Altorientalische Siegelbilder* (Ancient oriental seals). 2 vols. Illus. Leipzig: J. C. Hinrichs, 1920.

Weichardt, Carl Friedrich Wilhelm. *Pompeji vor der Zerstörung: Reconstructionen der Tempel und ihrer Umgebung* (Pompeii before its destruction: reconstruction of its temples and their surroundings). Pocket ed. Illus. Leipzig: K. F. Koehler, n.d.
Stamped on title page: E. Prass. Neapel, 59–60 Piazza dei Martiri.

Woolley, Sir Charles Leonard. *The Royal Cemetery: A Report on the Predynastic and Sargonid Graves Excavated between 1926 and 1931.* 1 vol. in 2. Illus. London: British Museum and University of Pennsylvania, 1934.

————. *Vor 5000 Jahren: die Ausgrabungen von Ur und die Geschichte der Sumerer* (Five thousand years ago: the excavations of Ur and the history of the Sumerians). Trans. Heribert Hassler. 4th ed. Illus. Stuttgart: Franckh, n.d.